IMAGES
of America

COPIAH COUNTY

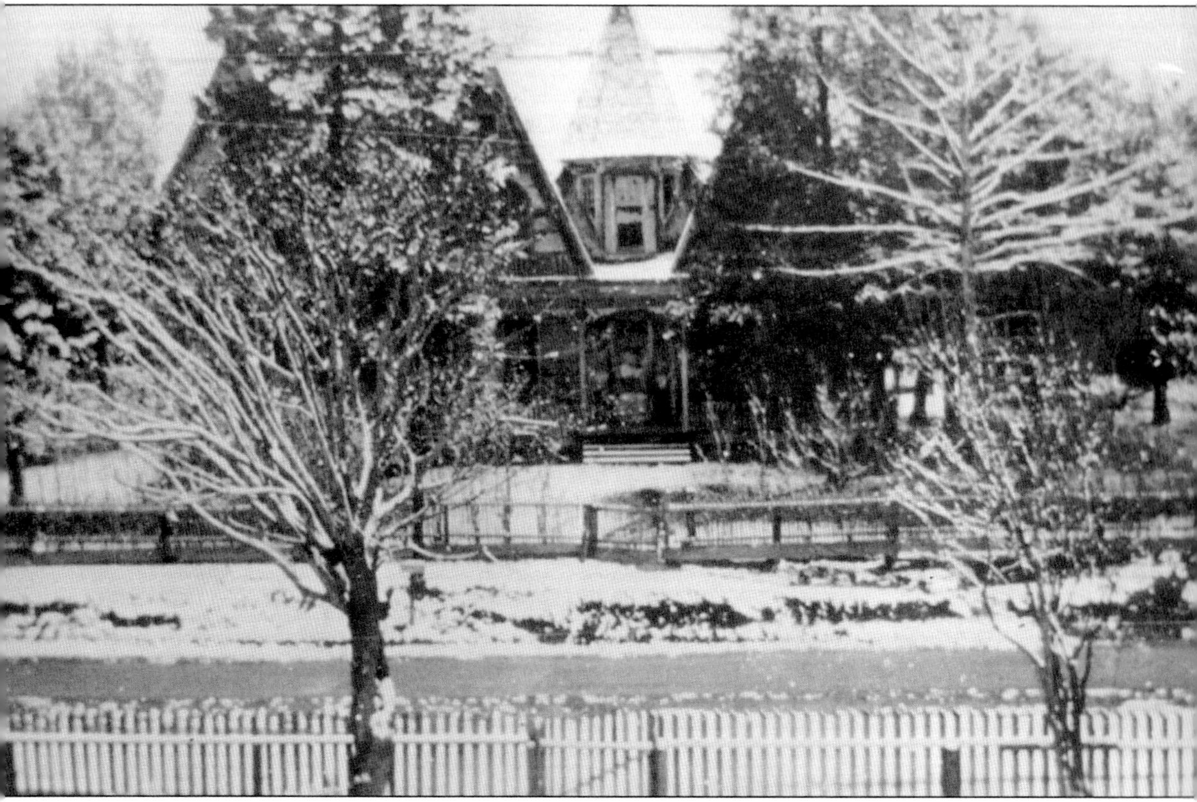

This 24-room Victorian house, built *c.* 1870, was the home of Dr. Elias Alford Rowan; his wife, the former Julia Lamb; and their seven children. Located between Wesson and Beauregard, Dr. Rowan originally planned to hospitalize patients there. However, its only service as a hospital occurred after the tornado of April 1883. Dr. Rowan died December 10, 1912 in his 75th year after being struck by a southbound Illinois Central train. After family members died or moved away, the huge house remained vacant yet furnished. Tales of ghosts at the house circulated in the neighborhood, and the Rowan house became known as the "Haunted House." The property was later sold, and the house was demolished, the materials being sold for salvage. (Photograph from the Estate of Jeanelle Wright Harvey.)

ON THE COVER: Cotton and produce were the mainstays of Copiah County. As in this picture, taken in the late 1800s, farmers would spend a day traveling to sell their goods to buyers staked along the railroad shipping points. (Courtesy of J. T. Biggs Jr. Memorial Library.)

IMAGES
of America

COPIAH COUNTY

LaTricia M. Nelson-Easley

ARCADIA
PUBLISHING

ISBN 978-0-7385-5300-9

Published by Arcadia Publishing
Charleston, South Carolina

Printed in the United States of America

Library of Congress Catalog Card Number: 2007934712

For all general information contact Arcadia Publishing at:
Telephone 843-853-2070
Fax 843-853-0044
E-mail sales@arcadiapublishing.com
For customer service and orders:
Toll-Free 1-888-313-2665

Visit us on the Internet at www.arcadiapublishing.com

This book is dedicated to my family, including my mother and father, who have always supported my endeavors, and my husband, Charles, who tolerated my absence in mind and body.

Contents

ACKNOWLEDGMENTS

I wish to thank Sally Garland and the individuals who donated photographs to the Tomato Museum at Chautauqua Park. If not for their donations, this book would not have been possible. I also wish to thank the librarians who provided photographs and materials to which I would not have had access otherwise. I also wish to thank my editor at Arcadia Publishing, Kate Crawford, who permitted me the time to condense the vast amount of information that was initially submitted.

I also wish to thank the community for supporting the Copiah County Historical and Genealogical Society. Being president and having contact with individuals interested in seeing this book published has helped make an eight-year dream a reality. I especially need to thank Dan Johnson for his encouragement and help in forming the society and in proofing the book. His knowledge of the history of Copiah County has proven invaluable.

There are two other individuals who did not live to see this book published, both having passed away while it was being written. If not for Dorothy Alford and her articles about Crystal Springs and Hartwell Cook and his book about Hazlehurst, much of the information you are about to read would have been lost forever. For this, I humbly remain an editor, not an author, of this pictorial history of Copiah County.

INTRODUCTION

The Mississippi Territory was organized on April 7, 1798, from territory ceded by Georgia and South Carolina. It was later twice expanded to include disputed territory claimed by both the United States and Spain. The central portion of the state was settled by the Choctaws, and the northern portion was settled by the Chickasaws. This land was purchased from the Native Americans through a series of treaties from 1800 to 1830. On December 10, 1817, Mississippi became the 20th state admitted to the Union. On October 18, 1820, in the Treaty of Doak's Stand, the Choctaws gave part of their homeland to Mississippi in exchange for land in Arkansas. From this land, Hinds County was formed in 1821. In 1823, the counties of Copiah and Yazoo were carved from Hinds County. In 1824, Simpson County was formed from the eastern portion of Copiah County, east of the Pearl River. *Copiah* is Native American for "calling panther."

The only roads that existed were Native American trails. One of the earliest settlers in the county was Elisha Lott, a preacher, who came from Hancock County around 1820 with his companion, Thomas Cottingham. Interested in passing along his spiritual message to the Choctaws, Lott moved his family to Old Crystal Springs and eventually built a lumber mill and a gristmill. With the help of Wesley Cottingham, Lott built the Old Crystal Springs Methodist Church. The land for the church was donated by Pleasant Moore, another early settler of the county.

From January 1823 to January 1824, the home of John Coor was the county seat. When Simpson County was formed, the county seat was moved to Gallatin, and a courthouse was built. The county seat was moved to Hazlehurst after the New Orleans, Jackson, and Great Northern Railroad bypassed Gallatin by four miles in 1858.

Education was not stressed until the 1870s, when a universal system of education was supported by the state legislature. Until school consolidation was achieved, many children attended private schools and one-room schoolhouses. Crystal Springs Consolidated School was, at one time, the largest consolidated school in the United States.

Cotton was the predominant way to earn a living. Some farmers made daylong excursions to sell their cotton at the markets. The existence of the Wesson cotton mills allowed Wesson to have electricity before any other town in the state. With the decline in cotton prices, vegetable shipping began to take hold in the late 1800s, and soon the county was known as the "Tomatopolis of the World."

Early on, springs were discovered in the county. This is how the town of Crystal Springs earned its name. Brown's Wells, which existed in the 1800s and early 1900s, capitalized on the idea and sold spring water that was claimed to heal several types of ailments. Many rich and famous people visited the wells, including Eudora Welty.

Religion has always been important to the South, and Copiah County was no different. When a community formed, one of the first tasks was the establishment of a church. The Hennington Campgrounds became a refuge for the Methodists to pray in peace and be surrounded by nature. Soon the Mississippi Chautauqua Assembly formed and used the campgrounds for its annual events. People from all over the state would gather for this multi-day event. Like Brown's Wells, the campgrounds had several cottages and a hotel. World War II brought these and other activities to a close.

Today there are faint reminders of the days of old. One might notice the mural on the post office in Crystal Springs, or the log wagon on Extension Street in Hazlehurst. A visit to the Tomato Museum and the Hazlehurst Depot Museum would be a good start in learning more about some of the information mentioned in this book. So sit back and enjoy and let the pictures tell a story about a county that has endured many changes over its 185-year life.

One

Forming the County

Copiah County was formed from the southern portion of Hinds County on January 21, 1823, and included part of what is now Simpson County. By act of the state legislature, the home of John Coor was designated as the temporary seat of justice. When Simpson County was formed from the eastern portion of Copiah County on January 23, 1824, the county seat was moved to Gallatin. When the railroad came in 1858, Hazlehurst began to thrive, and soon the county seat was moved there. This chapter discusses the three county seats, some of the smaller communities, and some of the people who helped shape the county.

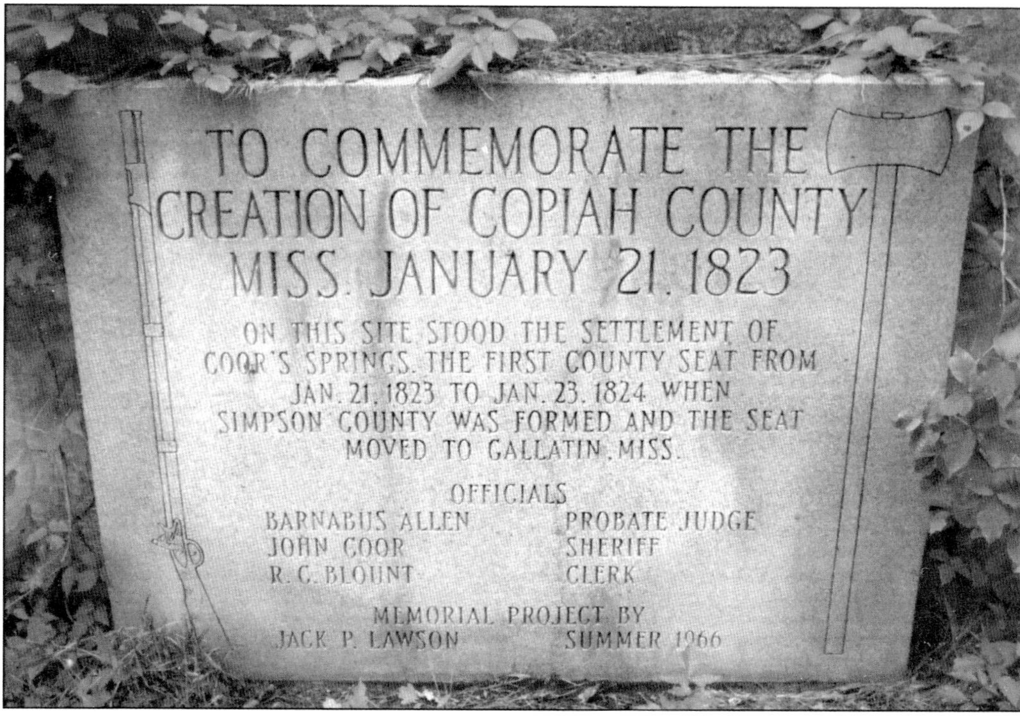

Coor Springs was established in 1819 by John Coor and his family. When Simpson County was formed from the eastern part of Copiah County in 1824, the county seat was moved to Gallatin. This monument is now at the site of Coor Springs. (Courtesy of Copiah County Historical and Genealogical Society [CCHGS].)

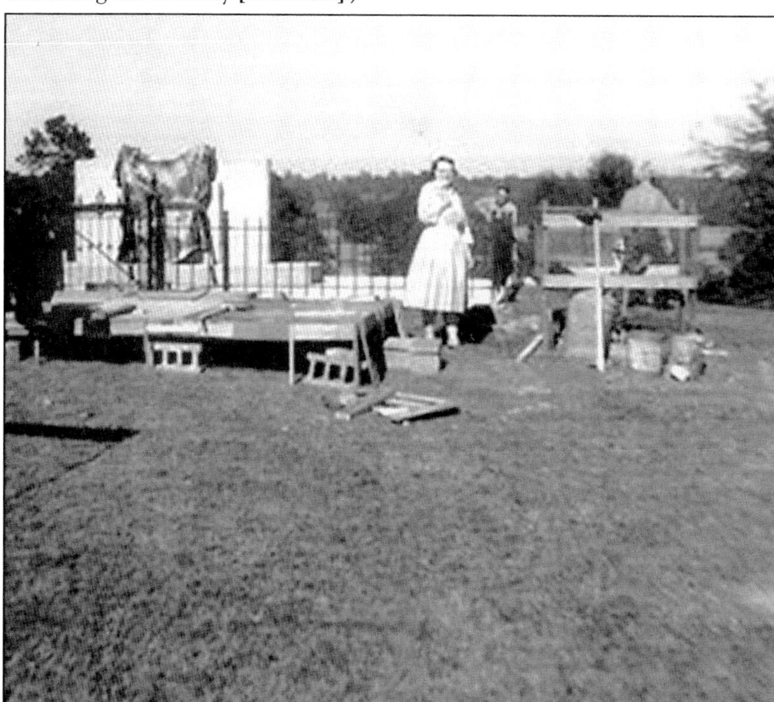

In 1966, Jack P. Lawson of Hazlehurst worked with the Coor family to have a road cut, grounds cleared, and a marker placed at the site. This image was taken a few days before October 9, 1966, when Dr. William McCain dedicated the marker to the founders of Copiah County and to the site of its first government. Over 1,000 people attended the ceremony. (Courtesy of Odie and Elsie Rutledge.)

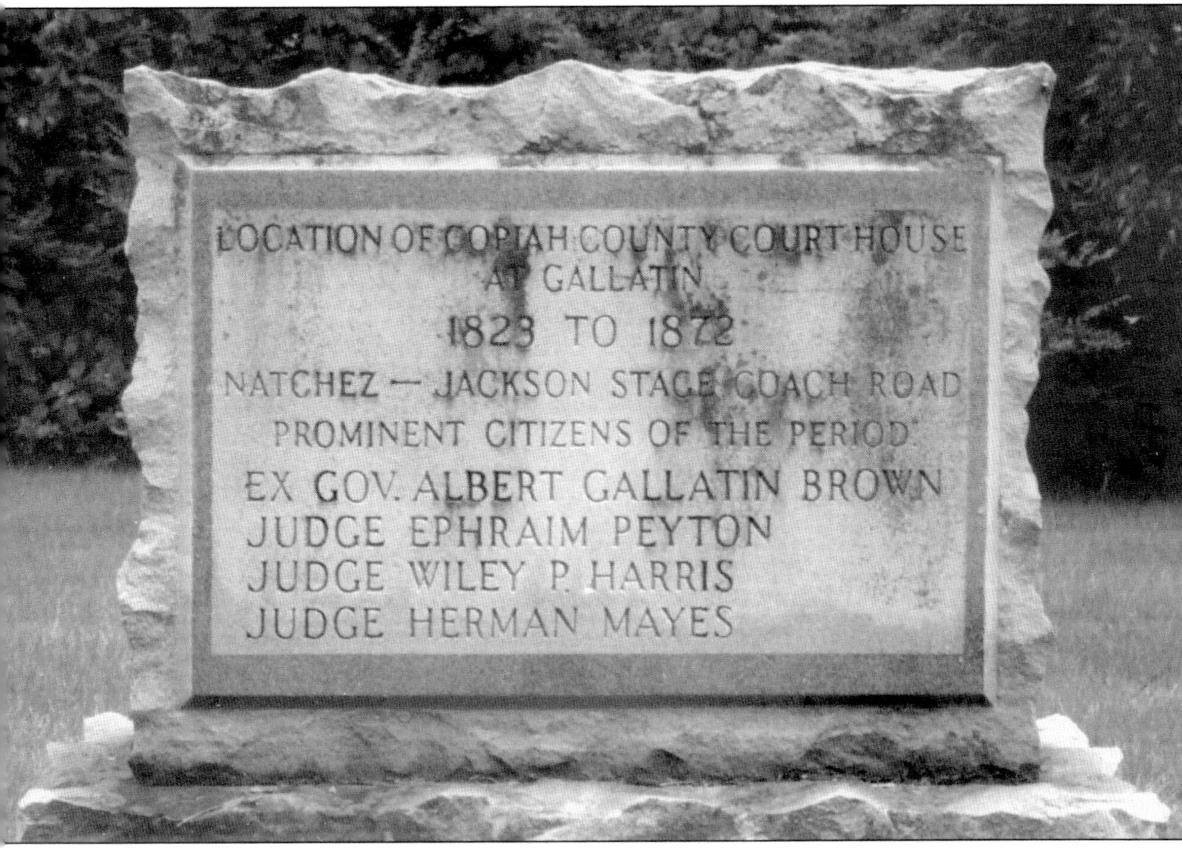

Gallatin, located four miles west of Hazlehurst, was settled in 1819 by two lawyers who were also brothers-in-law named Walker and Saunders from Gallatin, Tennessee. The land was very fertile, and the principal crop was cotton. Other settlers soon came, and in 1829, the legislature incorporated the town. Gallatin soon became the county seat. The town thrived for many years but began to decline when Hazlehurst was established in 1865 along the New Orleans, Jackson, and Great Northern Railroad. The more Hazlehurst flourished, the more Gallatin declined. Gallatin's charter was revoked in 1862, and in April 1872, the legislature ordered the county board of supervisors to hold an election to decide if the county seat should be moved from Gallatin to Hazlehurst. A majority voted for the change, and the courthouse was torn down and reassembled in Hazlehurst, the present county seat. Gallatin continued to decline. This marker is the only reminder of the town. (Courtesy of CCHGS.)

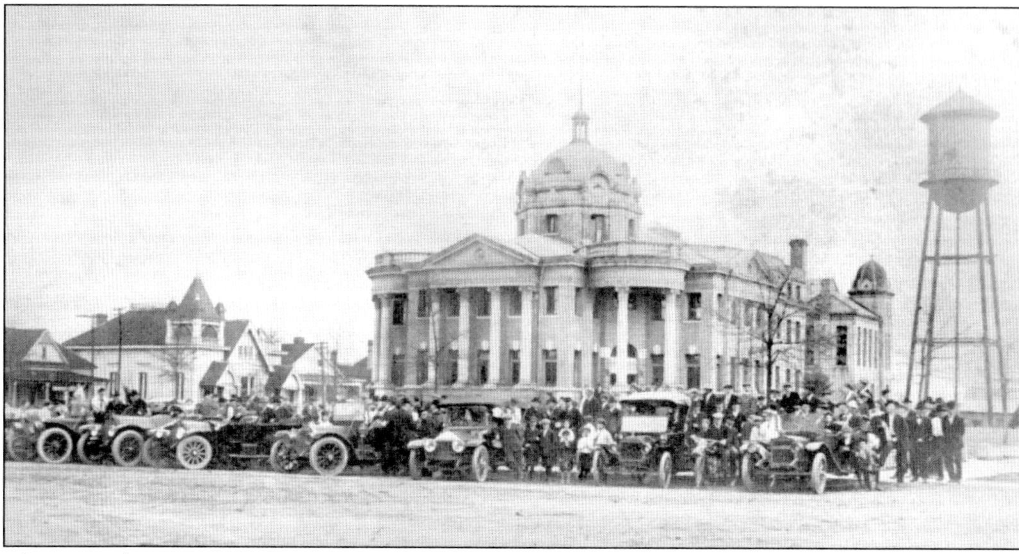

The Copiah County Board of Supervisors on January 7, 1902, approved a construction bid submitted by G. T. Hallas and Company for $44,603 to build a new courthouse. The original courthouse had been moved from Gallatin but was said to be in poor condition. The structure was completed in 1903. (Courtesy of George W. Covington Memorial Library.)

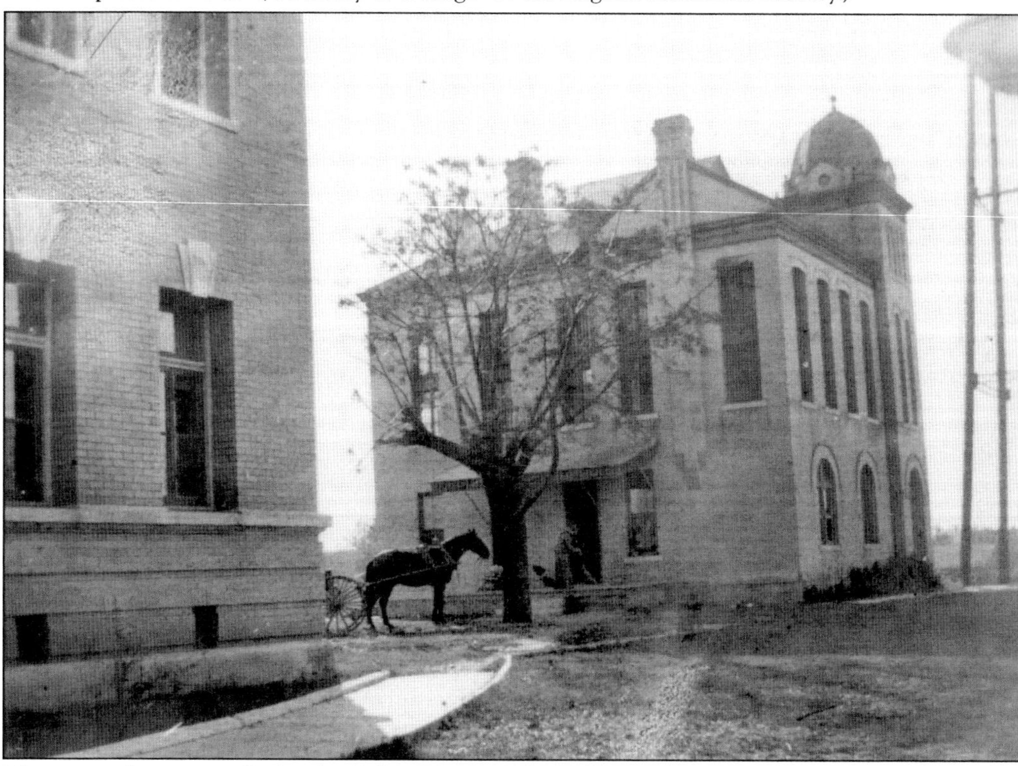

The original structure had a third-floor dome and clock, which were removed in 1934 when the dome began to leak. A stained-glass window in the dome illuminated the courthouse; the window is now sealed from view. Two wings were added in 1950. This is the jail, which was behind the courthouse and was torn down in 1981. (Courtesy of George W. Covington Memorial Library.)

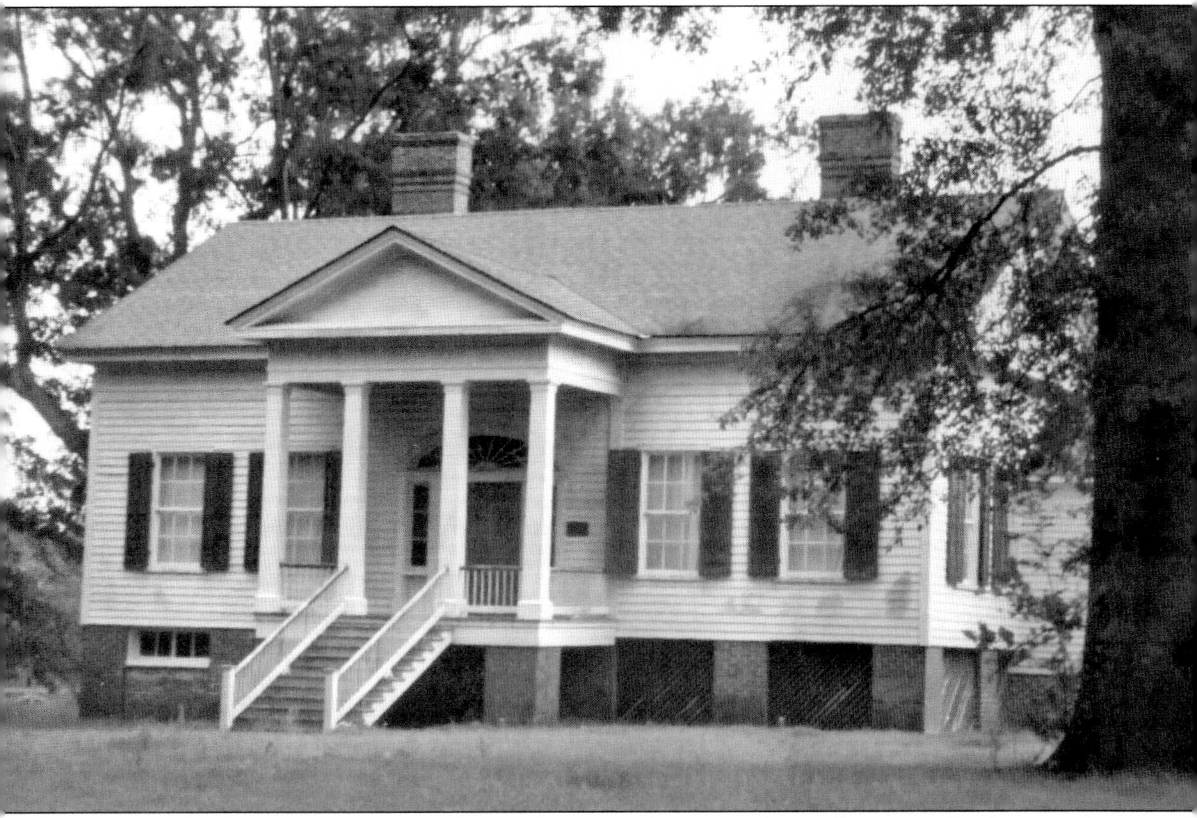

The County Line community is on the Hinds–Copiah County line. The Mims family owned the Line Store, located two miles north of County Line Baptist Church. With the post office located in the store, it became a stopping point for a stagecoach line that ran from Gallatin to Jackson and was operated by Capt. W. D. Terry. A mile from the store going east was a home built by William H. Didlake, an architect from Virginia. Cherry Grove, as it is known, dates to 1837. Most of the house was built by William, his nephew Jim, and a slave named Dick. They made the brick, the hand-planed boards, and the hand-carved windows and doors. It also features a hand-carved cherry circular stairway and a fan-shaped transom over the front door, the partitions of which are hand-carved with fitted glass. William died in 1869 and was buried in the cherry grove on the grounds of the plantation between two trees he had planted when he first moved to Mississippi. (Courtesy of CCHGS.)

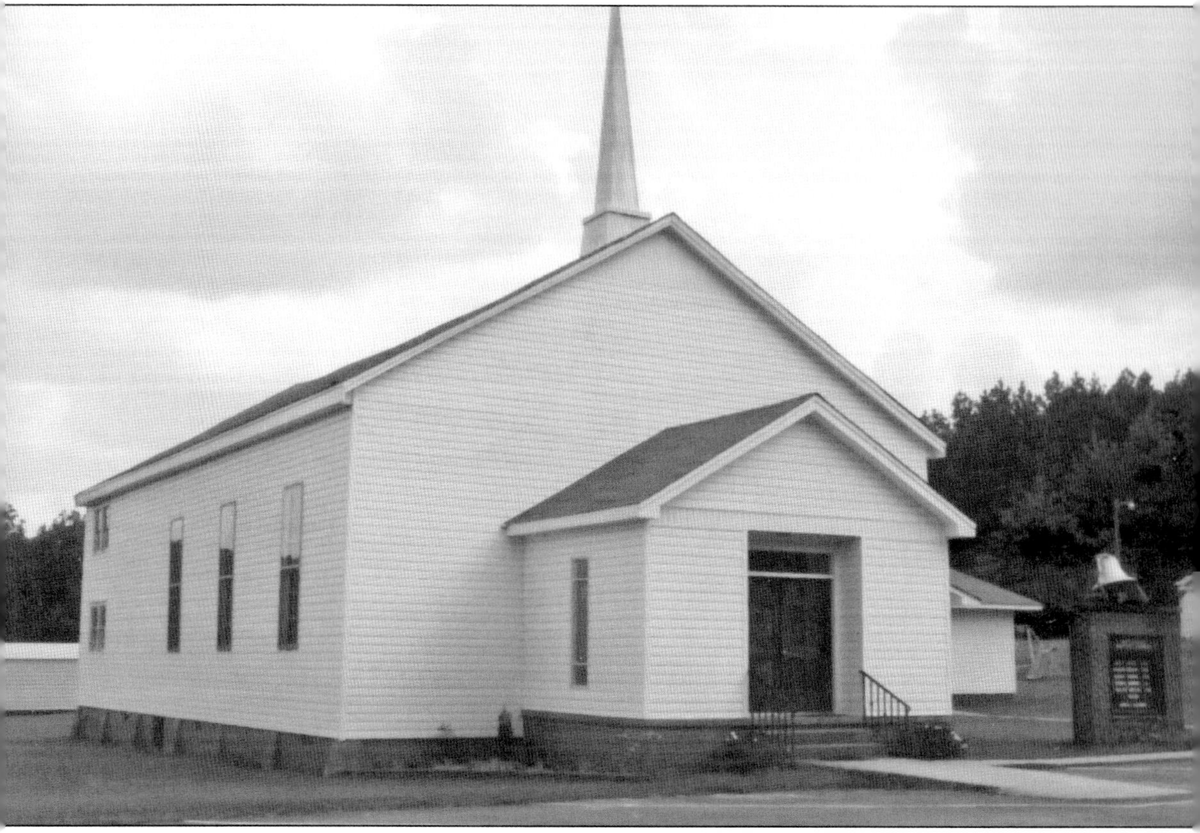

Gatesville was formed in 1907, when the railroad came through. Less than one mile west was the Beech Grove community. The railroad bought the right-of-way from D. W. Gates, for whom Gatesville was named, and paid him $15 to $50 per acre for it. Gates owned all the land that became Gatesville. The post office was in a store owned by G. L. Manning. The first church, known as Mount Pleasant Church, was Methodist and was located in Beech Grove. The church was later moved from the area. The second church, known as Pilgrims Rest Baptist Church was also in Beech Grove. This church, too, was later moved to another area. A large shipping shed was operated by Gatesville Produce Company, and Mrs. V. Grantham ran a boardinghouse across the street. L. Carmichael owned a large grist and feed mill and Carmichael's Grocery. Gatesville Gravel Company at one time owned a 300-acre gravel pit in the area. Pictured is Gatesville Baptist Church, which organized in 1917. (Courtesy of CCHGS.)

William Burt, born January 30, 1797, was an orphan in Georgia. When he discovered he was a Burt and might have a sister, he came to Mississippi to find her. He eventually settled in Copiah County in the Harmony Community. When the county seat was established at Gallatin, it is believed he was the first citizen to pay taxes in the county. Burt died May 19, 1900. William Burt's granddaughter, Gertrude, always said she was going to live longer that her grandfather—and she did. When Gertrude Burt Taylor died April 14, 1993, she was 104 years, 8 months, and 17 days old. She is seen holding a picture of her grandfather. (Courtesy of Ted Dear.)

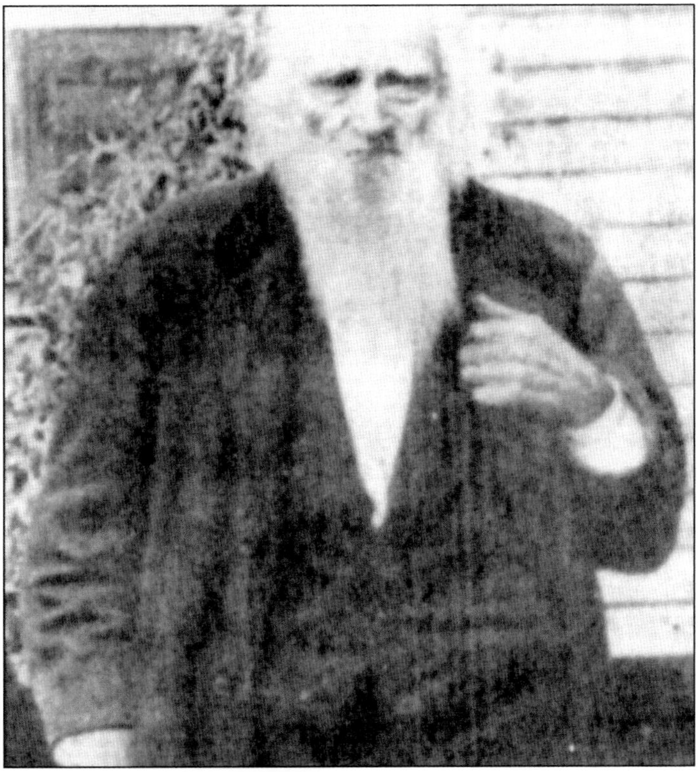

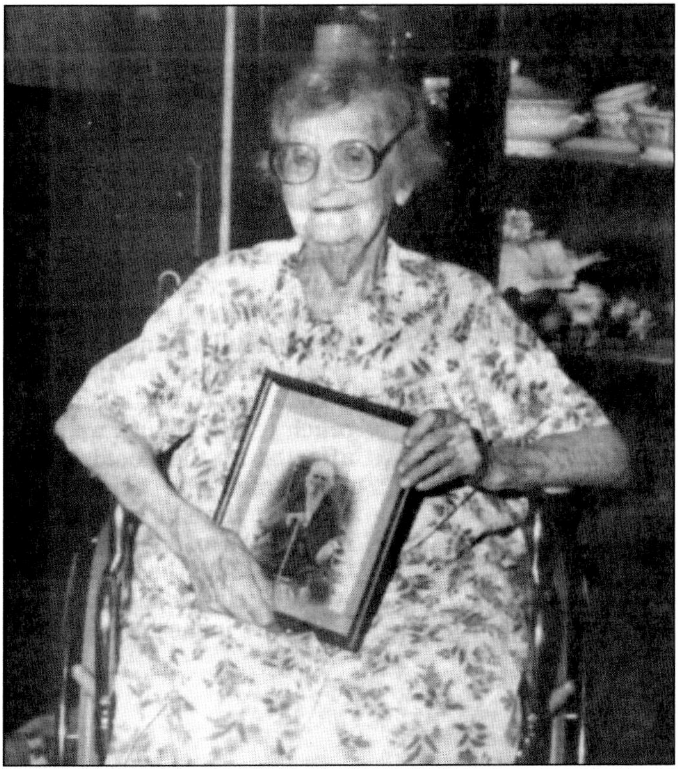

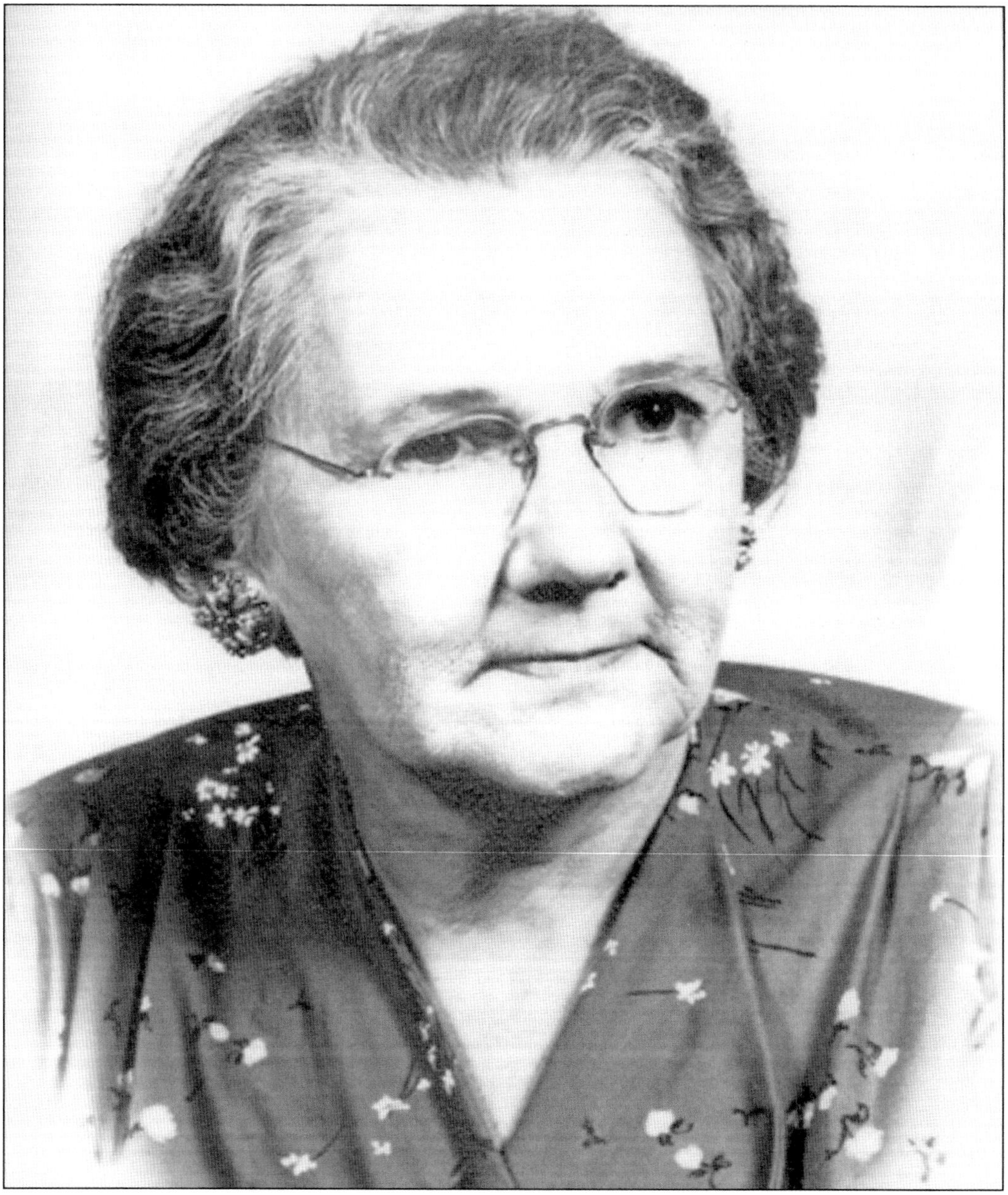

M. A. Howard was the last postmistress of Hopewell. In 1850, settlers from the Carolinas settled about 10 miles east of Crystal Springs, close to the Pearl River. Albert Gates owned the first store and named the settlement Ruby, after his daughter. In 1840, there was a sawmill, owned by Billie Sandifer. Other first settlers were named Roberts, Riley, Burt, and Sojourner. The first post office was established in 1876 and was located in a corner of Albert Gates's store. The first school was a very small structure, and the first professor was Rev. Martin W. Trawick, a Presbyterian minister. In the early 1900s, the railroad came through one mile east of the settlement, and a depot was built in 1909. The townsfolk soon migrated toward the railroad and established a new town, named Hopewell by W. T. Sandifer, Daniel Young, and a Mr. Barron. It is not known how they came up with this name. The first church to be established was the Baptist church, and soon thereafter, a Methodist church was built. (Courtesy of Rita Howard Sullivan.)

Ashley was settled by Elihu Ashley who was born November 5, 1825, to George S. Sanders and Susanah Dickens. He married Ann Terry, and they had six children by the time she died at age 27 in 1859. In 1862, he married Delilah Jones Beck, and they had three children. Pictured are Elihu and three of his children, Emma (left), Martha (center), and Elizabeth, in 1855. (From scrapbook of Thelma Ashley Litton, courtesy of Martha Ashley Girling.)

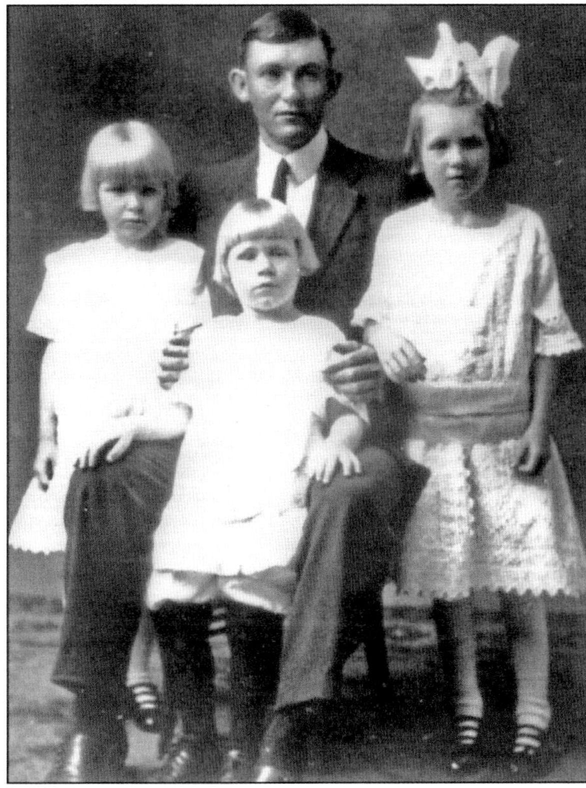

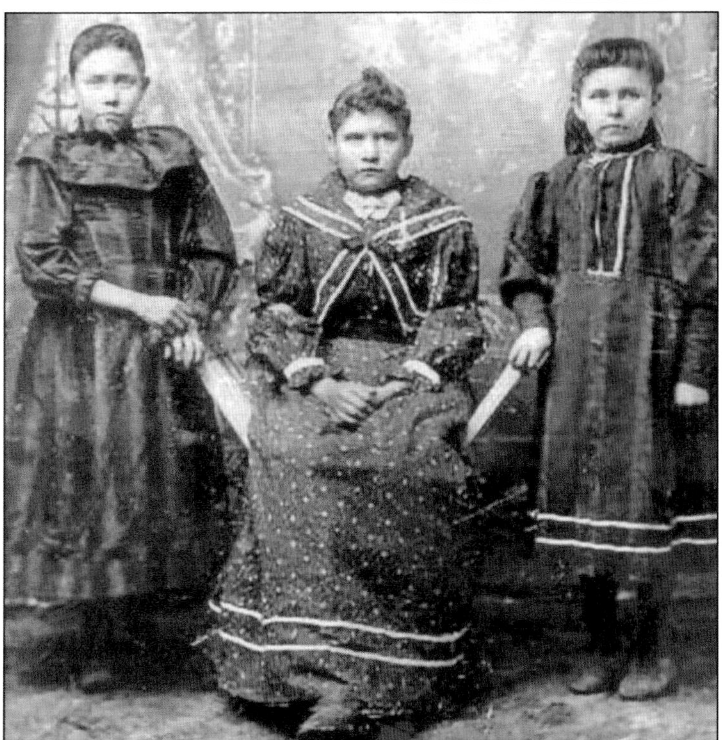

Elihu Ashley farmed and owned a chair shop. He would take the chairs to Wesson, 17 miles away. He also made caskets and horseshoes. Pictured are Elihu's second wife, Delilah (center), and her two sisters Martha (right) and Susanna (left). Their parents were Thomas P. and Susanna Jones. (From scrapbook of Thelma Ashley Litton, courtesy of Martha Ashley Girling.)

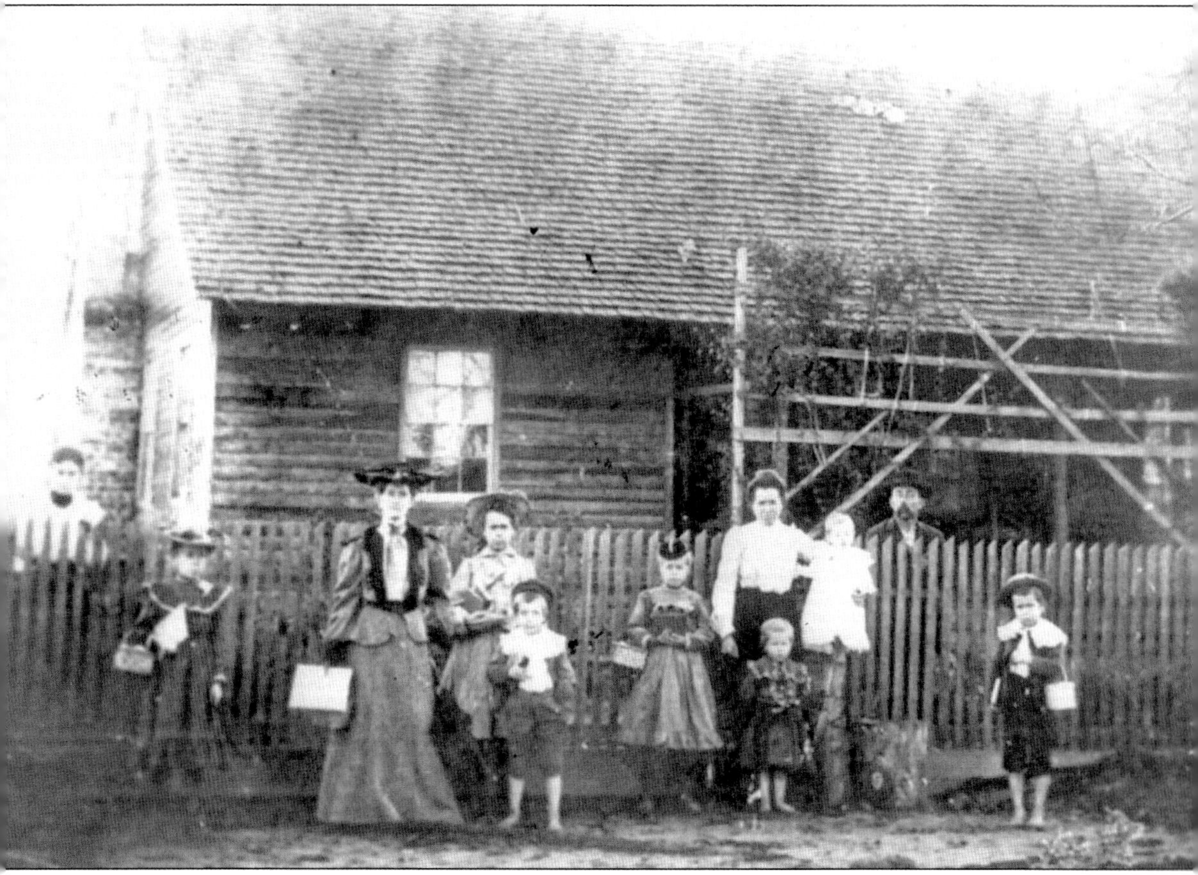

Elihu's daughter-in-law, Permelia, was the first buried in the Ashley cemetery. A bad winter in 1877 prevented her from being buried anywhere but near the home, so Elihu donated some land on a hill for her to be buried. This is the same place he was buried when he died on February 28, 1900. Elihu also established the Ashley School in 1886. It lasted until it consolidated with the Union School. It is not known where Elihu received his education, but it is said he had beautiful handwriting and was knowledgeable of legal affairs. He wrote his own will and his father George's petition to probate. The youngest of Elihu's children was David G., who is pictured here (on the right behind the fence) with his family in front of his home in 1904. The town of Ashley still exists, though not many residents reside there. (From scrapbook of Thelma Ashley Litton, courtesy of Martha Ashley Girling.)

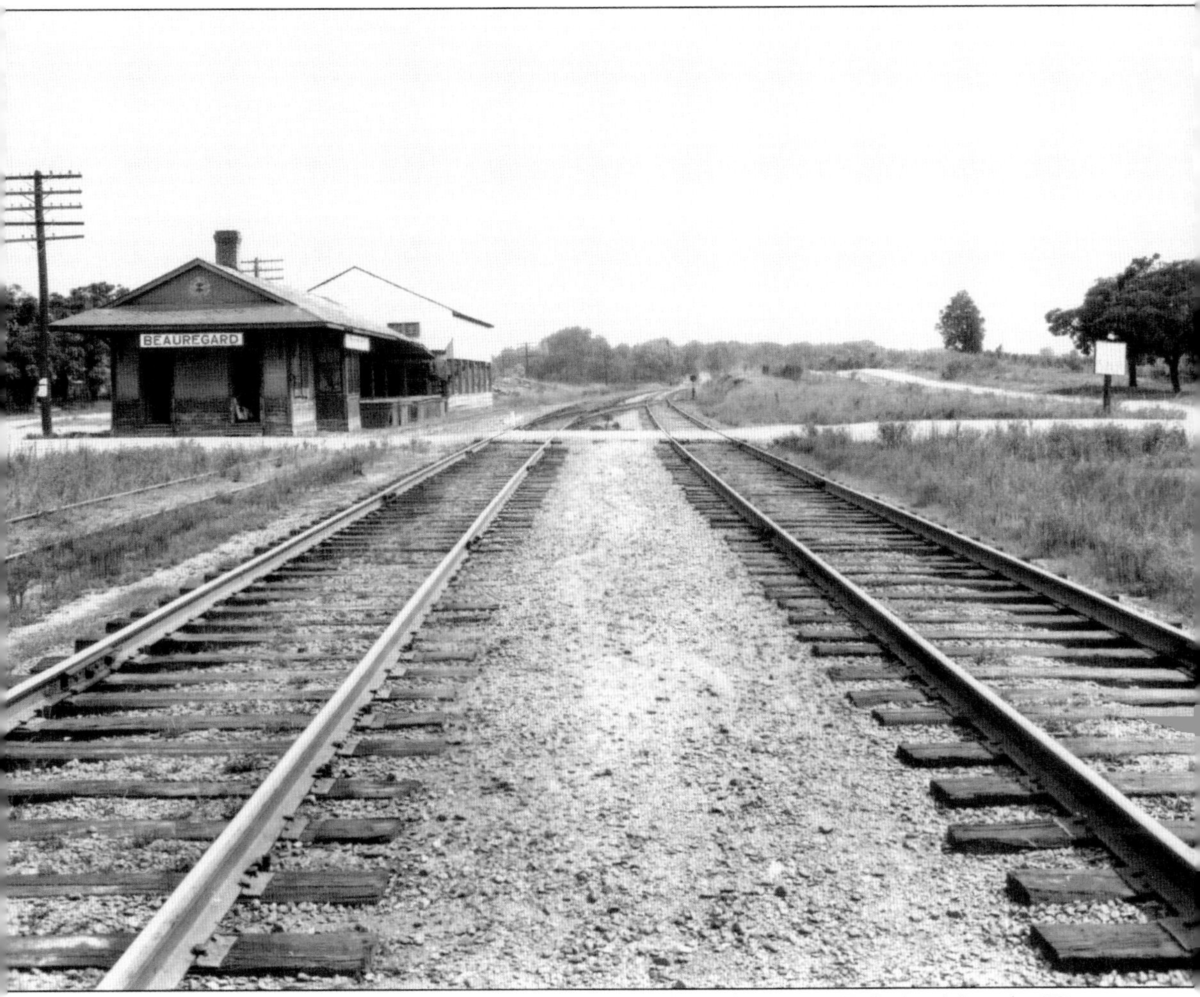

This depot was in Beauregard. In the 1850s, Beauregard was known as Bahala. After the War Between the States, the name was changed to honor P. G. T. Beauregard, one of the great Confederate generals. The town became the largest center for buying cotton between Memphis and New Orleans. By the 1860s, there were five stores, a post office, and a Methodist church. Soon a Baptist church followed, and a school was built as well. The Wesson Mills were close by, and this kept the saloons quite busy. The town was said to have more saloons than any other town of its size in the state. Some believed that is why a tornado in April 1883 wiped out most of the town except for three houses. Dr. Elias Alford Rowan's spared house was used as a hospital. It was three stories tall and had 23 rooms and 11 porches. When built two years prior, he had planned to use it as a hospital. That plan soon came to fruition. (Courtesy of Mississippi Department of Archives and History [MDAH].)

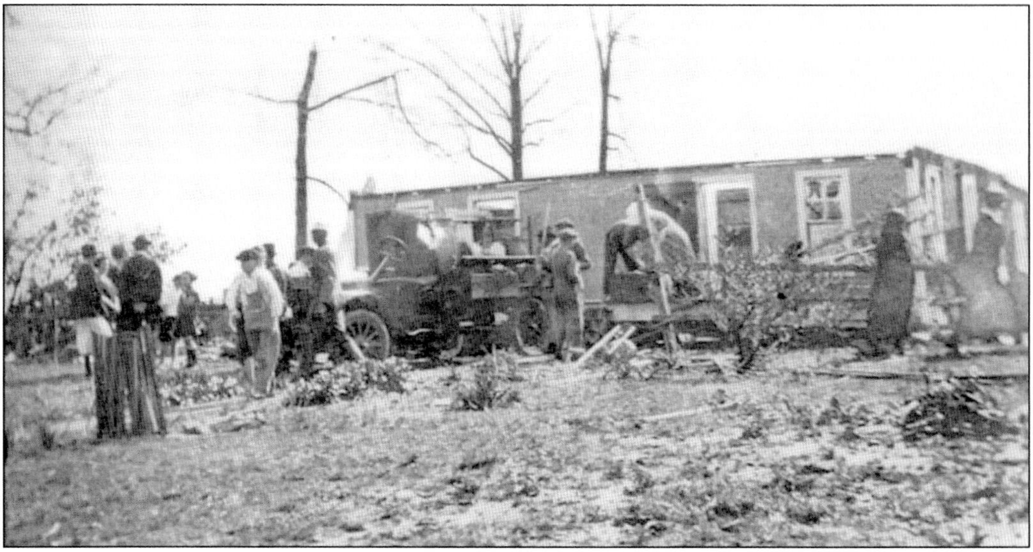

According to the *Monthly Weather Review* of March 1908, on January 31, 1908, a tornado "of remarkable energy and duration" formed in the eastern part of Jefferson County, Mississippi, and made its way in an easterly direction across Copiah County and into central Simpson County. The heaviest losses occurred at Martinsville. The tornado crossed the railroad a half-mile north of the depot. "Twelve families were left homeless, and it was in this place that 6 of the 7 persons killed met death." It continued its course in a nearly straight line, passing north of Ashley and crossing the Pearl River at Georgetown. Sixteen people were injured at Georgetown. The tornado was reportedly the worst in the area since the Beauregard tornado of 1883. (From scrapbook of Thelma Ashley Litton, courtesy of Martha Ashley Girling.)

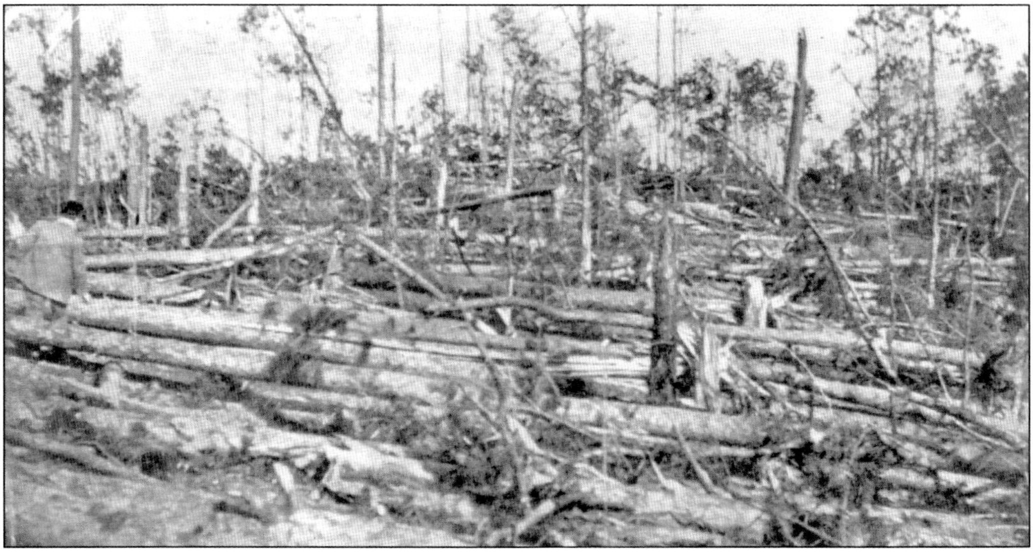

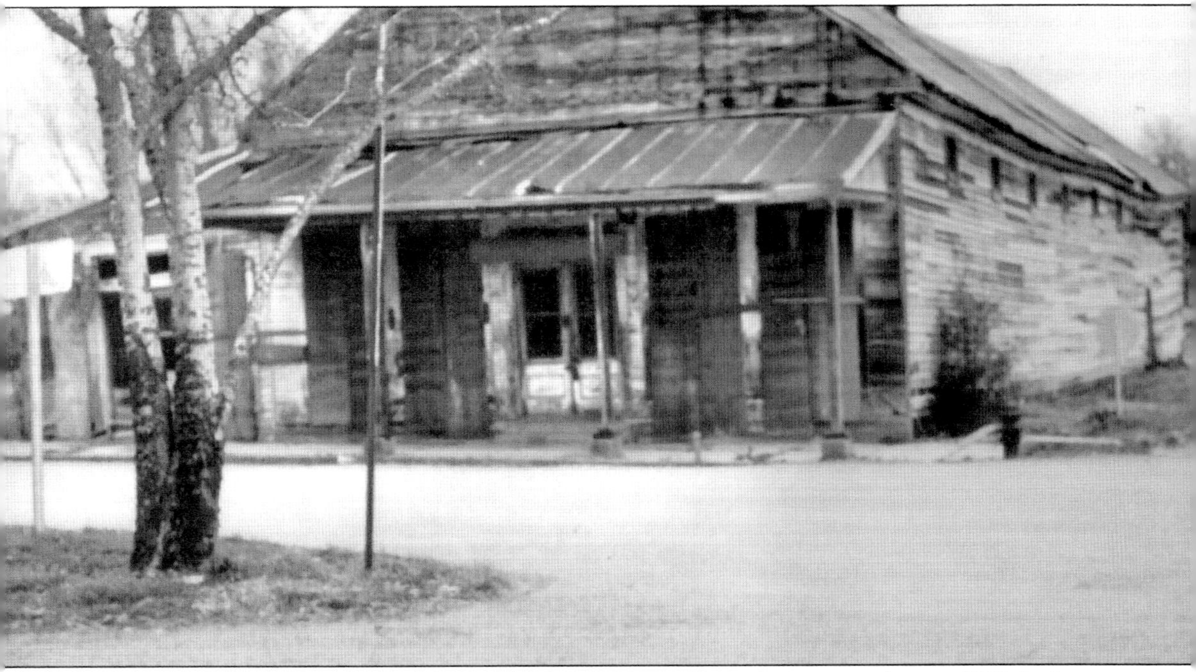

This photograph of Georgetown Mercantile Company in Georgetown was taken in 1971, before the structure was torn down. It is thought to be the Brown Store referred to in early census records. It was in business from around 1840 until 1953. Originally it was located on the Pearl River some two miles from this location, but when the Gulf, Mobile, and Ohio Railroad built a rail line through Georgetown, everything moved to the railroad. The men contracted to move the building used logs as rollers and oxen to pull it as they moved it. It is said they went bankrupt in the process of moving it, and another man had to finish the job. Georgetown was one of the first settlements in the county. George Briley had a ferryboat that crossed the turbulent Pearl River. In 1818, Dr. Phil Catchings bought acreage from Arthur Woods and established a plantation. In 1908, the New Orleans, Jackson, and Great Northern Railroad came through, and in 1909, the city incorporated. (Courtesy of Patrick Roper.)

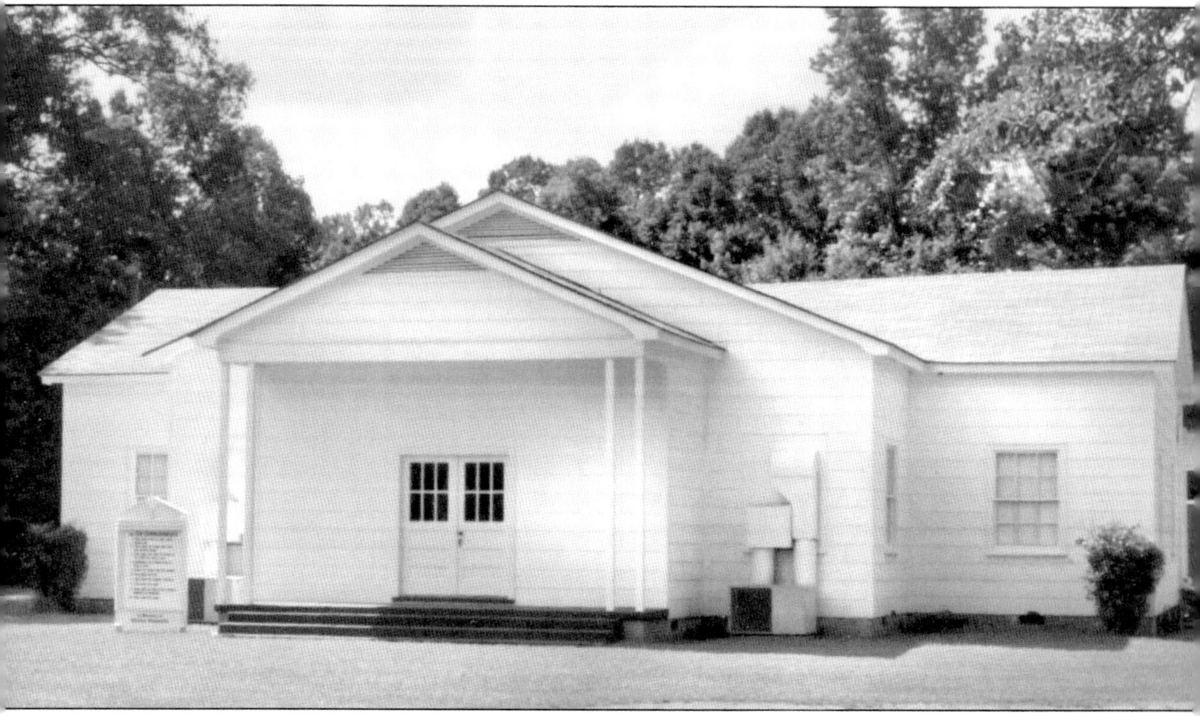

Rockport, established in 1849 and located on the Copiah County side of the Pearl River across from Bridgeport on the Simpson County side, was a railroad flag stop. West of the railroad tracks and north of the street were the post office, the drugstore, Sea Berry's barbershop, and Roy Berry's home (still standing). South of the street was the S. K. Armstrong Store, and behind the store was the Rockport Hotel, now a home owned by Ruby Clyburn. East of the old railroad tracks was M. L. Ashley, Bascom Beasley Estate Store, and H. J. Jones Store, and in the curve was the W. D. Fleming Store, later known as Paul Little's Store. By 1937, the only commercial buildings left were one small store, a gasoline station, and the post office. This is Galilee Baptist Church, which organized in 1825 in Rockport. (Courtesy of CCHGS.)

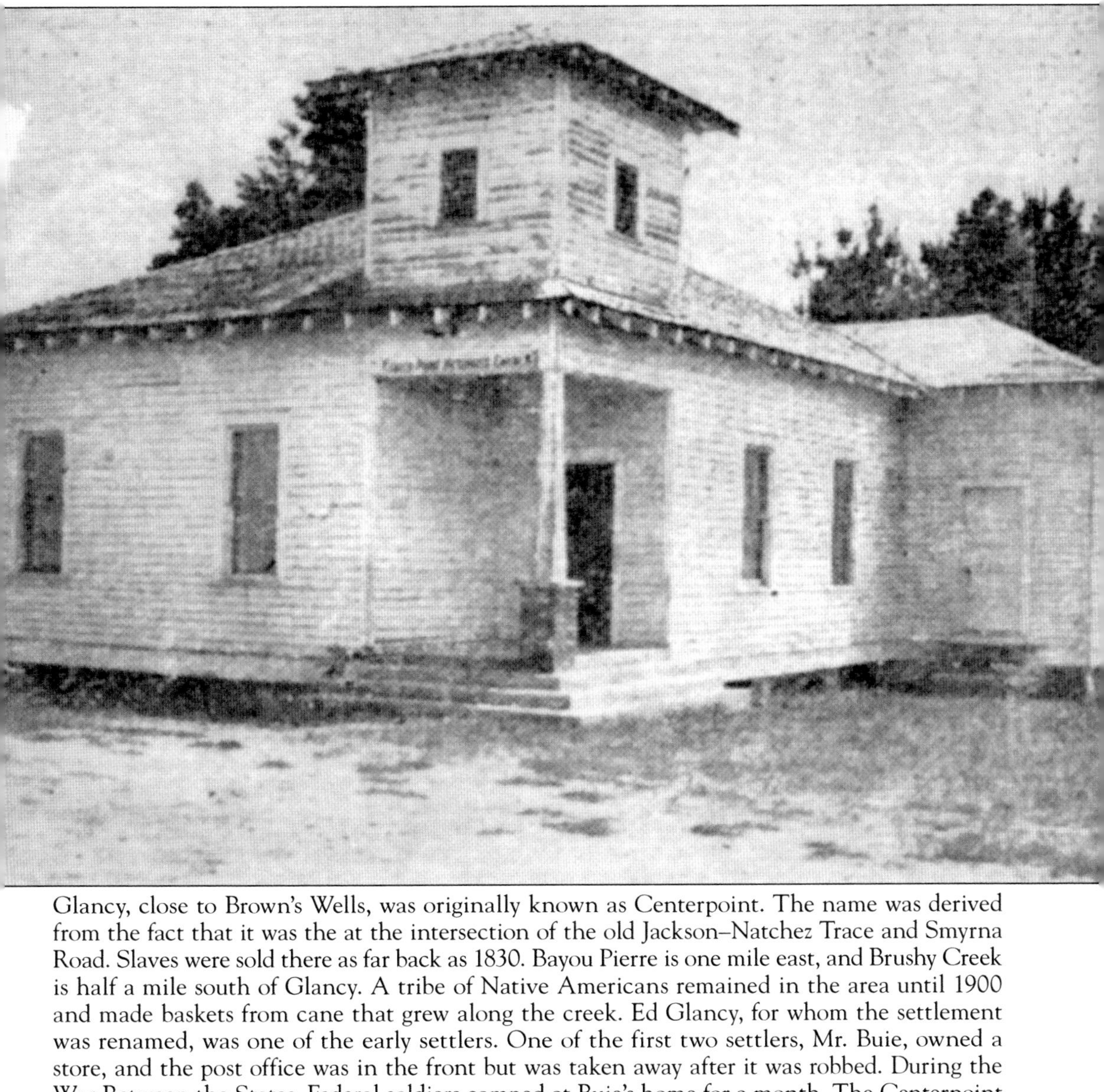

Glancy, close to Brown's Wells, was originally known as Centerpoint. The name was derived from the fact that it was the at the intersection of the old Jackson–Natchez Trace and Smyrna Road. Slaves were sold there as far back as 1830. Bayou Pierre is one mile east, and Brushy Creek is half a mile south of Glancy. A tribe of Native Americans remained in the area until 1900 and made baskets from cane that grew along the creek. Ed Glancy, for whom the settlement was renamed, was one of the early settlers. One of the first two settlers, Mr. Buie, owned a store, and the post office was in the front but was taken away after it was robbed. During the War Between the States, Federal soldiers camped at Buie's home for a month. The Centerpoint Gin and Manufacturing Company operated for several years, making boxes. They eventually consolidated with Southern Package Company. The Centerpoint Methodist Church, pictured, was the first church in the area; it was organized around 1910 and rebuilt in 1924. (Courtesy of George W. Covington Memorial Library.)

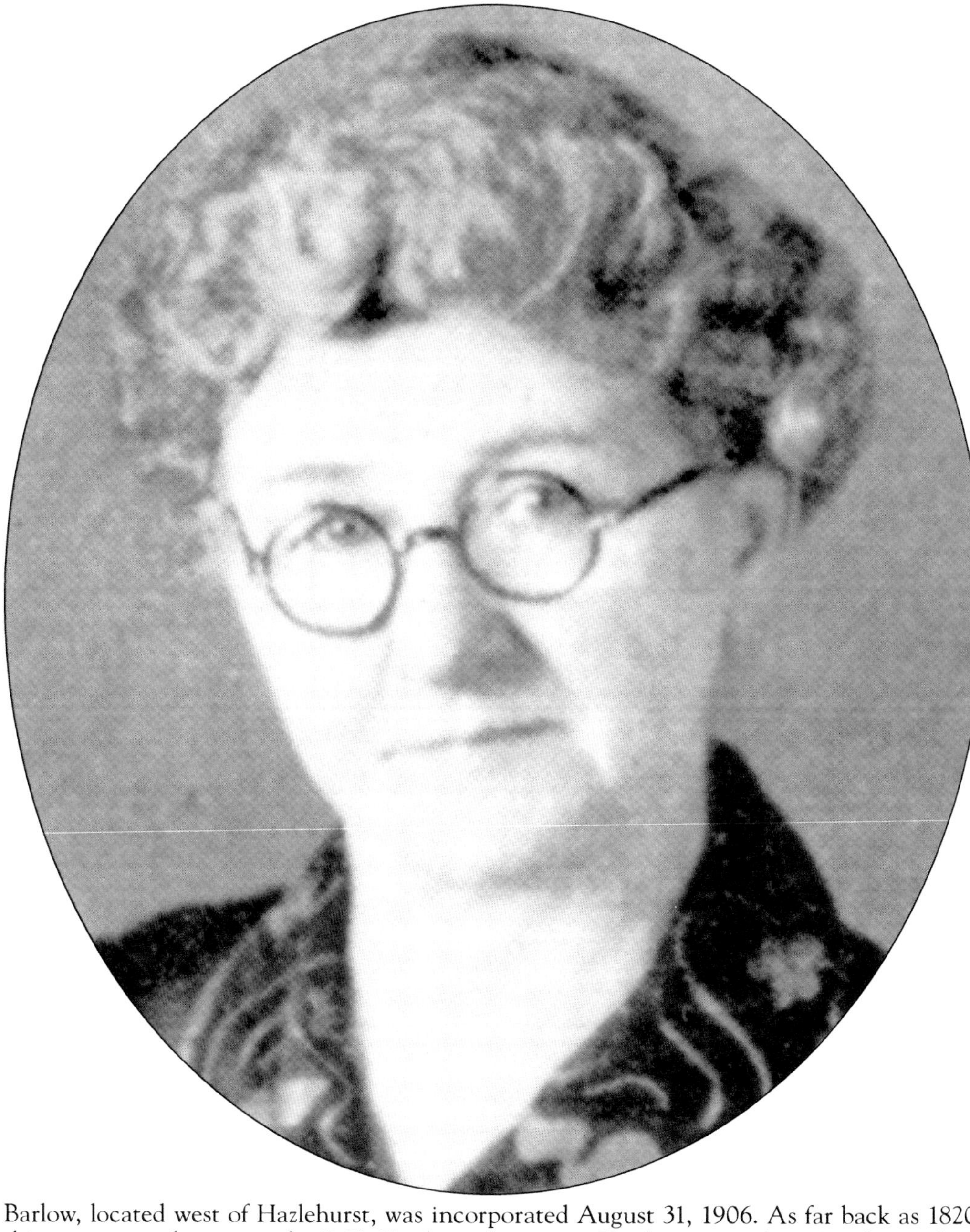

Barlow, located west of Hazlehurst, was incorporated August 31, 1906. As far back as 1820, this section was known as the S. K. Hawkins plantation. Hawkins came from South Carolina, purchased land, and built a beautiful two-story home of hand-made brick. In the early 1890s, the home was foreclosed on, and it was subsequently purchased by Harmon Howard Barlow. Barlow had not been married to Kate Downer long when he bought the property. He was a medical doctor, and Kate served as a dietician and matron at Copiah-Lincoln Agricultural High School until her retirement. She is pictured here in the 1926 Copiah-Lincoln annual. Barlow had a post office, a school, and an oil mill for around 10 years in the early 1900s. Sadly the town eventually declined into nothing, just like many other small towns in the county. (Courtesy of Evelyn W. Oswalt Library.)

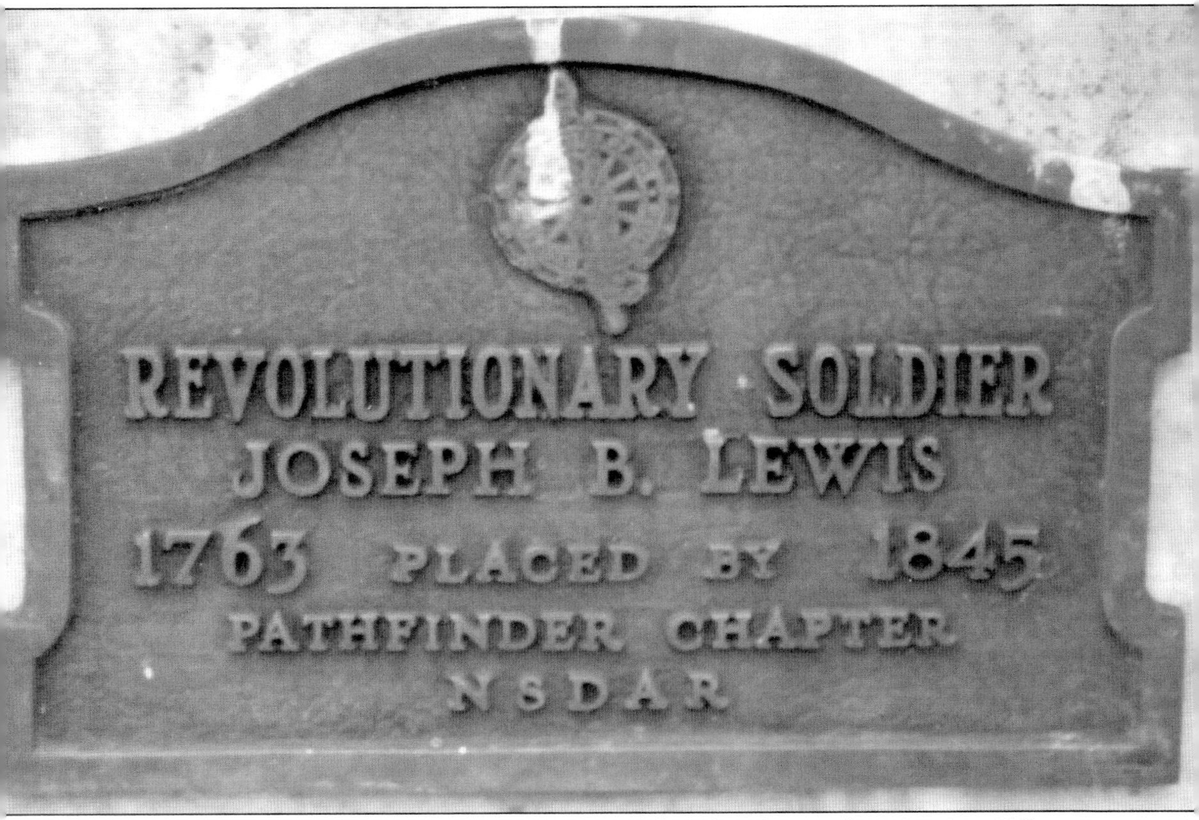

In 1859, Warren R. Dent, for whom Dentville is named, bought 650 acres from Stephen Tillman. In the old days, there was a high bluff above the Bayou Pierre, two miles long, and on it stood a tall pine tree, taller than any other. The Native Americans named it Pine Bluff. When time came to name the post office, another post office already existed by the name of Pine Bluff. Since Warren Dent had the largest plantation in the area, the decision was made to name it Dentville around 1889. Dent owned the first store and was the first postmaster. The first school, named Union Ridge Cabin, was a one-room facility with one teacher and was located one mile north on Bayou Pierre. Joseph B. Lewis, a revolutionary soldier, is buried at Pine Bluff Cemetery. His grave was marked by the Pathfinder Chapter of the Daughters of the American Revolution. (Courtesy of CCHGS.)

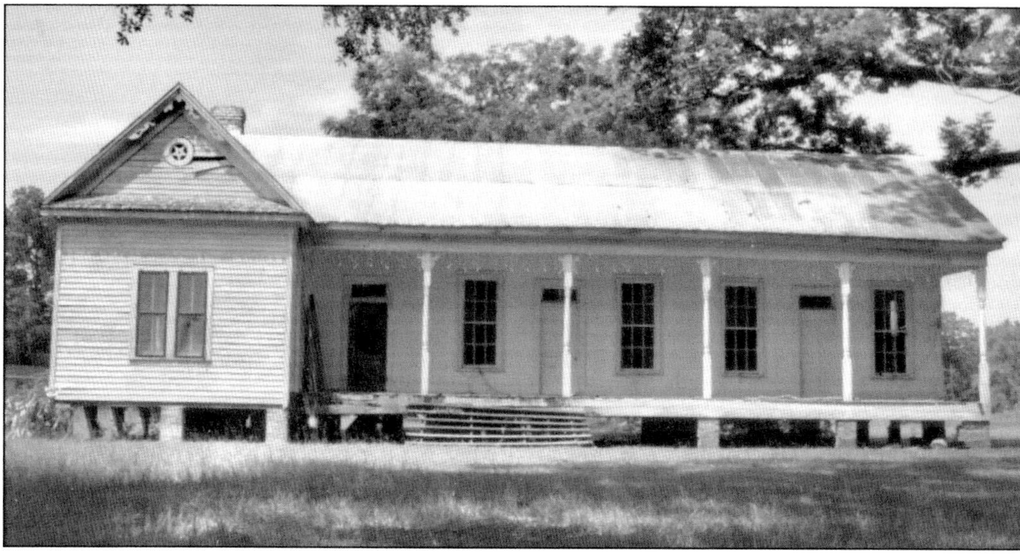

Carpenter was named for J. N. Carpenter, president of the Natchez, Jackson, and Columbia Railroad in 1883. Early settlers were the Ritches, Craigs, Lloyds, and Fulfams. The first school was built on the Craig plantation. William L. Lloyd was the first railroad agent and postmaster. This was his home built in the 1800s. (Courtesy of CCHGS.)

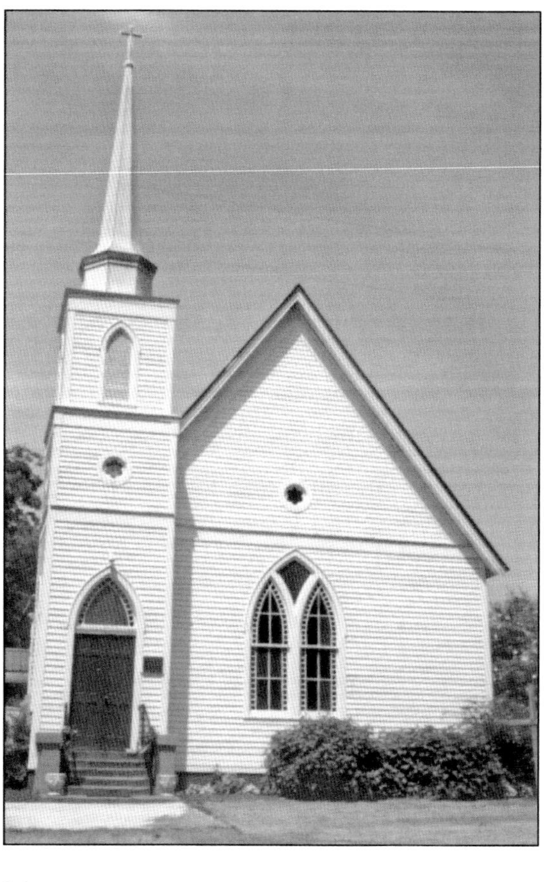

W. A. Price helped establish the first church in Carpenter in 1901. Pictured is the Carpenter Methodist Church, which is on the National Register. The architecture reflects the late Federal style, which was prevalent which was prevalent at the start of the 20th century. The Baptist church, built in 1903, burned and was not rebuilt. The depot was torn down in the 1970s. Little remains of the town. (Courtesy of CCHGS.)

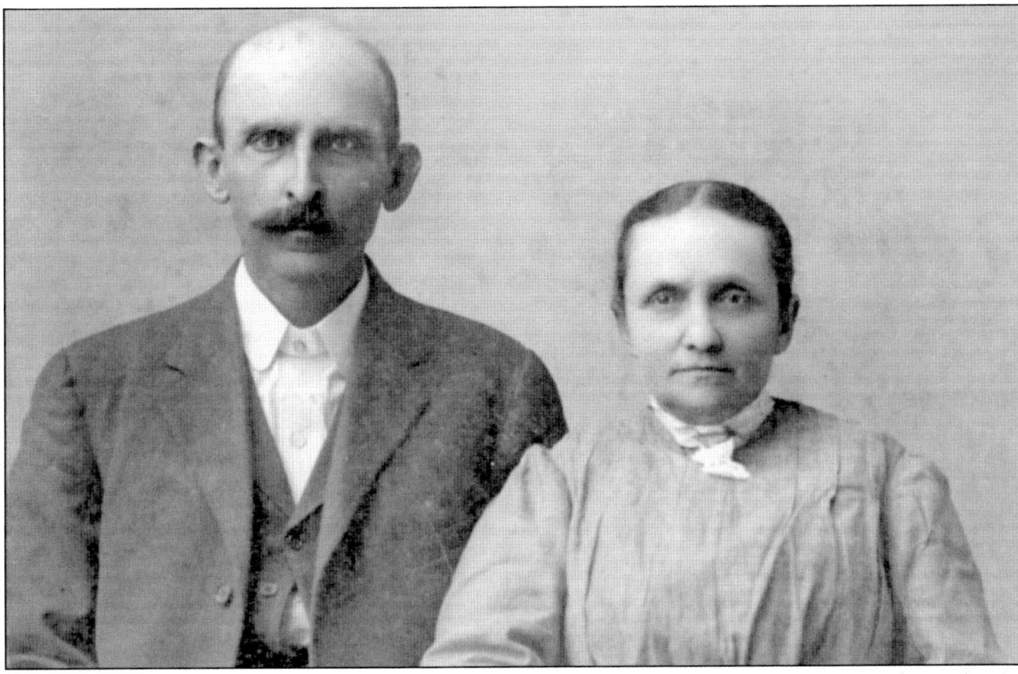

John Riley Taylor Sr., born March 28, 1824, in Alabama, arrived in Copiah County in the mid-1830s with his mother, Mary M.; stepfather, John Lee; and half-brother, Richard. John Lee purchased land in Copiah County on November 10, 1837. The Taylors were married January 6, 1847, in Rankin County, and briefly lived in Simpson County before settling in the New Zion community in Copiah County. They reared eight children: Richard Franklin, William Zackary, John Riley Jr., Robert Cornelius, Margaret Saphoronia, Mary Elizabeth Ann, Nancy Amanda, and Lourina Isabel. Above is one of John Riley Taylor Sr.'s sons, John Riley Jr., and wife, Sarah. Below is one of Riley Jr.'s sons, Riley H. Taylor and his wife, May. (Courtesy of Mary Taylor Guy.)

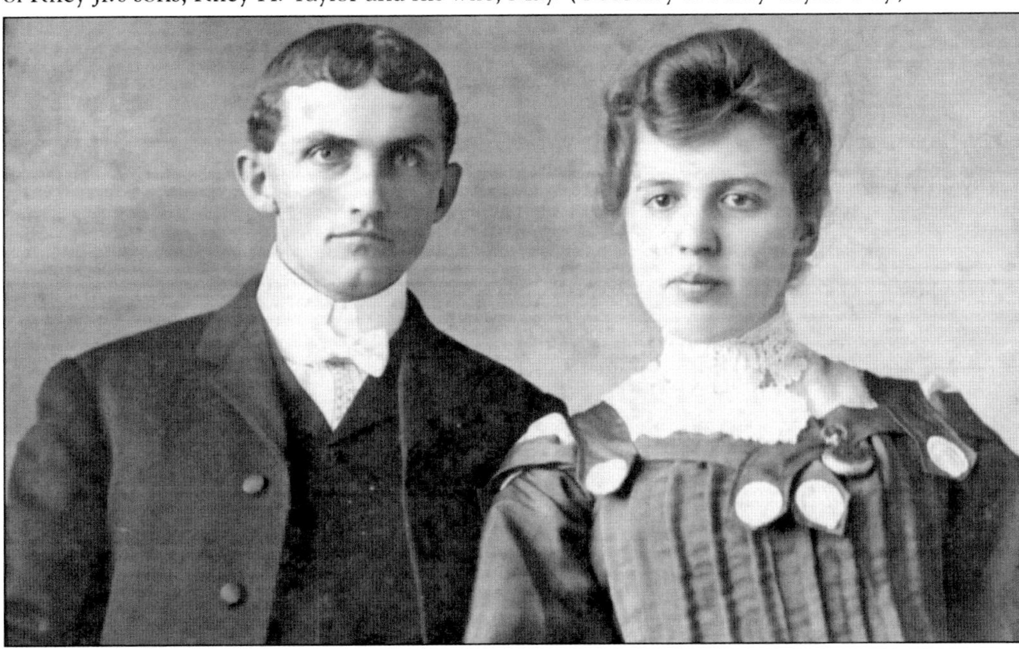

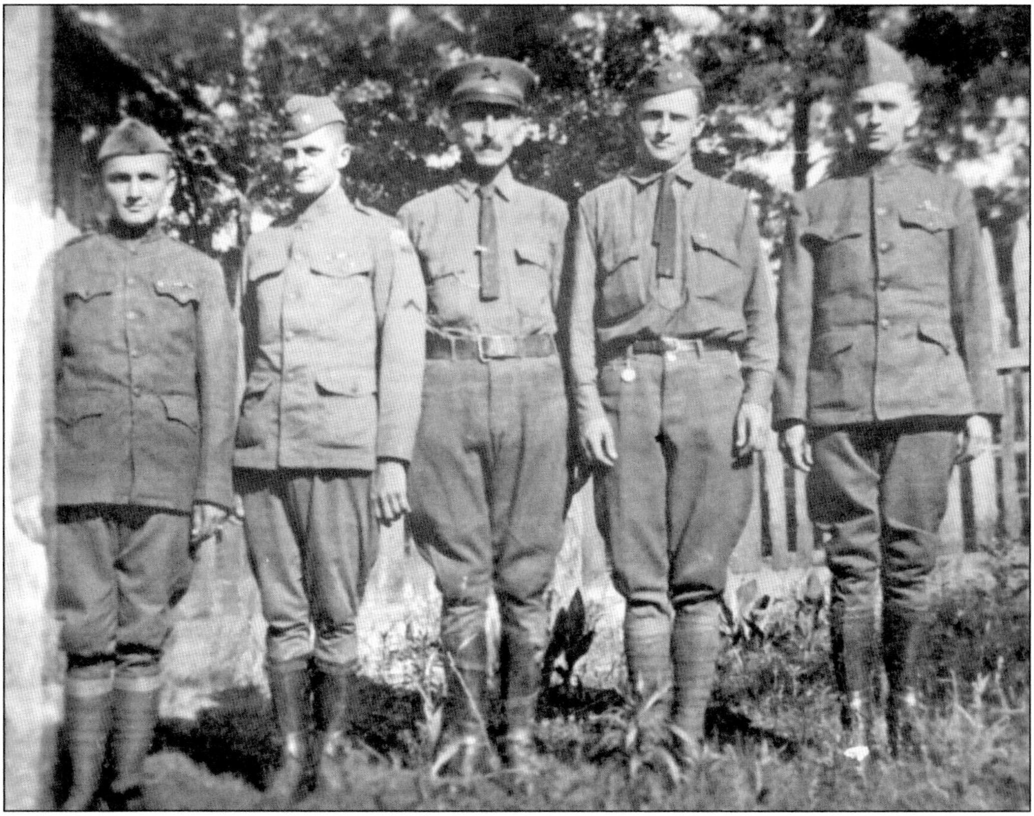

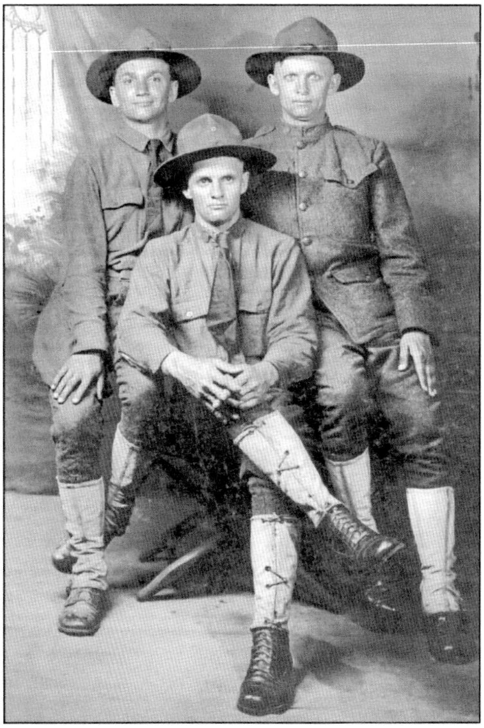

John Riley Taylor Jr., the third son of John Riley Taylor Sr., was born on April 24, 1857, and married Sarah Malissie Thornton on September 27, 1877. They produced 16 children—10 sons and 6 daughters—all of whom survived to maturity. The five younger sons all served in the U.S. Army during World War I, making the family a five-star family. Benjamin Theodore was the first to die, as the result of influenza contracted during the epidemic of 1918. Pictured above are four of the sons with their father, John Riley Taylor Jr. (center, wearing Benjamin Theodore's uniform). The sons are, from left to right, John Vernon, Robert Joseph, Frank Cecil, and James Monroe. Pictured left are Frank, Monroe, and Joe in their World War I uniforms. (Courtesy of Mary Taylor Guy.)

Two

When the Railroad Came

The construction of railroads was the top priority throughout the South in the 1850s. Organized in 1852, the New Orleans, Jackson, and Great Northern (NOJ&GN) Railroad was completed in Copiah County on March 31, 1858. This had a significant impact on the development of the county. Three lines eventually came through the county. The Natchez, Jackson, and Columbus came through in 1882, and the New Orleans Great Northern was completed in 1909. The Illinois Central Railroad purchased the assets of the NOJ&GN in 1877, merging that line with the Mississippi Central to form the Chicago, St. Louis, and New Orleans Railroad. It was controlled by the Illinois Central and subsequently consolidated into that system in 1882. Although three lines ran through Copiah County, only the NOJ&GN (now Illinois Central) line has not been abandoned. Depots were built on the NOJ&GN line at Crystal Springs, Hazlehurst, Beauregard, and Wesson. The only remaining depot is in Hazlehurst and has been designated a historic structure.

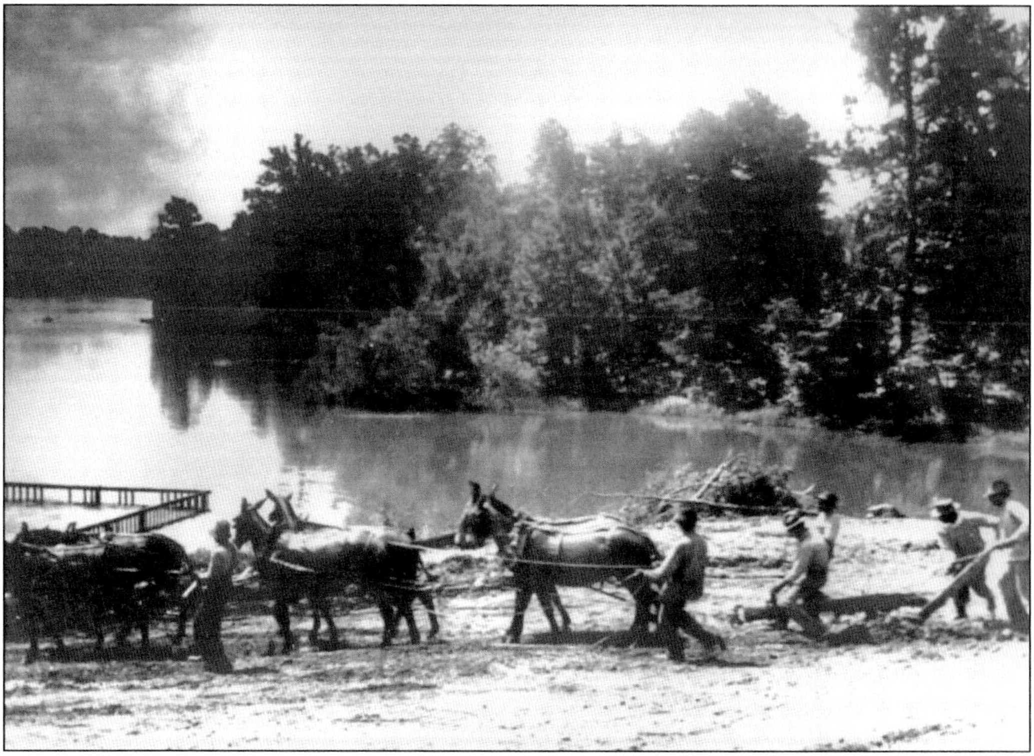

The railroad needed water for its steam engines, so the small creek that meandered through the Hennington Campgrounds was used to build Lake Chautauqua. Capt. Frederick Y. Dabney designed the lake and supervised the construction, which began in 1895 and was completed in 1897. The lake was dug with four mule plows and two mule team slips to move the dirt. A diesel pump was used to carry water to steam locomotives that stopped in Crystal Springs to load locally grown produce for shipment throughout the United States. A wooden pipe carried the water from the lake east to an elevated tank at the side of the train tracks in downtown Crystal Springs. (Courtesy of Tomato Museum.)

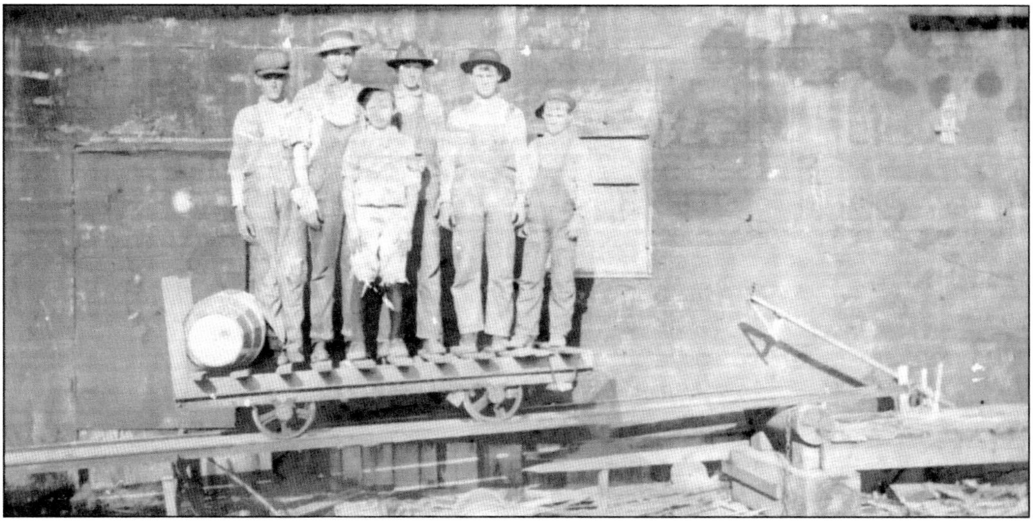

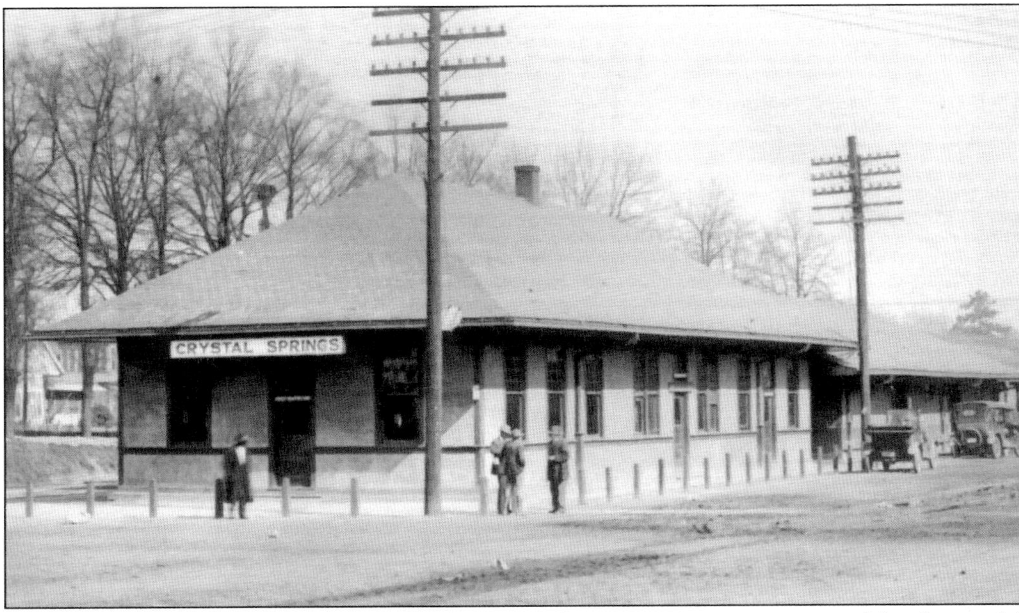

The Crystal Springs depot was once a bustling area of activity. Many passenger and freight cars left the depot. Boxcars by the dozens carried produce to all parts of the United States. Unfortunately, the depot's fate was sealed when the railroad decided to close it. With no upkeep, it met its demise and was torn down. All that is left is the "Crystal Springs" sign, saved by two city workers, Tally Jackson and Robert Sims, which now hangs in the Tomato Museum at Chautauqua Park. In 1951, the Illinois Central Railroad presented markers to Crystal Springs and Hazlehurst, symbolizing a century of service to mid-America. (Courtesy of MDAH and CCHGS.)

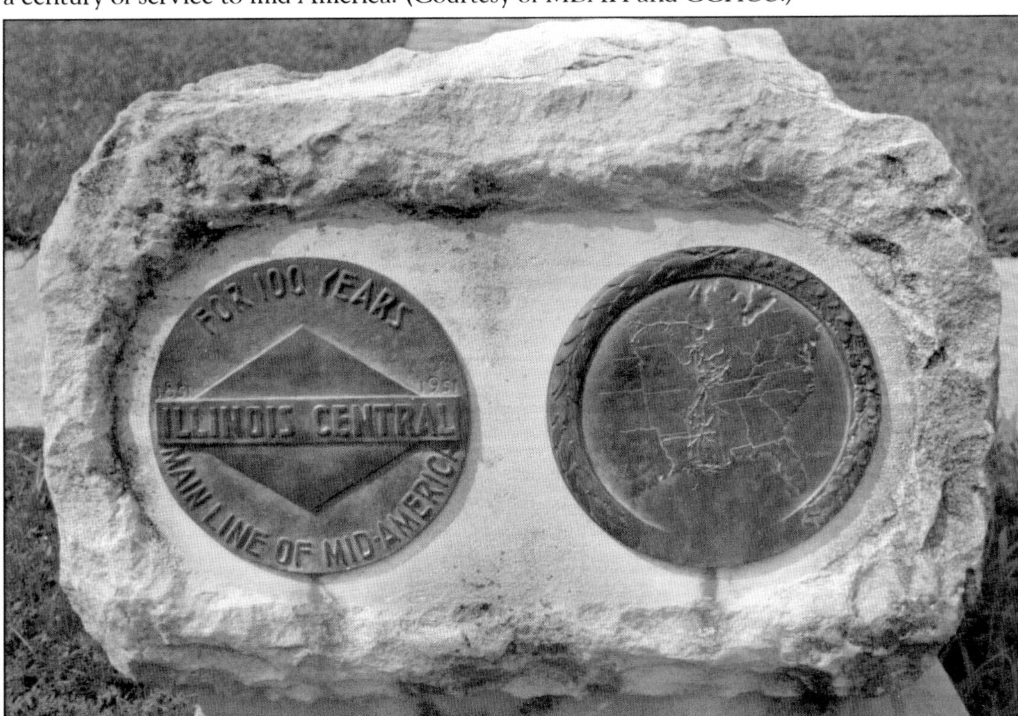

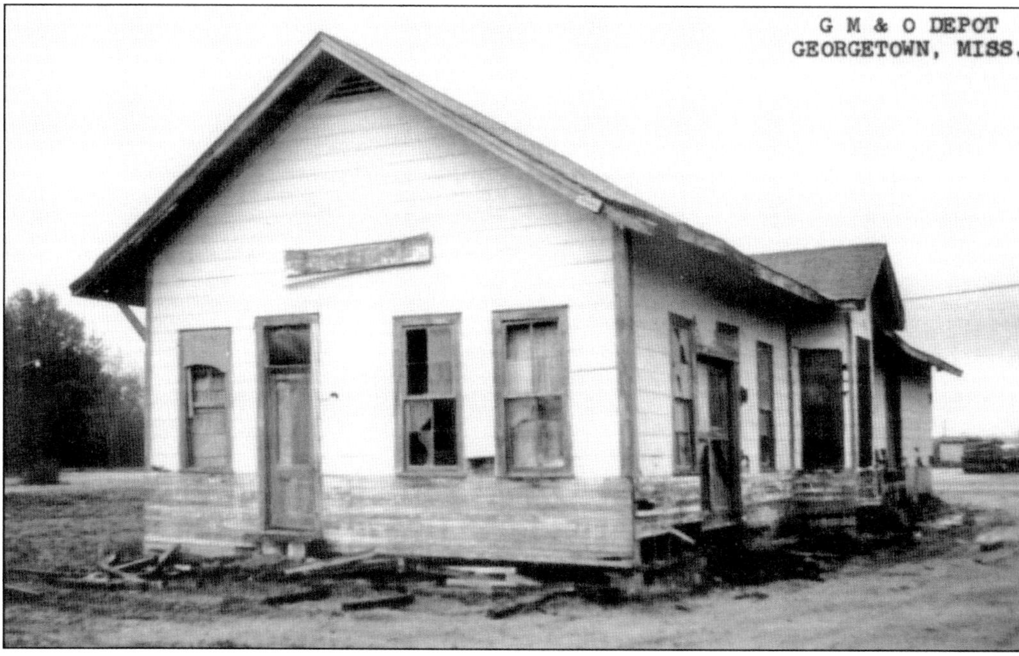

Depots were an essential part of the railroad. Most people traveled by rail during this time, so depots were usually full of activity. The depots along the NOJ&GN were no exception. There were also the rails that branched from the main line, which required depots as well. Crystal Springs, Hazlehurst, Beauregard, Wesson (pictured below), Carpenter, and Georgetown (pictured above) all had depots. The Wesson depot, built in 1884, was one of the first passenger stations built of brick. In the photograph, the smoke from the Wesson Mills is visible in the background. (Courtesy of MDAH.)

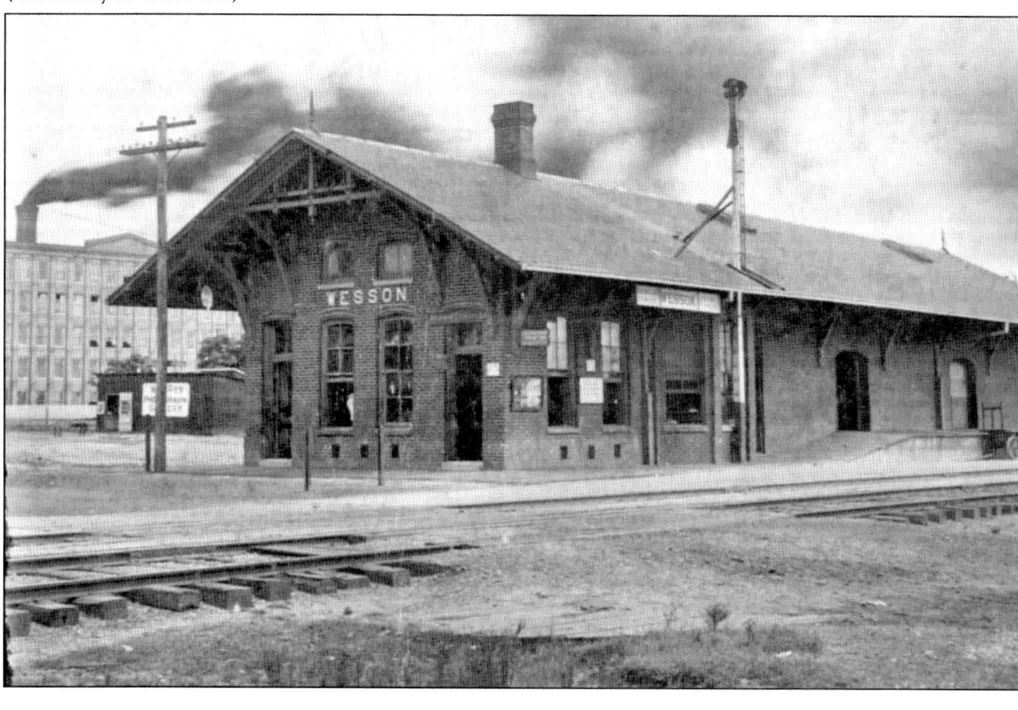

Three

Cotton and Tomatoes are King

Cotton was a dominant element in the state's agricultural economy from the time of statehood until the Civil War. In 1870, Copiah County ranked 13th of the state's 65 counties in the production of cotton. Immediately after the war, the Mississippi Mills was established in Wesson. In 1886, cotton prices fell as low as 8¢ per pound, which led many to venture into vegetable production. Although commercial fruit and vegetable production was important to other parts of the state, Copiah County became the focus of this industry. In 1879, the first carload of tomatoes was shipped from Crystal Springs, which became know as the "Tomatopolis of the World." As the number of vegetable farmers grew, the fear of over-production spread. Copiah County farmers tried to time the tomatoes to come in before those of Florida and Texas, but this had disastrous consequences, and eventually Copiah County had too much competition to remain a major competitor in the industry.

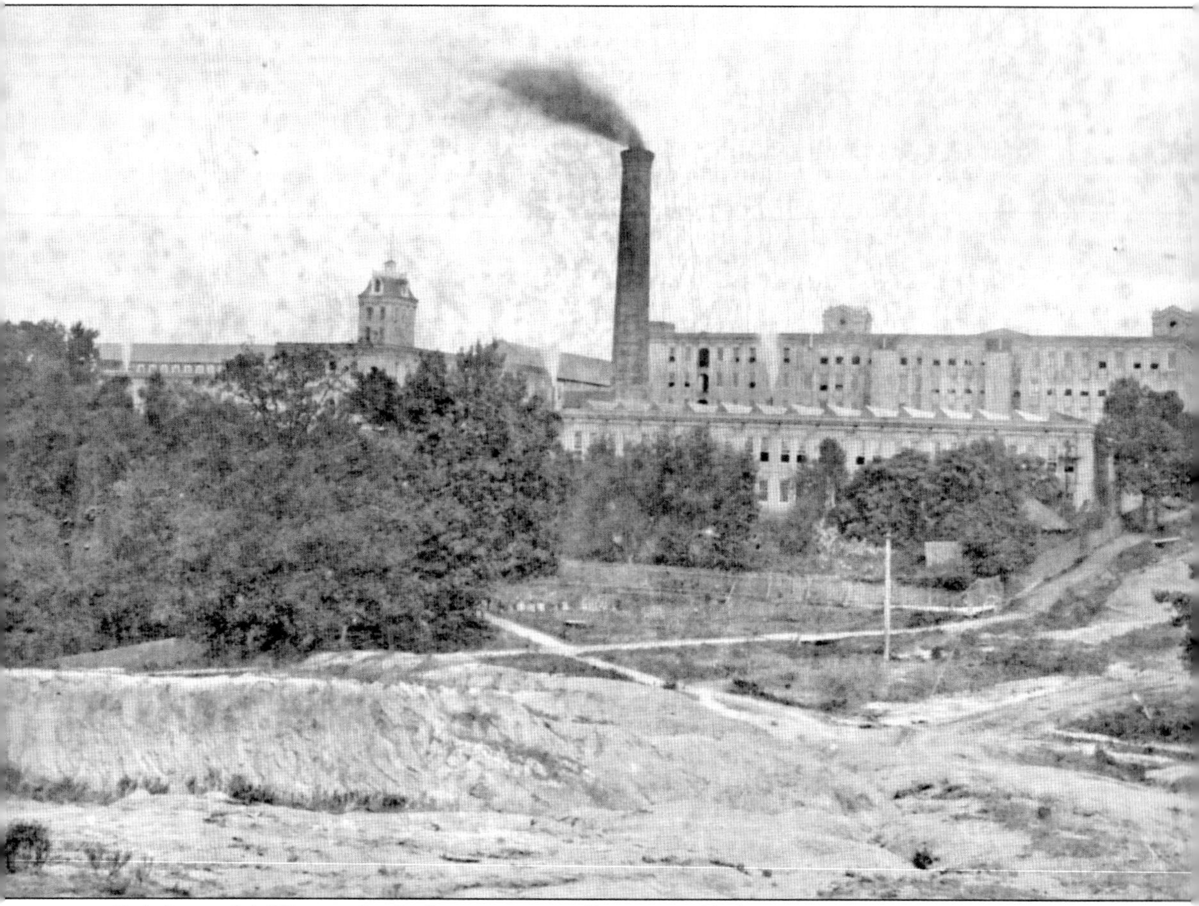

Col. James M. Wesson built the Wesson Mills, originally known as Mississippi Manufacturing Company, in 1867 after his first mill in Bankston was burned by Federal troops in 1864. The mills soon became the most famous post–Civil War manufacturing plant in the state. Wesson scouted the county, incorporated the town of Wesson in 1864, and began work on his new mills. Three years later, the cotton mill and 75 houses for workers were completed. He donated the land for the first three churches. The town grew rapidly and around 1905 had a population of 4,000 and was the state's 14th largest city. In 1871, having problems with Reconstruction, Wesson sold the company. Capt. William Oliver, one of the new owners, assumed the management role. After a fire destroyed the mills two years later, Oliver persuaded Edmund Richardson, the largest cotton planter in the world, to buy into the business. (Courtesy of MDAH.)

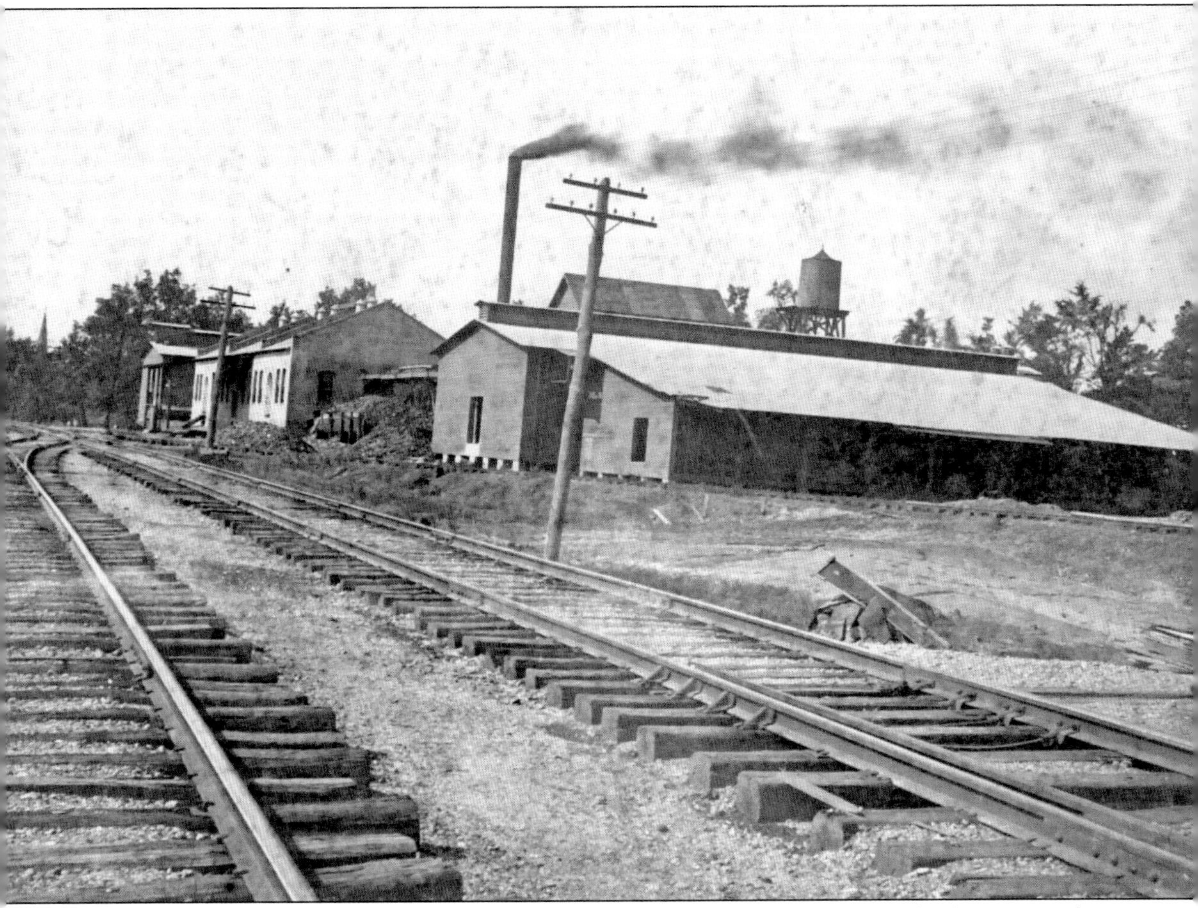

With Richardson as president and Oliver as general manager, the mills were rebuilt on a much larger scale. The four mills were built between 1873 and 1894. Now named the Mississippi Mills, the new mills were powered by steam engines and electricity. Being the largest manufacturing enterprise of any type in Mississippi, it should be no surprise that the mills were the first in the state to receive power in 1882. People came from miles around to see the giant, illuminated, five-story plant glow. The mills produced a variety of high-quality, award-winning fabrics affectionately termed "Mississippi silk." When Oliver died in 1891, the mills would begin to decline. Oliver's son, John, took over and brought in a manager from the North. In January 1910, the price of cotton dropped to $5.85 a bale, which forced Wesson and several other mills to shut down. Within a year, the population of Wesson went from 5,000 to 1,000. Pictured is the cottonseed oil mill and cotton gin in Wesson. (Courtesy of MDAH.)

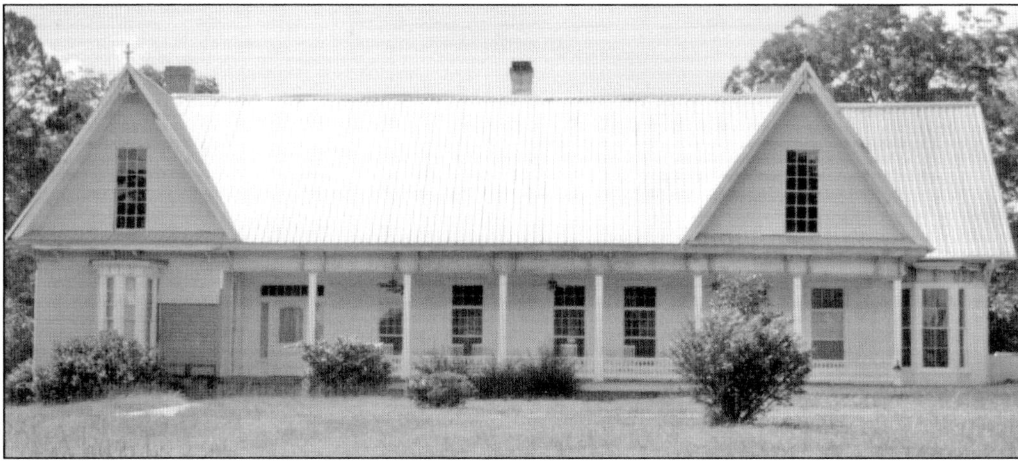

Col. James M. Wesson had this home built of cypress and select pine. The windows are 9 feet by 42 inches, and the entire house is 97 feet, 5 inches long, with a depth of 98 feet, 4 inches on the north side. The front porch runs almost the entire length of the house. Some rooms have ceiling medallions made by Jules la Branch, a mulatto bricklayer from the mills. (Courtesy of Longie Dale Hamilton Memorial Library.)

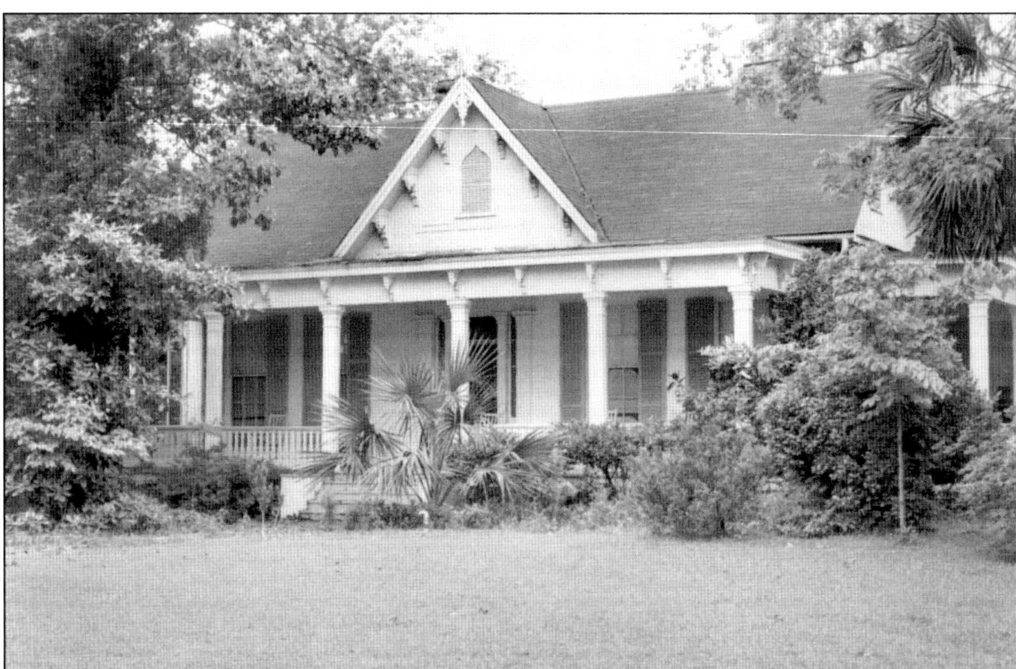

This house was built by Capt. William Oliver and his wife for their daughter, Rilla Oliver, and Dr. Robert W. Rea as a wedding gift. The couple married in December 1874 and spent the first year of their marriage with their parents in their house. Several descendants of the Reas lived in this house until their deaths. (Courtesy of Longie Dale Hamilton Memorial Library.)

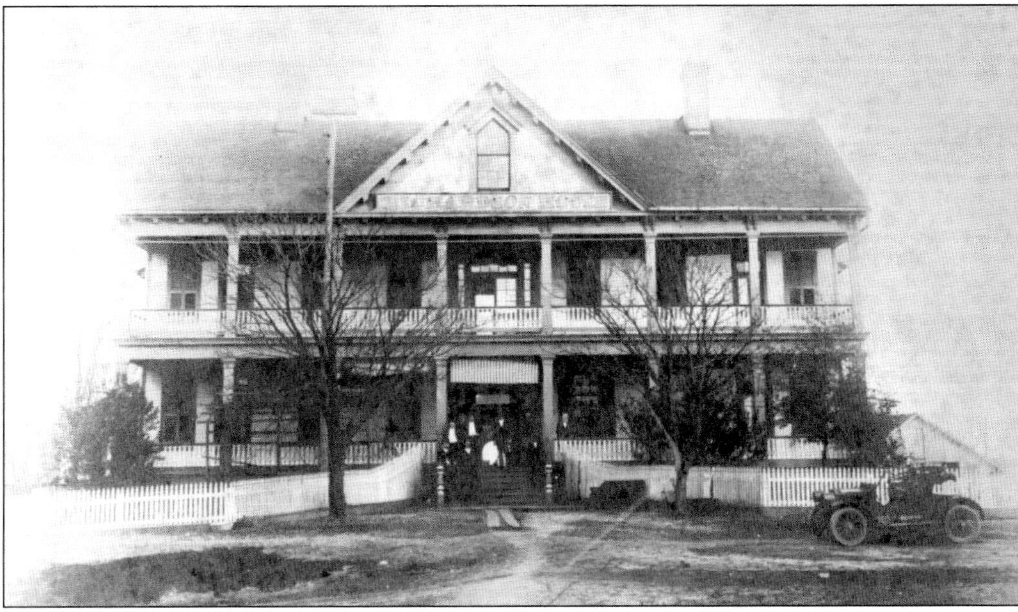

This is the Richardson House, owned by Edmund Richardson, who was president of the Mississippi Mills at one point. He was said to be the largest cotton planter in the world. Later it became the Wesson Hotel. Once on the National Register of Historic Places, the structure is no longer standing. (Courtesy of Longie Dale Hamilton Memorial Library.)

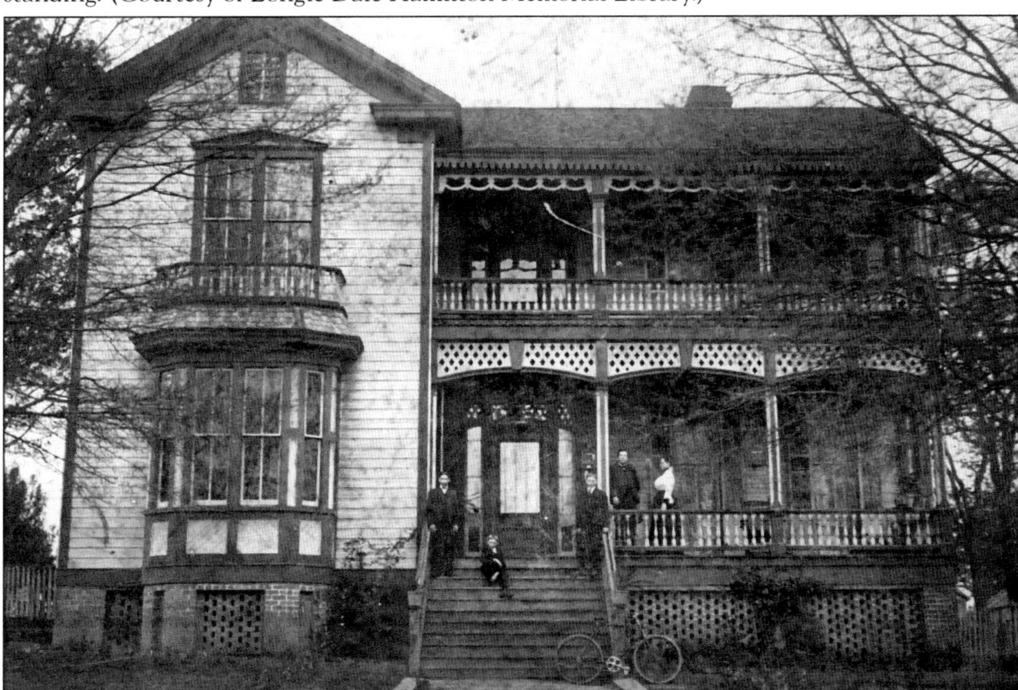

The Highlands, built in 1881, was the home of Major Hamilton, the secretary-treasurer of the Wesson Mills at one time. The house is made of select long-leaf yellow pine and has two stories and a cellar. It has 20-foot ceilings with two long halls and a wide front porch. The Hamiltons were among the organizing members of the Wesson Presbyterian Church. (Courtesy of MDAH.)

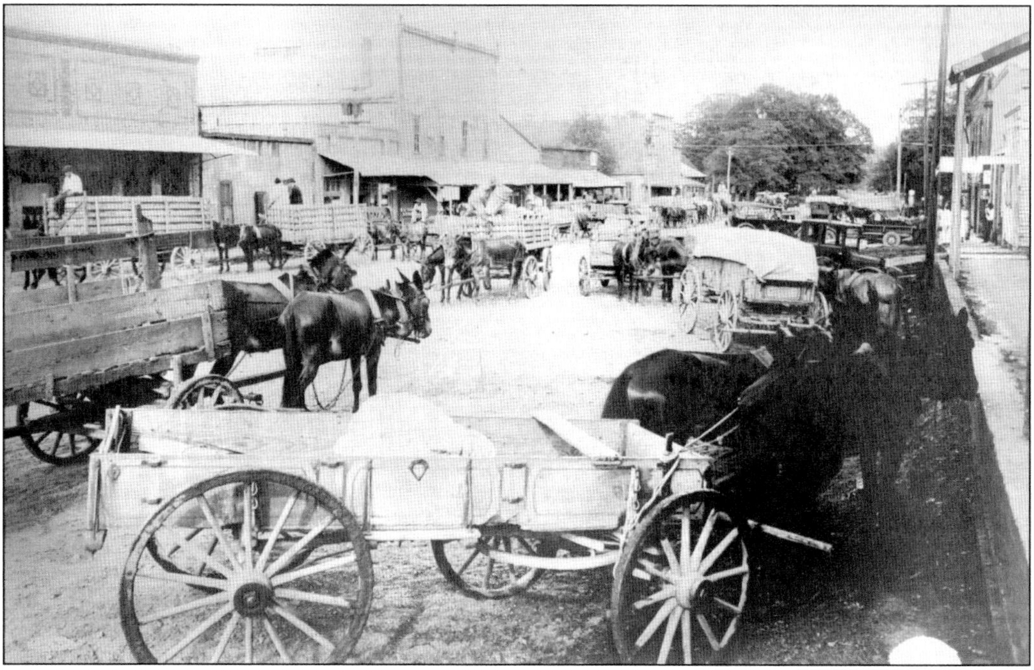

Many farmers were growing cotton, but sales had begun to decline. The tomato days began when N. Piazza received some tomato seeds from his native Italy. The notion to grow tomatoes caught on, and in 1883, the first railroad car of tomatoes was shipped by Augustus Lotterhos. Soon, with the county's newfound crop, tomatoes were in high demand in the eastern markets, and a new industry was born. (Courtesy of Tomato Museum.)

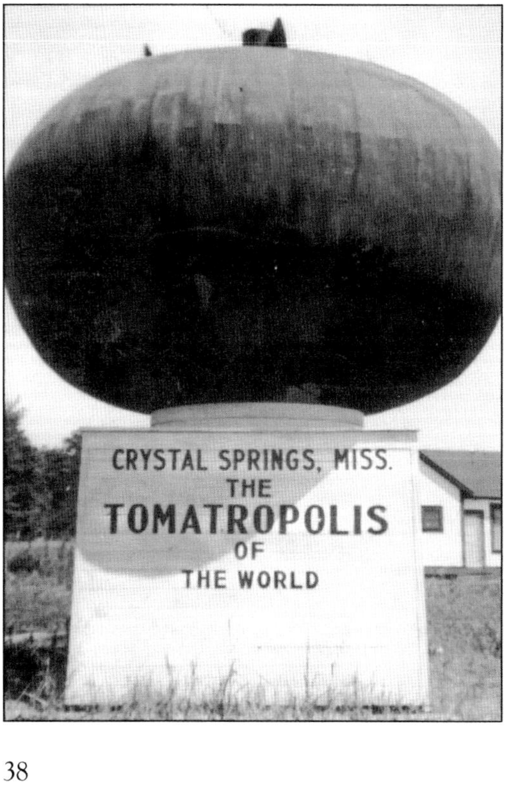

The Lotterhos family was influential in the vegetable-growing industry, developing new growing techniques and introducing modernized transportation methods. At one time, the firm of Lotterhos and Huber, incorporated in 1905, gained prominence as the largest shipper of tomatoes in the United States. (Courtesy of MDAH.)

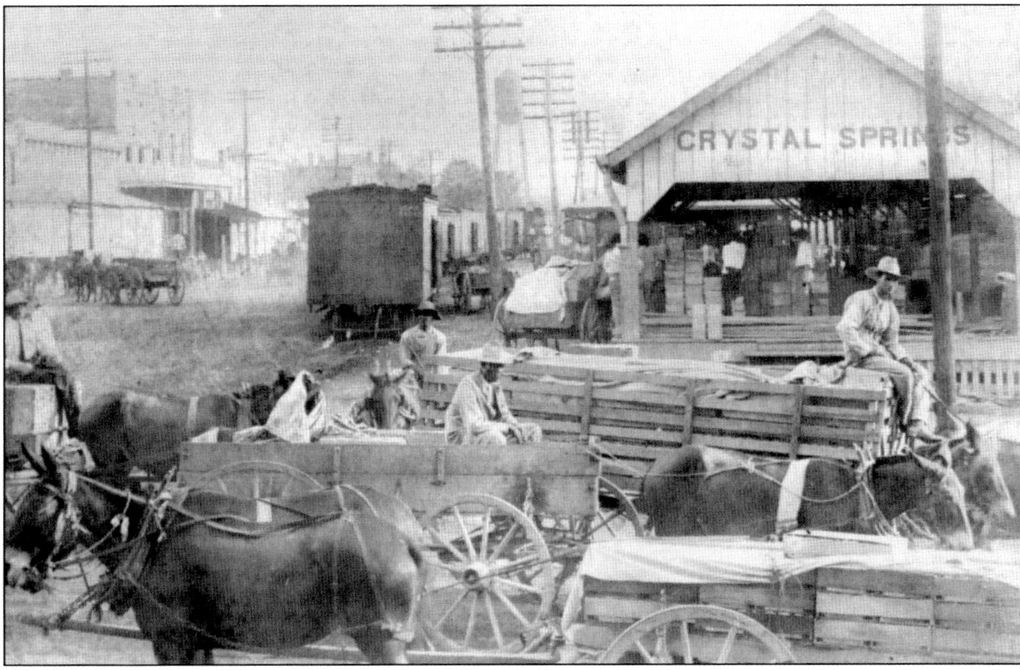

Lotterhos began the practice of warning farmers of a potential freeze, which could damage crops. It is said that his first warning technique was to discharge a cannon. Later he ordered the sounding of a steam horn, referred to as the "squeedunk," which was connected to the town powerhouse. This saved the farmers' crops and meant more money when they were able to provide early spring vegetables. (Courtesy of Tomato Museum.)

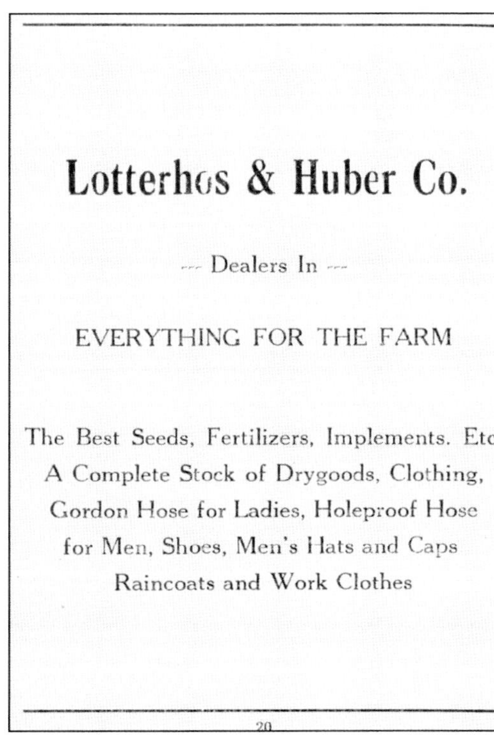

C. M. Huber, nephew and partner of Augustus Lotterhos, advanced Lotterhos and Huber in many ways. He worked to develop more varieties of tomatoes, more desirable packaging, better distribution of products, better transportation, and more favorable freight rates. This is one of the company's advertisements during the Copiah County Fair in 1931. (Courtesy of J. T. Biggs Jr. Memorial Library.)

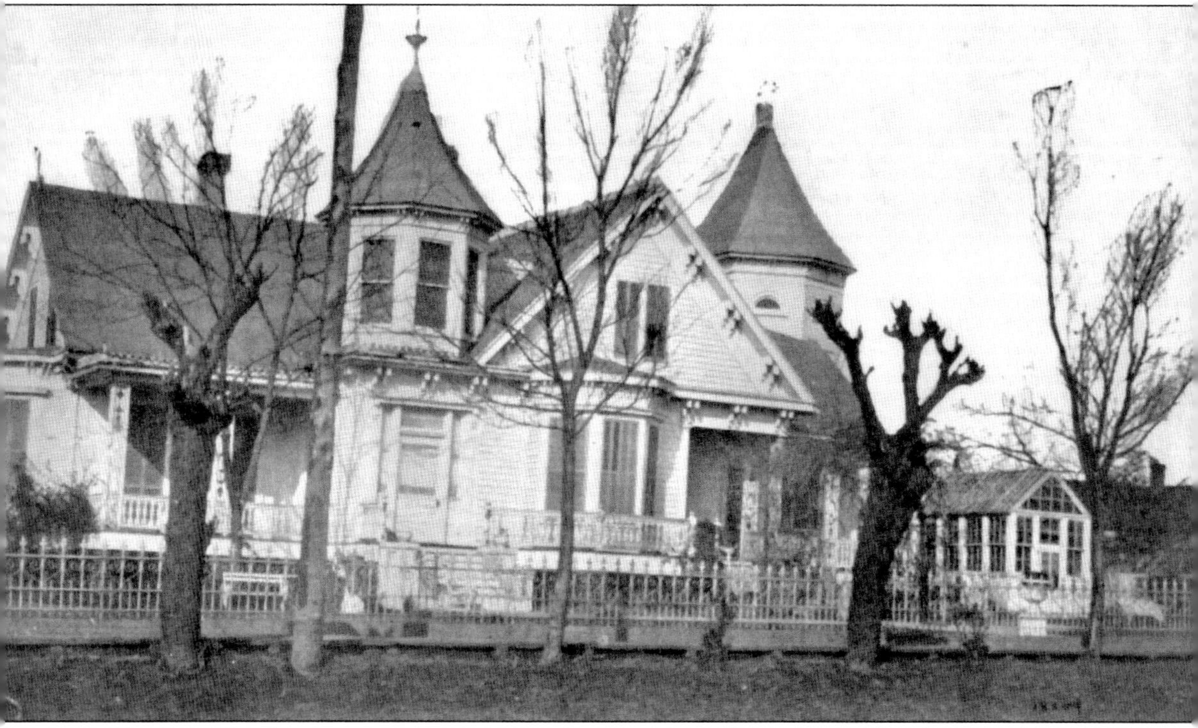

The Lotterhos home was on Georgetown Street in Crystal Springs on four lots bought from W. H. Garland in 1876. It was here Augustus Lotterhos brought his bride, Magdalena Lieb. The house was said to be a showplace with an east tower, intricate carvings, and numerous porches. It had double parlors and a third front parlor. Each of the bedrooms had its own fireplace. Many of the windows had stained glass. One room housed an inside garden, and outside there was a glass-enclosed conservatory. There was a brick patio along the back of the house. The lawn was surrounded by a beautiful iron fence and enclosed was a beautiful fountain. The Crystal Springs Methodist Church eventually bought the property, and the house was torn down. The beautiful fountain was moved to Railroad Park in Crystal Springs. Augustus Lotterhos is buried in the Crystal Springs Cemetery. (Courtesy of MDAH.)

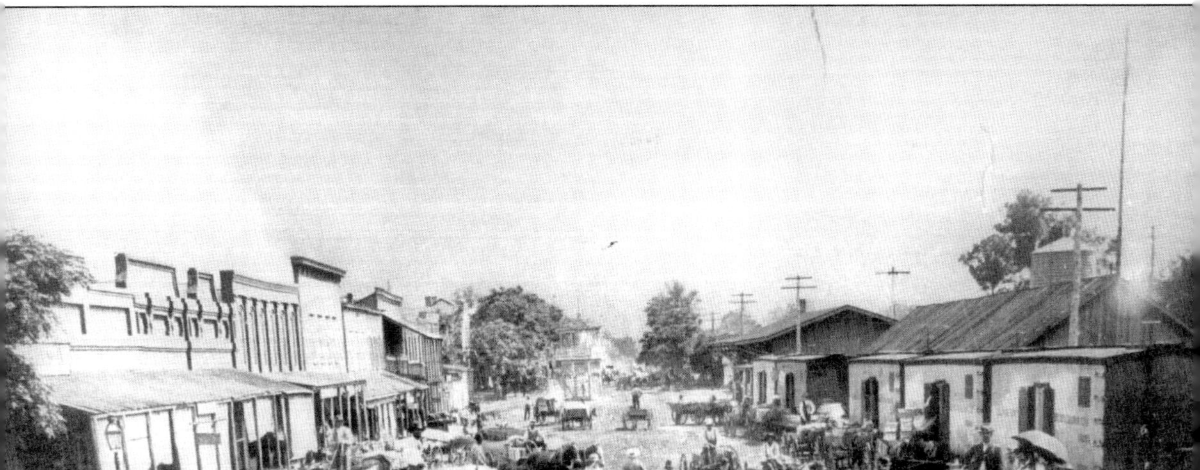

Many people were instrumental in the vegetable and trucking industries in the county. William Warren Alford began growing vegetables at Gallman prior to 1880. At one time he had over 500 acres, mainly in strawberries. W. B. Alford Jr. was president and general manager of Alford and Miller Company, Inc., and was considered a pioneer of vegetable shipping in Hazlehurst. W. L. Redding and D. C. Simmons, of Utica and Terry respectively, both promoted the growing and shipping of vegetables in Copiah County. J. S. Youngblood was a pioneer in the tomato business in Wesson. Wilbur S. Catchings Sr. was a pioneer and early grower of vegetables in the Georgetown area. He had many acres and hauled his produce 18 miles to market. Catchings Jr. followed in his father's footsteps. (Courtesy of Dan Rogers.)

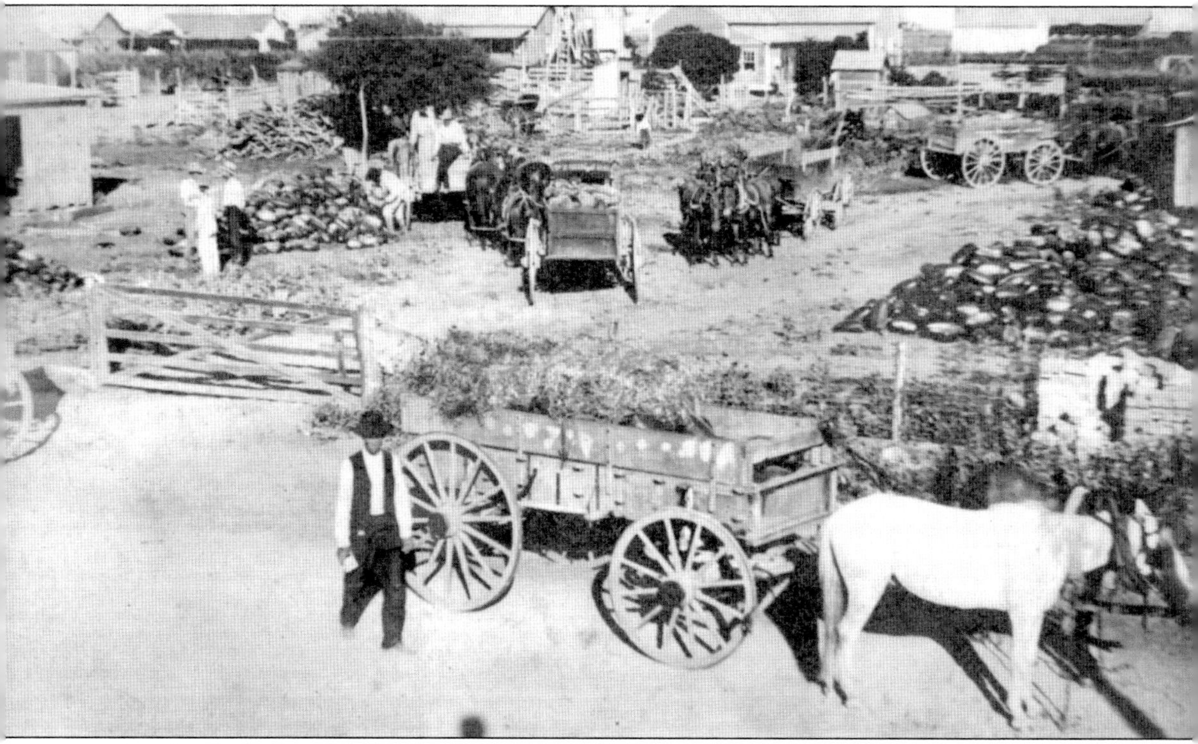

The "Tomato King," S. R. Evans, also known as "Uncle Sing," was a grower of tomatoes for almost 40 years. R. B. Thomas also grew tomatoes for many years after first being in the lumber business. He was active in the religious, civic, educational, and business interests of the county. Benjamin R. Ford was another vegetable grower. After entering the Confederate army at the age of 17 and being wounded in the Battle of Shiloh, he returned to the county and first grew peaches and grapes, then tomatoes and beans, and in later years corn and cotton. N. L. Hutchison was one of the earliest growers and shippers of cabbages, tomatoes, and peaches, among other things. He also operated a large poultry farm. He was one of the charter members of the Truck Growers Association. (Courtesy of Georgetown Public Library.)

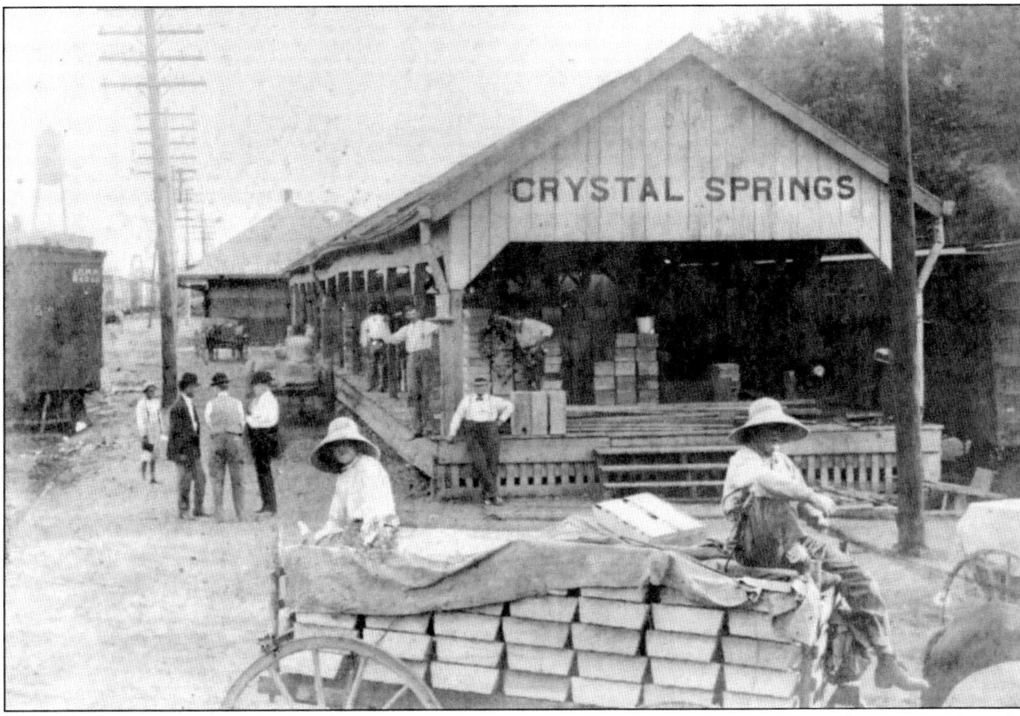

W. H. Barron was one of the first to ship green, wrapped tomatoes. For 40 years, he engaged in the mercantile and shipping business. He served as alderman and for a number of years was director of Chautauqua and was largely instrumental in developing the Hennington Campground and Lake Chautauqua. C. Glen Erving of Crystal Springs was another prominent grower for many years. He was affiliated with the Truck Growers Association from its beginning. John W. Day had a beautiful home and large farm near Crystal Springs. He was among the earliest growers and shippers of peaches. He farmed on a large scale, raising peaches, tomatoes, and beans, among others things. (Courtesy of Tomato Museum and George W. Covington Memorial Library.)

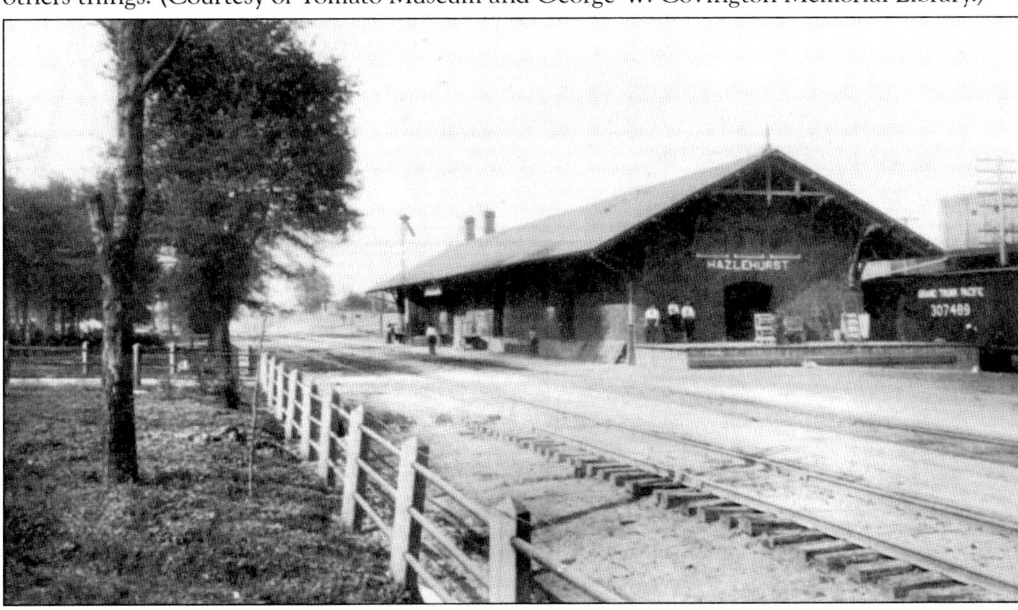

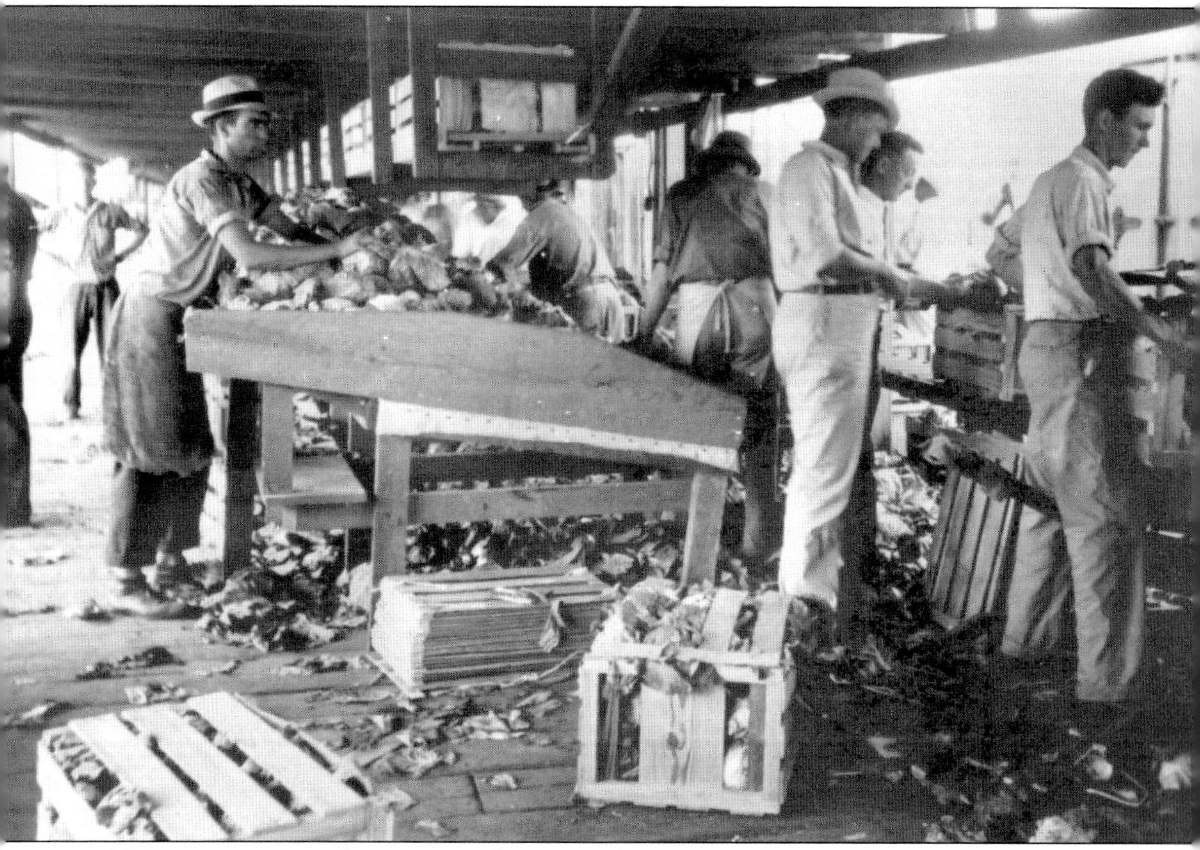

N. Piazza is given credit as a scientific grower of tomatoes. He improved seeds brought from his native Italy. He was also a pioneer in the shipment of peaches. B. W. Mathis, later known as the "Cabbage King," first grew strawberries and tomatoes. He was a large cotton and corn grower, also. F. M. Brewer Sr. was a pioneer in the Crystal Springs area and was especially known for growing beans. He had advanced ideas in farming and laid the foundation for trucking interests. His son, Randall Brewer, was known as the "Carrot King" and grew cabbage and tomatoes on a large scale. Farmers all over the county worked hard to prepare their land and cultivate their crops. Eventually they would harvest the crops and take them to the shipping towns along the railroad such as Crystal Springs and Hazlehurst. (Courtesy of J. T. Biggs Jr. Memorial Library.)

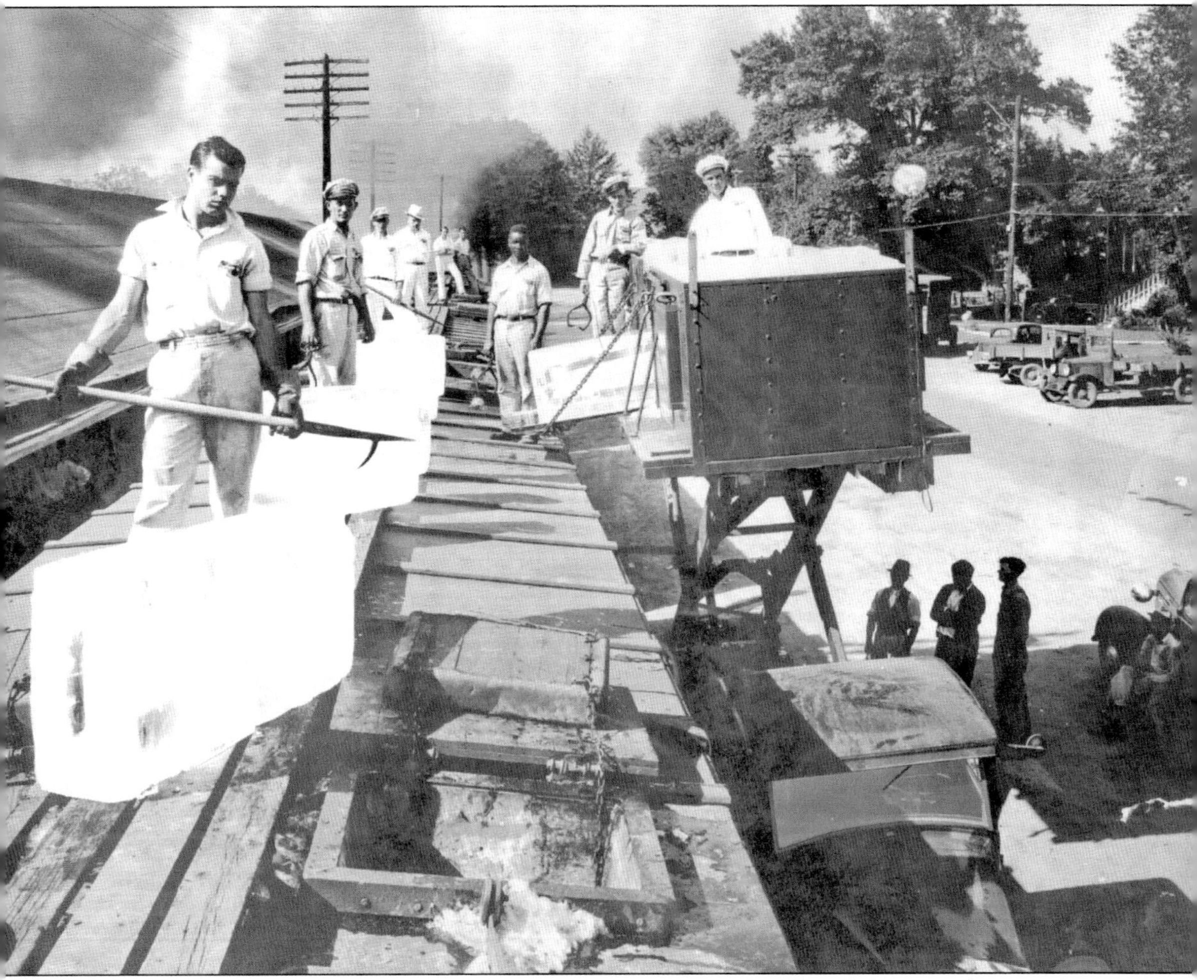

Lines would form in front of the buyer so long that it could easily take all day to make it to the "hotspot," as it was named in Hazlehurst. Once the produce was bought, it was unloaded at the packing sheds. Then workers would pack the produce in crates and load the crates into the freight cars. Packing sheds such as this one in Crystal Springs were very busy. Women were seen with blue tissue paper wrapping green tomatoes and then packing them in lugs. Young boys could be seen gluing labels on crates, and older boys and men were seen nailing the tops on the lugs. The containers were then pushed down the chute, where the freight cars were waiting to take them to all parts of the United States. Seen icing a vegetable car are Louis Sturgis and James Freels around 1938. (Courtesy of J. T. Biggs Jr. Memorial Library.)

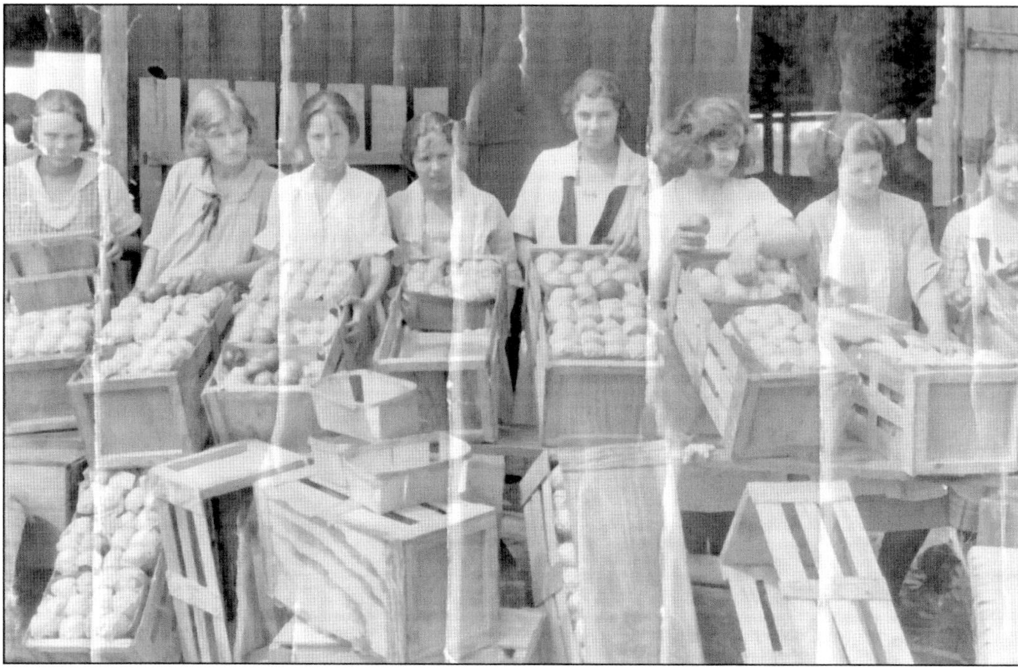

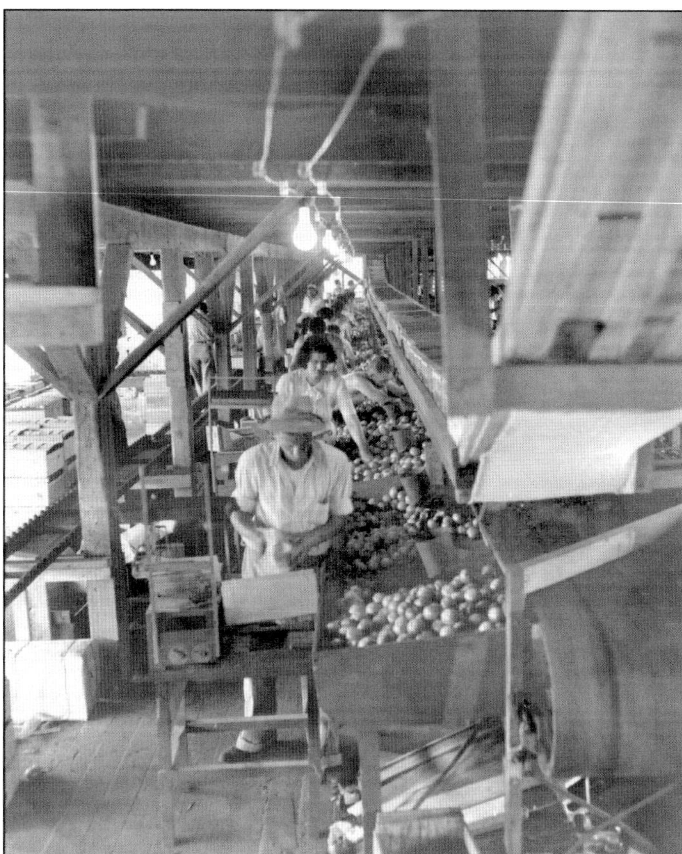

By 1930, many vegetable-packing sheds appeared. Thousands of tons of cabbage, beans, tomatoes, and other crops were shipped. In 1927, a total of 3,331 refrigerated railroad cars were shipped from Copiah County. By 1936, the number had increased to 4,130. Packers were paid well. Jewel Myers Taylor packed tomatoes and recalls receiving $150 a week. That was a good income for a female in the 1930s. Pictured above at a Hazlehurst packing shed are just a few of the many ladies who were packers. Third from left is Inez Hall Bufkin, and fourth from left is Betty Bishop Davis. (Courtesy of Billie Davis and J. T. Biggs Jr. Memorial Library.)

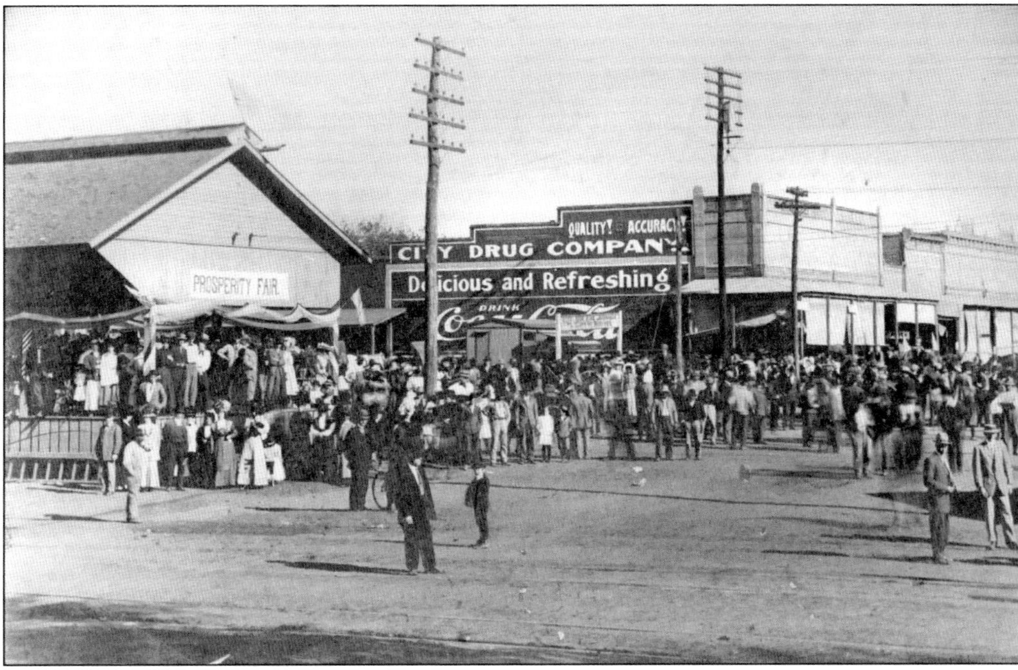

The Prosperity Fair in Crystal Springs may have been the forerunner of the Tomato Festival, which began in 1938 to afford growers a way to celebrate the harvest. At first it was called the Crystal Springs Tomato Festival, but the name was soon changed to the Copiah County Tomato Festival to acknowledge the importance of surrounding communities with regard to the tomato industry. Then the name was changed to the Mississippi Tomato Festival to acknowledge all the towns in the state involved in the tomato industry. For three years, Crystal Springs had a festival complete with a Tomato Queen. The first queen was June Garland in 1938, then Barnett Messer and Blanche Brewer. In 1996, the chamber of commerce revived the Tomato Festival. (Courtesy of J. T. Biggs Jr. Memorial Library and MDAH.)

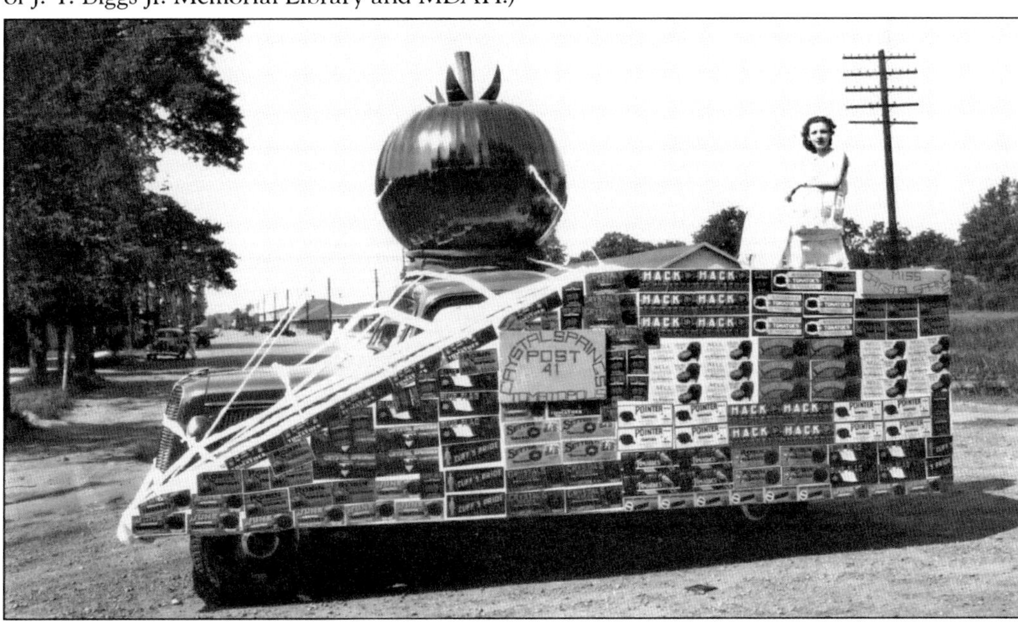

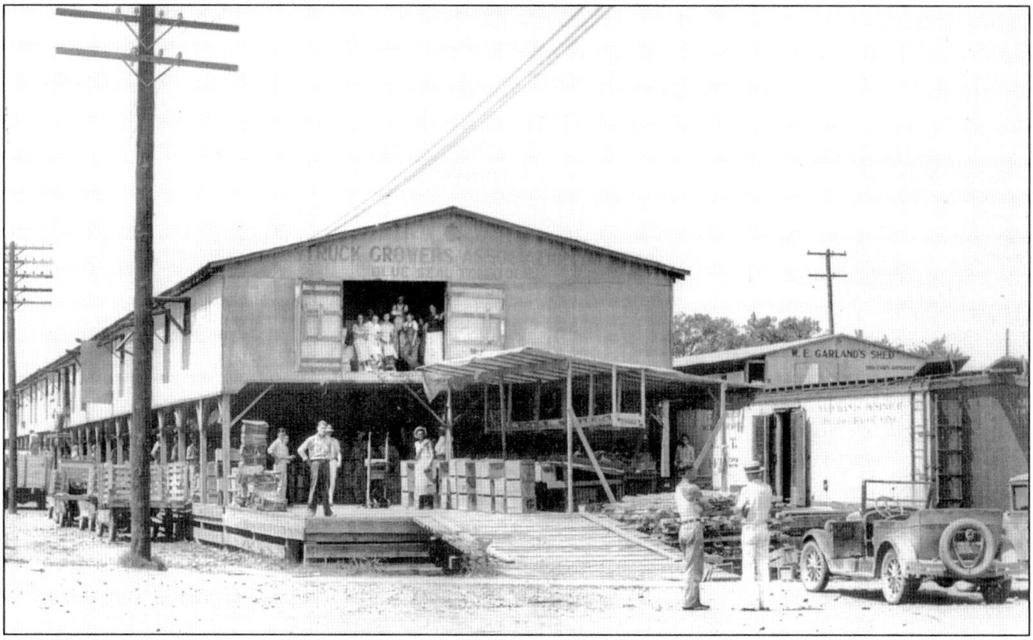

This is the Truck Growers Association, which organized in 1912 and incorporated in 1925. The purpose of the organization was "to encourage better and more economical methods of growing and harvesting vegetables. To cultivate a cooperative spirit and to perform any other work or service which might tend to further and safeguard the general interest of the business, the industry and the members of the association." (Courtesy of Tomato Museum.)

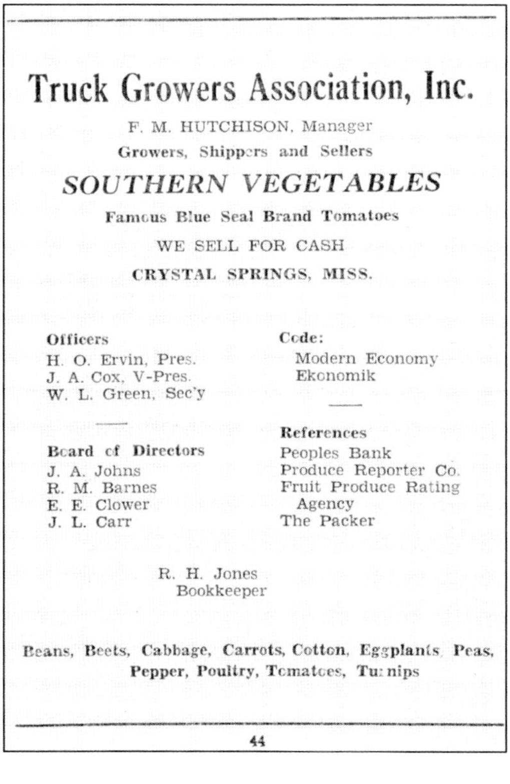

Truck Growers Association, Inc.

F. M. HUTCHISON, Manager

Growers, Shippers and Sellers

SOUTHERN VEGETABLES

Famous Blue Seal Brand Tomatoes

WE SELL FOR CASH

CRYSTAL SPRINGS, MISS.

Officers
H. O. Ervin, Pres.
J. A. Cox, V-Pres.
W. L. Green, Sec'y

Code:
Modern Economy
Ekonomik

References
Peoples Bank
Produce Reporter Co.
Fruit Produce Rating Agency
The Packer

Board of Directors
J. A. Johns
R. M. Barnes
E. E. Clower
J. L. Carr

R. H. Jones
Bookkeeper

Beans, Beets, Cabbage, Carrots, Cotton, Eggplants, Peas, Pepper, Poultry, Tomatoes, Turnips

44

The association ran strong for many years, selling over $250,000 worth of produce in 1937 alone. It ran longer than any similar organization in the United States but dissolved around 1942 after being in operation for 30 years. This is an advertisement from the list of advertisers during the 1931 Copiah County Fair. (Courtesy of J. T. Biggs Jr. Memorial Library.)

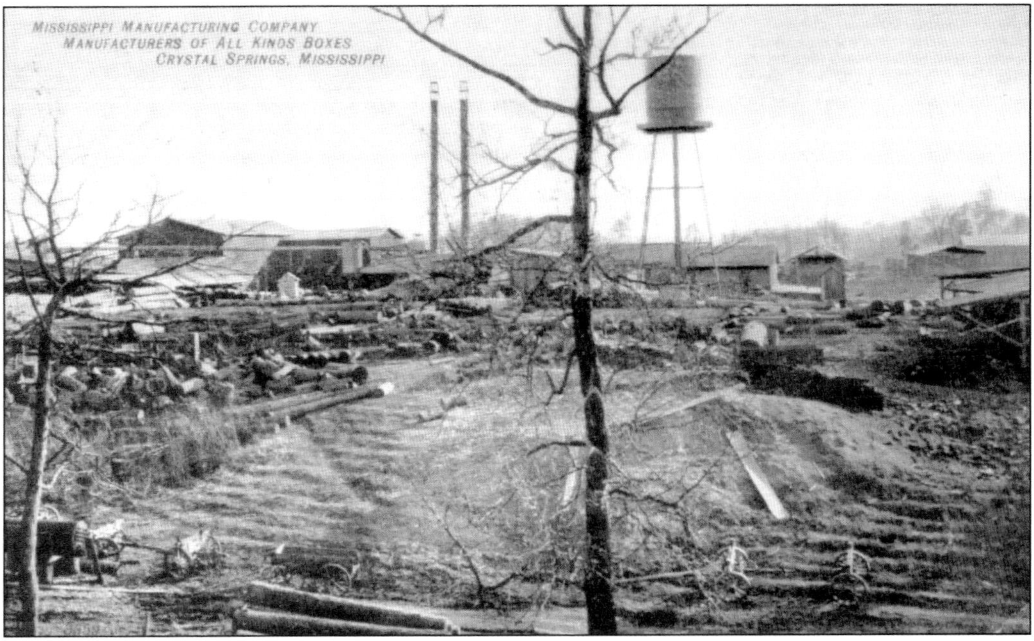

Several other types of businesses were associated with the produce industry as well. One such business was the Mississippi Manufacturing Company, which was at one point located west of the railroad near Cayuga Street in Crystal Springs. The company manufactured wire-bound wooden boxes for packaging fruits and vegetables. Tomato and strawberry baskets were said to often be made by hand by women and girls. (Courtesy of MDAH.)

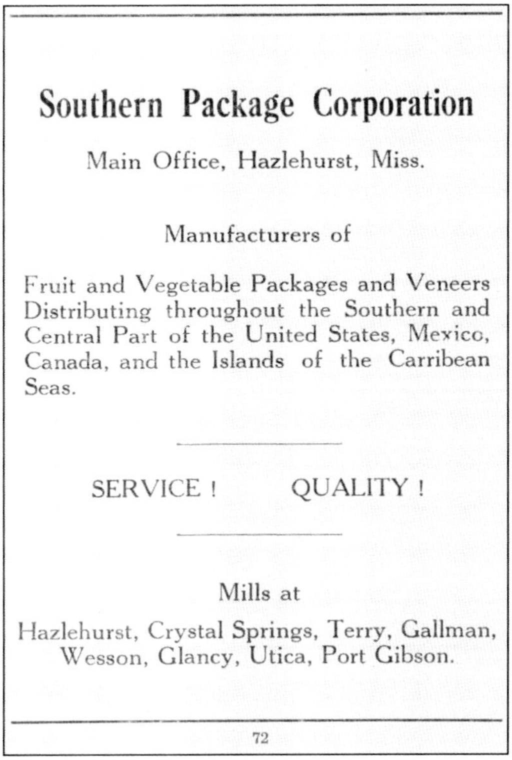

Southern Package Corporation

Main Office, Hazlehurst, Miss.

Manufacturers of

Fruit and Vegetable Packages and Veneers Distributing throughout the Southern and Central Part of the United States, Mexico, Canada, and the Islands of the Carribean Seas.

SERVICE ! QUALITY !

Mills at

Hazlehurst, Crystal Springs, Terry, Gallman, Wesson, Glancy, Utica, Port Gibson.

72

At one time, every community had at least one box plant. In Copiah County, most of these facilities eventually consolidated into the Southern Package Corporation, which became a large industrial complex owning several manufacturing plants and approximately 35,000 acres of timberland. The few remaining companies were closed by the late 1970s. (Courtesy of J. T. Biggs Jr. Memorial Library.)

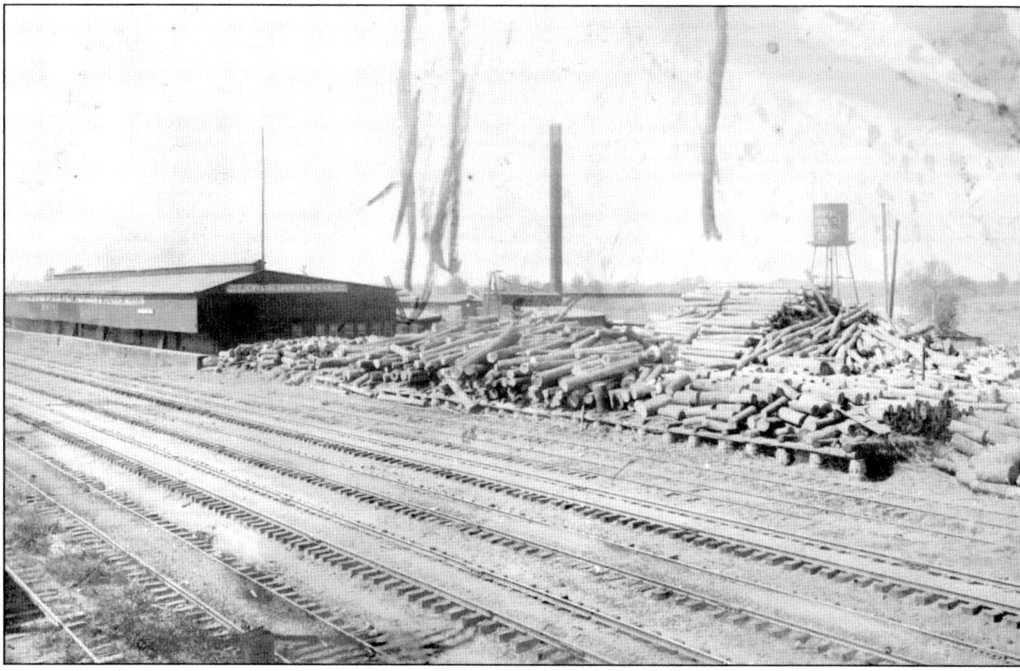

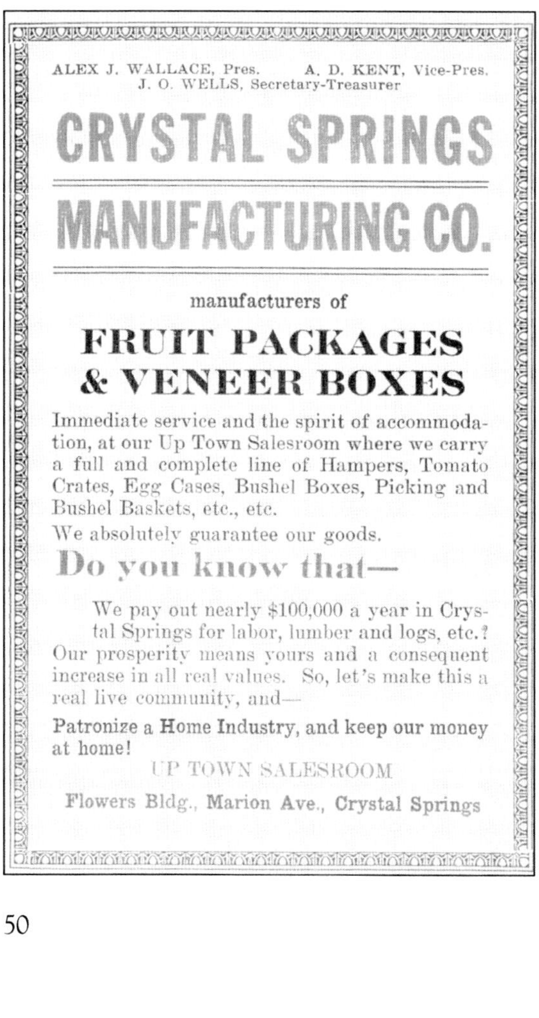

Pictured in 1920 is the Crystal Springs Manufacturing Company, which also consolidated with the Southern Package Corporation. Southern had mills in Hazlehurst, Crystal Springs, Terry, Gallman, Wesson, Glancy, Utica, and Port Gibson. This advertisement for the company claims that it pays out "nearly $100,000 a year in Crystal Springs for labor, lumber and logs, etc." The company made and sold "Hampers, Tomato Crates, Egg Cases, Bushel Boxes, Picking and Bushel Baskets, etc., etc." An abundance of trees made it easy for companies such as this to meet the demands of the produce shipping industry. Another company like this was the Hazlehurst Box Factory, which was chartered in 1912. (Courtesy of J. T. Biggs Jr. Memorial Library.)

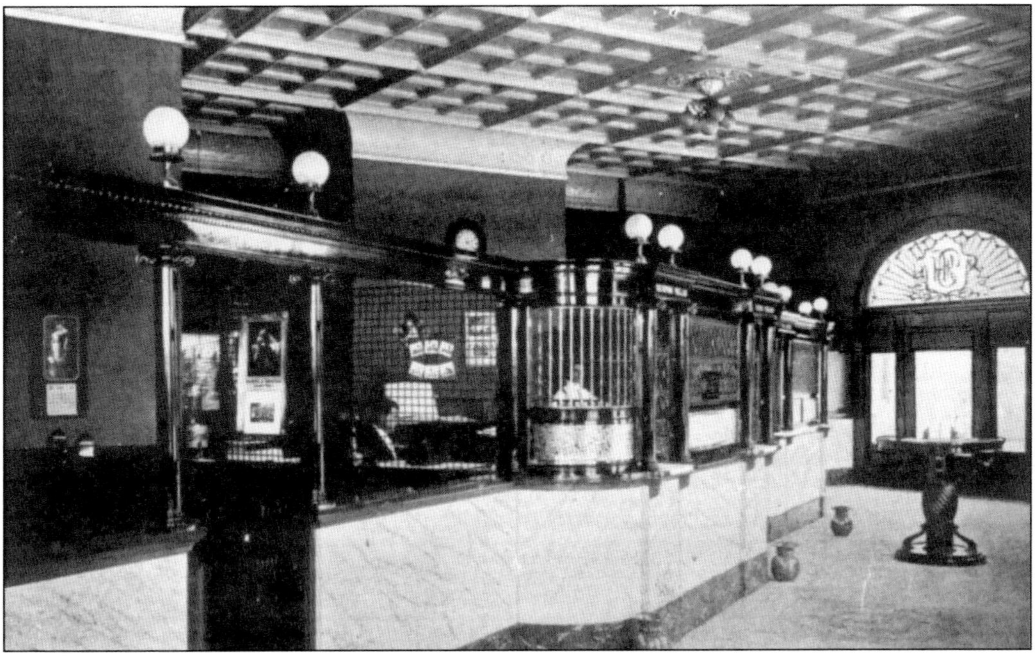

There were other businesses that flourished during these times. The Bank or Hazlehurst began serving the citizens of Hazlehurst and Copiah County on November 17, 1891. First it was on the southeast corner of Estelle Street near the overhead bridge, in the building that became known as the Watkins Furniture Company. By the 1930s, the bank had moved to a brick two-story building on Gallatin Street. The bank was founded by John A. Covington, who was president of the bank from 1891 to 1904. His son, George W. Covington, succeeded him and served until 1928, until which time George's brother, R. L. "Bob" Covington, became president. Bob served until 1960. In 1961, the bank underwent a major remodeling to coincide with the bank's 70th anniversary. This float passes the bank in the 1907 Floral Parade. (Courtesy of George W. Covington Memorial Library.)

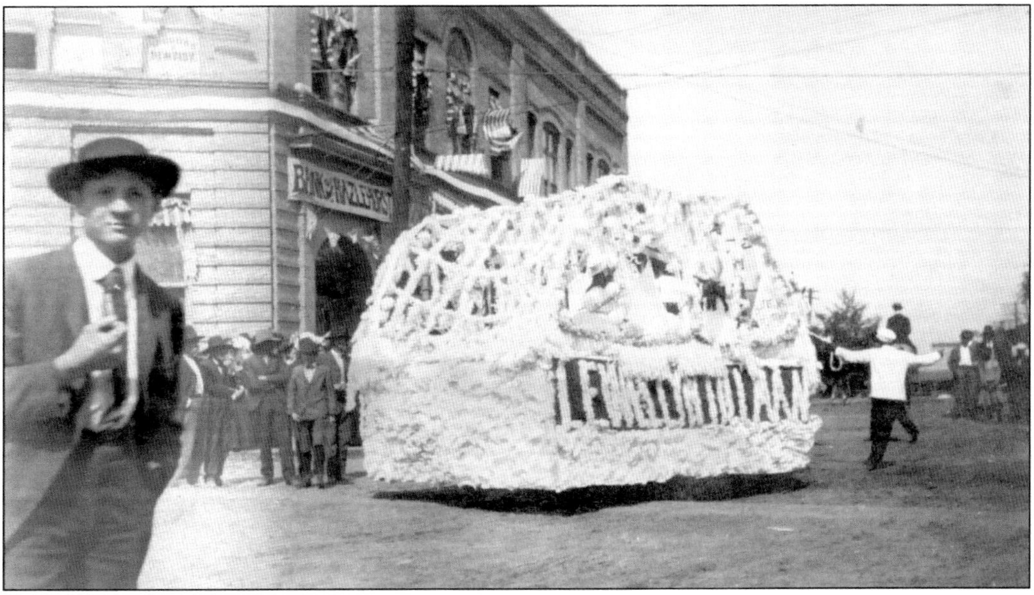

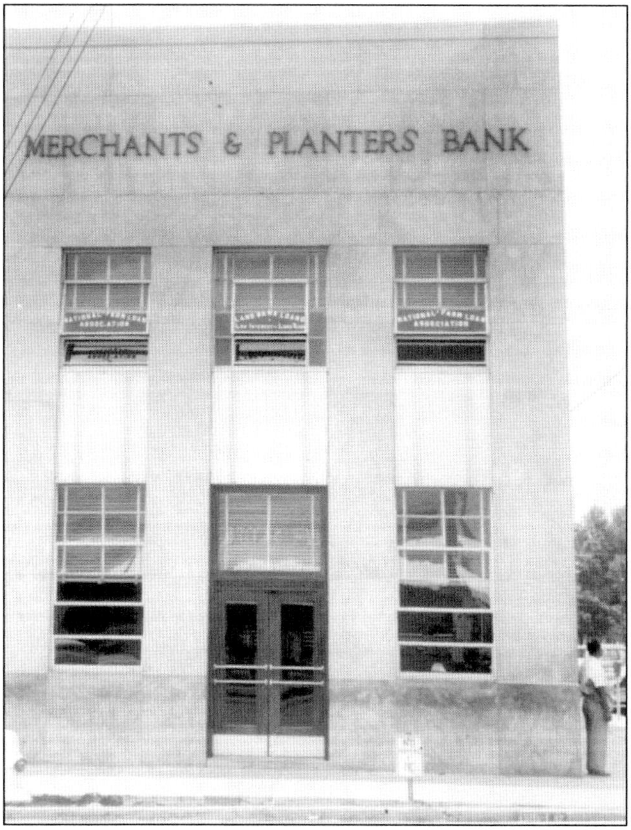

In February 1882, Isaac Newton Ellis and Maj. R. W. Millsaps started the Merchants and Planters Bank on Extension Street in Hazlehurst. Major Millsaps was president, and I. N. Ellis was vice president and cashier. The bank was owned solely by these two men until 1905, when they decided to increase the bank's capital by selling shares to new stockholders. When Major Millsaps resigned in 1916, I. N. Ellis became president, and his son Hal. R. Ellis became cashier. I. N. Ellis remained president until his death in 1930. H. R. Ellis was elected president to succeed him but was killed in an automobile accident in 1938. His brother, I. N. Ellis Jr., became president. They bought Georgetown Bank and made it a branch. Cliff Rawls stands in front of the building in Georgetown. (Courtesy of George W. Covington Memorial Library and Georgetown Public Library.)

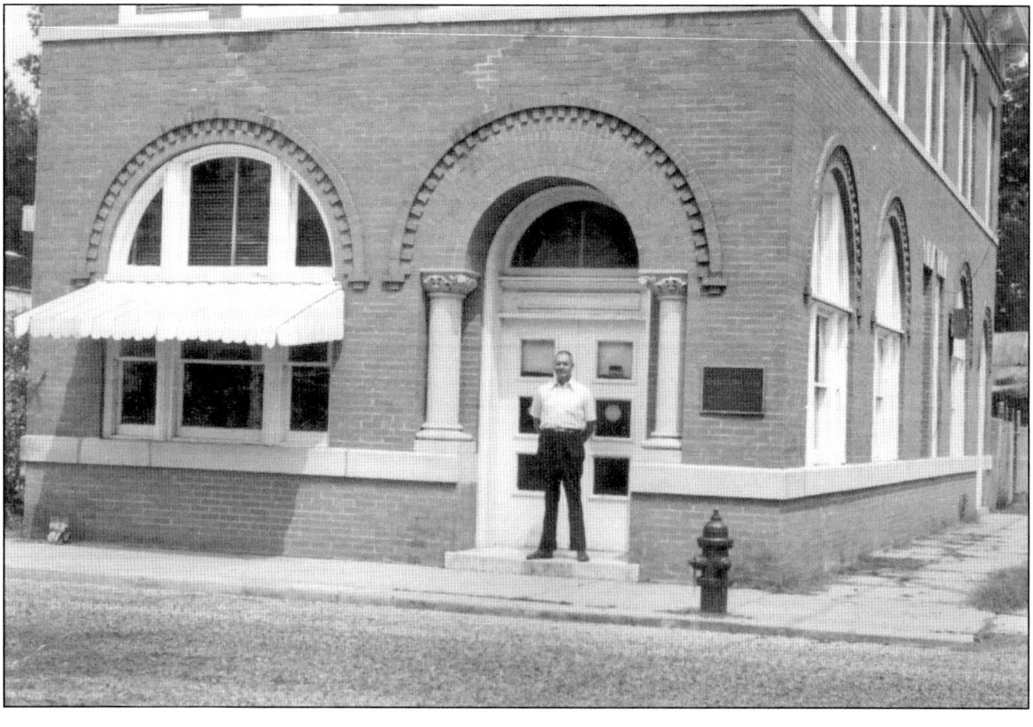

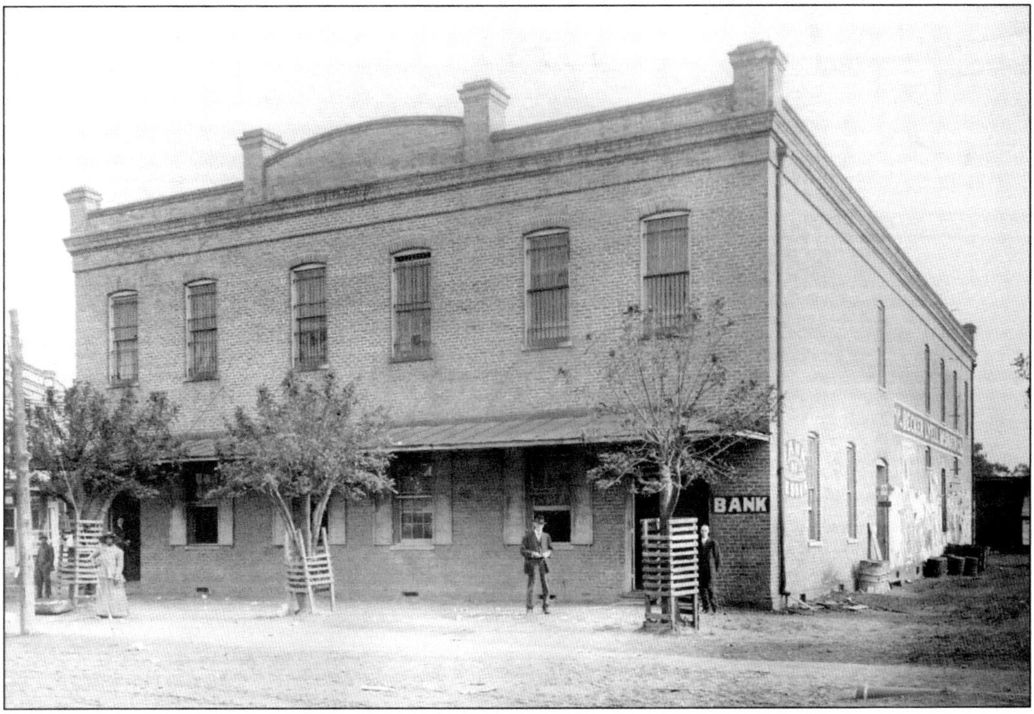

The Wesson Bank was incorporated January 5, 1893, and was located in one of the Wesson Mills buildings. This is the only mill building that exists today. Robert E. Rea was the head of the Wesson Bank for many years. He and his wife bought a house on what is now Highway 51 in Wesson in 1903, when they married. The structure, pictured below and now known as Porches, is most unusual in that the long, wide back porch makes a square, which allows for a courtyard in the center. The house was built in 1891 by Dr. Luther Sexton. (Courtesy of George W. Covington Memorial Library and Longie Dale Hamilton Memorial Library.)

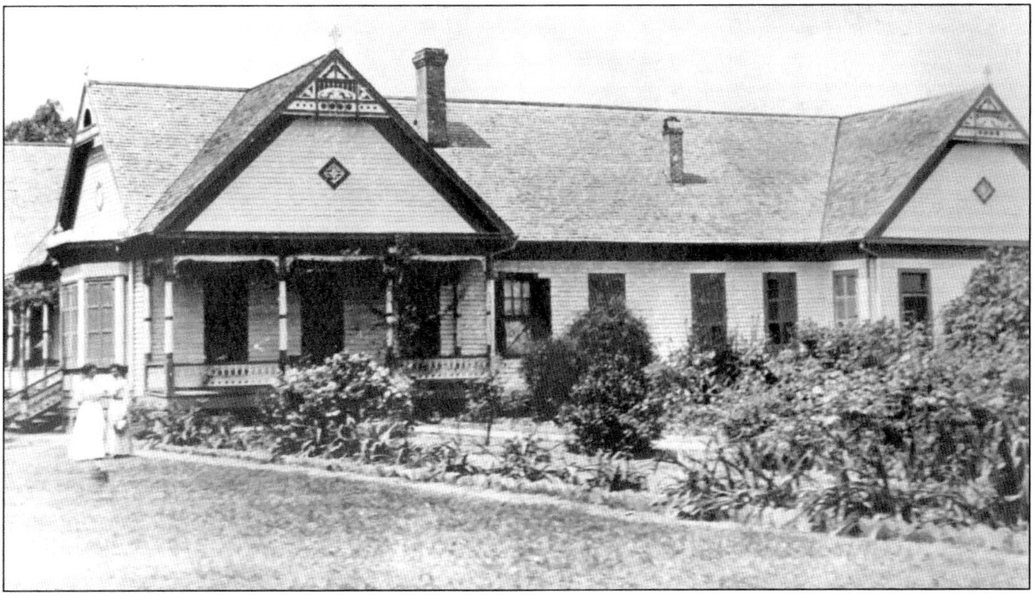

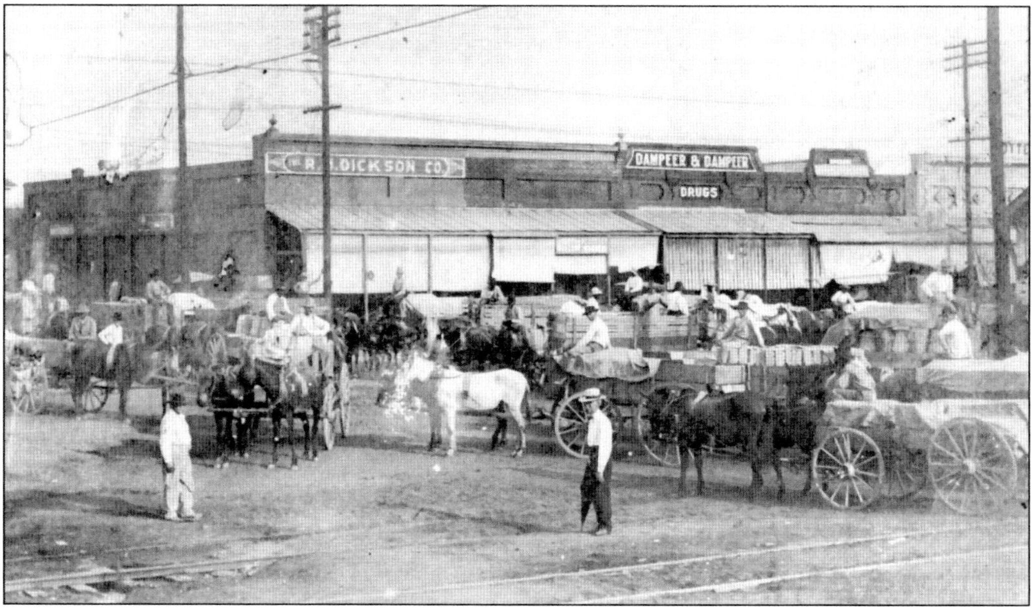

Dampeer and Dampeer Drugstore was established by L. M. Dampeer Sr., a druggist, in 1874 in Crystal Springs. L. M.'s brother, James Monroe (J. M.), was a well-respected doctor. J. M. and partner Dr. Robert E. Jones had an office in the back of the drugstore. J. M. married Lou Williams of Mount Carmel, Lawrence County, and in 1892, he studied medicine at Tulane University in New Orleans and served his residency at Mercy Hospital in Vicksburg. J. M. and Lou had two children: Mai, shown here in 1904, and Miles. Miles died while attending Mississippi College in Clinton. The family established a scholarship in Miles's name. In 1891, J. M. Dampeer Jr. became connected with the drugstore. (Courtesy of Tomato Museum and J. T. Biggs Jr. Memorial Library.)

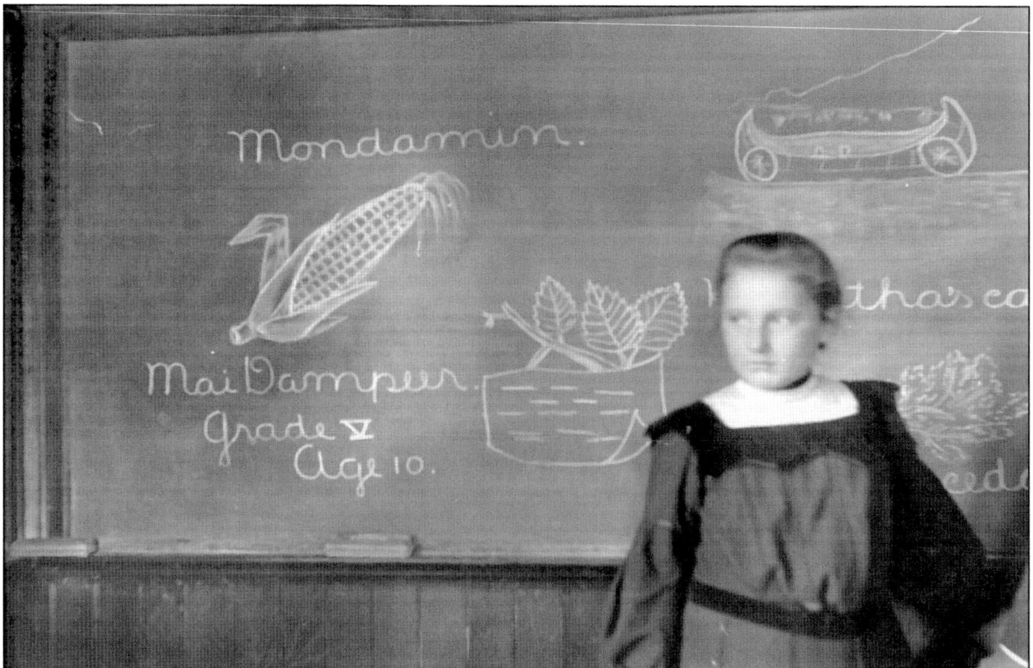

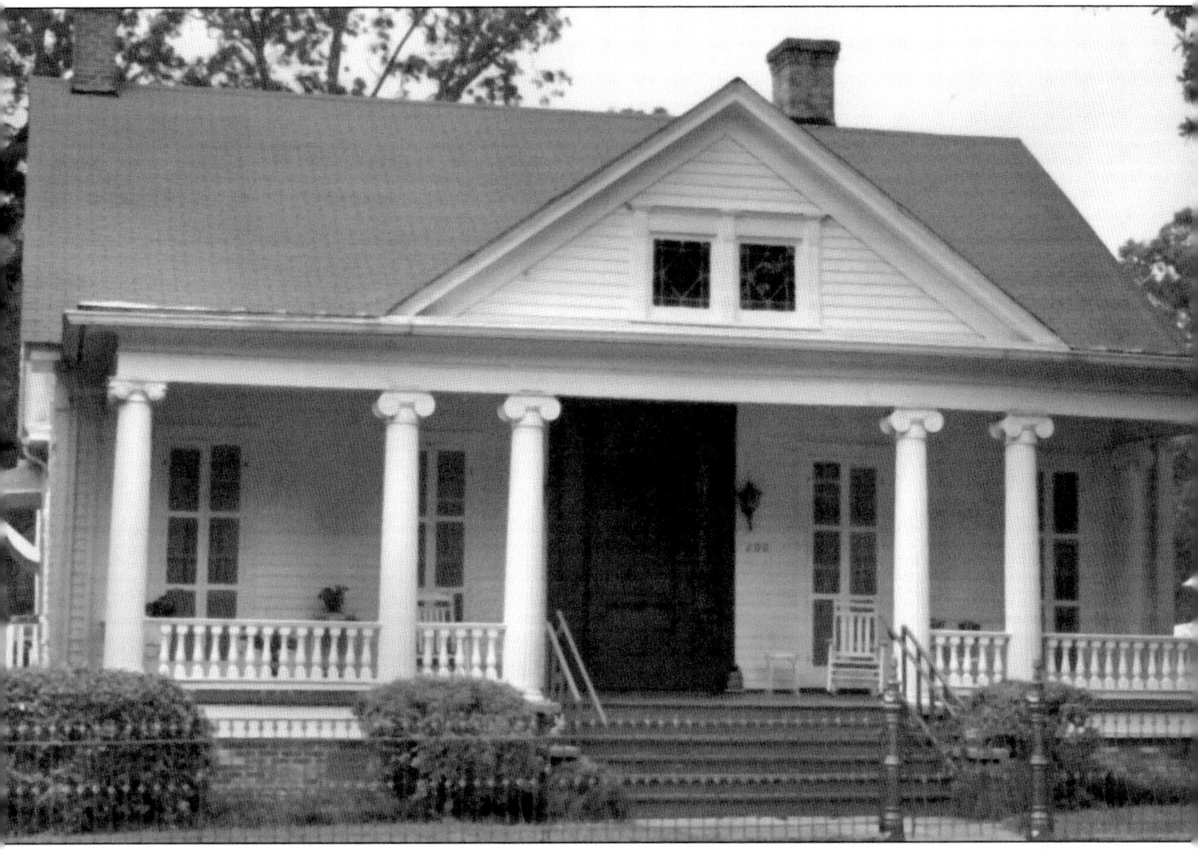

Robert Elam Jones, born October 5, 1843, in Utica, Mississippi, was in school at Mississippi College when the War Between the States began. He joined the army as a lieutenant in Company K, 36th Mississippi Volunteers. He was imprisoned twice, once at Vicksburg and once at Ship Island. He wrote in his diary of the dreadful conditions he underwent. As his troop traveled all over the state fighting the enemy, he once wrote of making it to Crystal Springs, where he camped near the site of the old Newton Institute. At the end of the war, he studied medicine at Tulane University in New Orleans and became a doctor in 1869. He would eventually partner with Dr. J. M. Dampeer. He was married to Elizabeth Ann McKey and had a home on Pearl Street that still stands today. Dr. Jones was once the president of the Mississippi State Medical Association. He died in 1921. (Courtesy of CCHGS.)

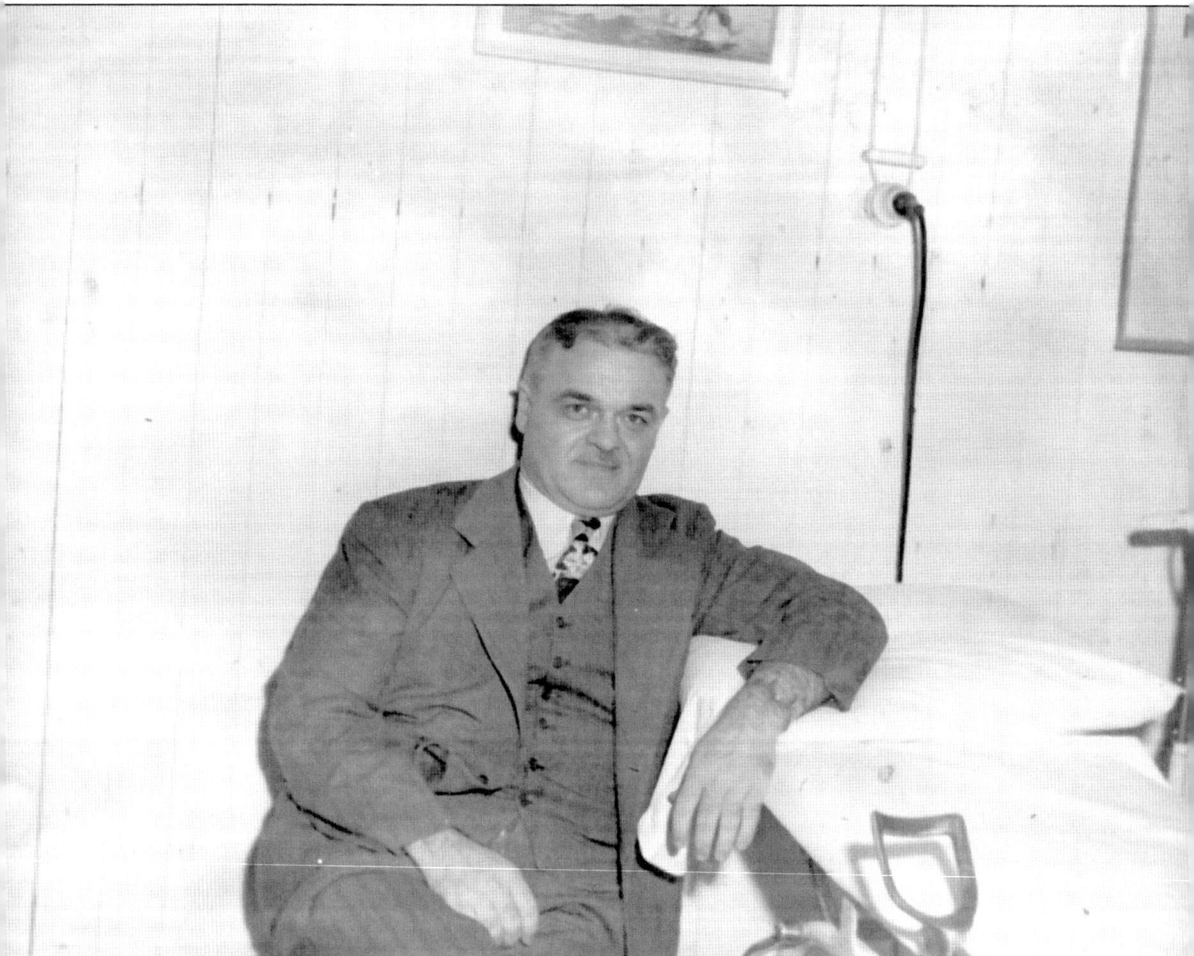

Dr. Oscar G. Eubanks, a native of Lucedale, Mississippi, was a graduate of Blue Mountain Heights Academy, the University of Mississippi, and Tulane University. He established his practice in Crystal Springs and occupied a five-room suite above Steve's Drugstore in the Howell Building for over 20 years. Two years after arriving in Crystal Springs, he married Q. T. Thomas, who was living in the Head House, which he eventually bought and used for his clinic. Soon, he was known as a great doctor all over the South. He would go to great lengths to ensure his patients were taken care of. Many nights he made house calls. His wife often accompanied him and spoke of the rough roads they traveled in the night. He would also travel to Jackson quite frequently to check on his patients. At one time he served as the president of the Central Medical Society of Mississippi. (Courtesy of Nurse Frances Ferguson and Tomato Museum.)

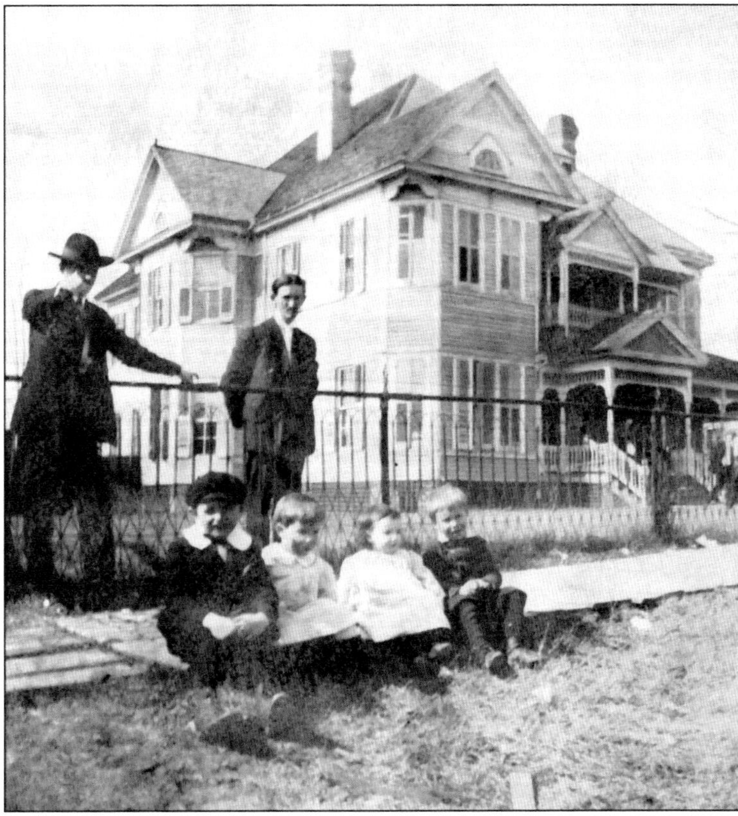

Allred Boarding House was located on Front Street in Hazlehurst behind Wise Motor Company. In the hat is C. B. Rea, and his son, Charley, is to his left. The identities of the children are unknown. Field Marx, the father of George Marx Sr. (who built many of the old buildings in Hazlehurst), was born in the house in 1879. (Courtesy of George W. Covington Memorial Library.)

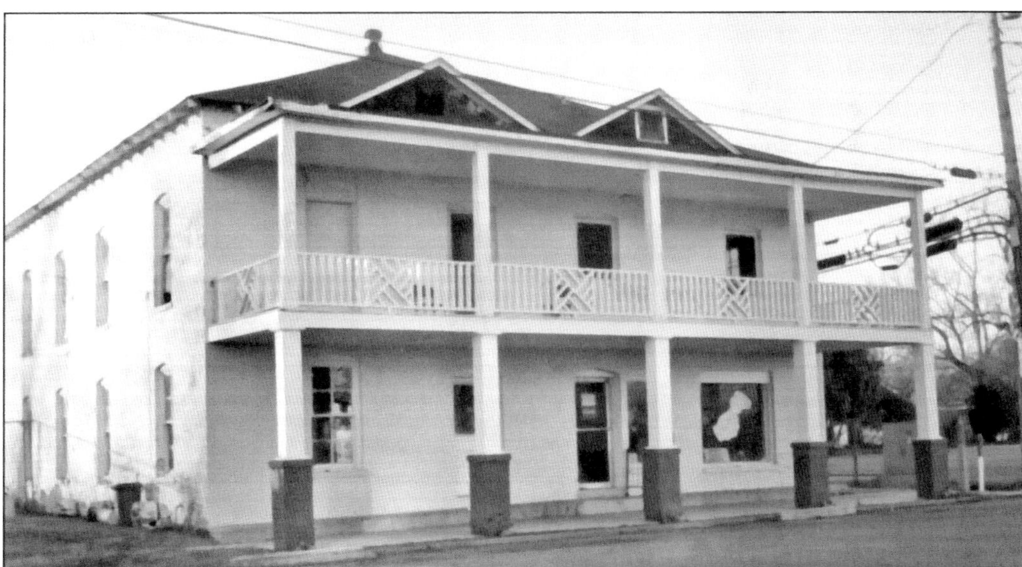

According to local residents, the Wolfe Hotel in downtown Crystal Springs was constructed before the War Between the States, possibly in 1861, when Henry Pickney Barnes moved to Crystal Springs from North Carolina and established his business as a builder. Rumored to be the first brick building in the Crystal Springs, it was once named the Roosevelt Hotel. In 1930, it was named the Crystal Springs Hotel. (Courtesy of CCHGS.)

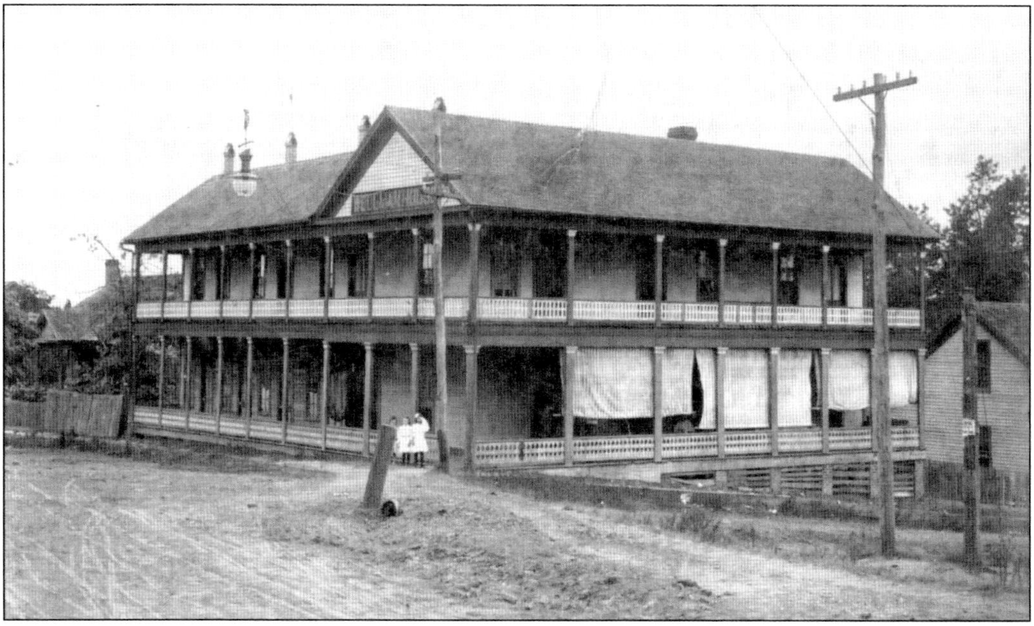

Two large hotels existed in Wesson and Hazlehurst. The one in Wesson was known as the Wellman House. It had long porches on the top and bottom floors and had many rooms. The one below in Hazlehurst was the Ford Hotel, owned by C. W. Ford. He had a hotel in Wesson for 11 years before moving to Hazlehurst in 1902 and establishing a hotel there. It had 22 rooms and boasted of electricity and cold and hot water. C. L. Ford, C. W.'s son, was the manager of the hotel, while C. W. personally attended to the guests' needs. The hotel was on Green Street, just one block from the depot. (Courtesy of MDAH and George W. Covington Memorial Library.)

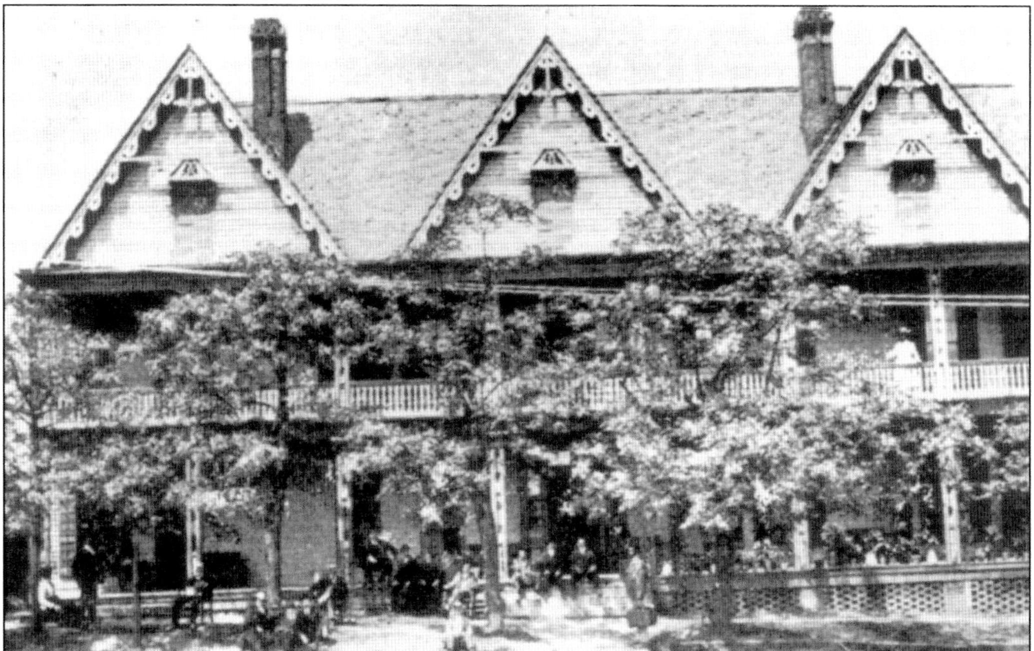

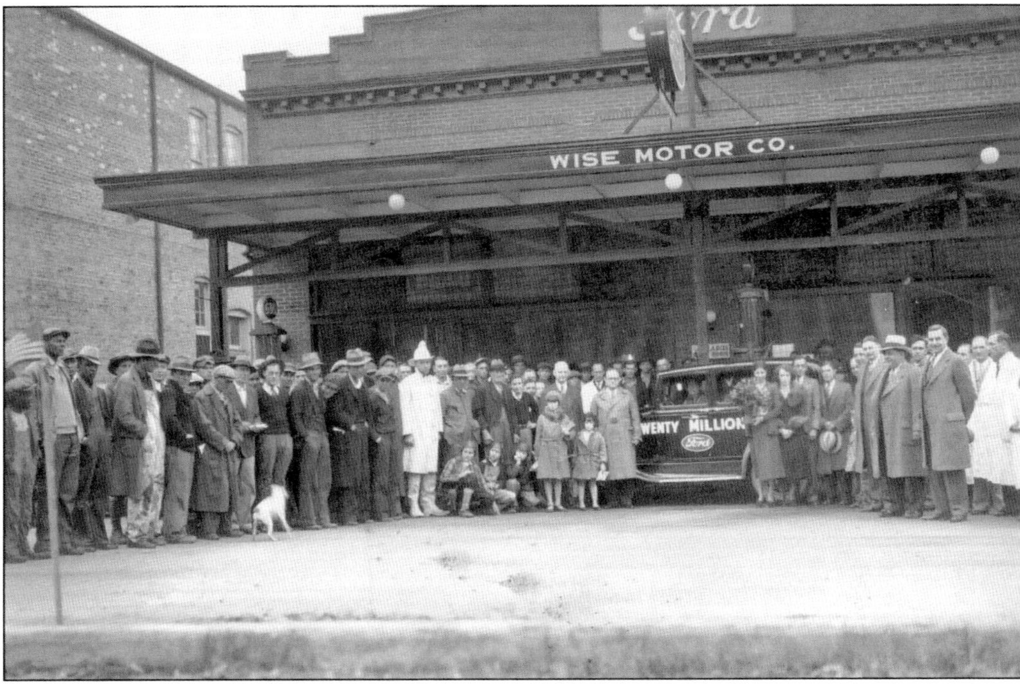

John A. Wise drove a jitney to supplement his income in the off months between vegetable seasons. The fare was 5¢. Around 1912, Wise started selling cars in addition to taxi driving. When the business began to grow, he and his brother, Joe S. Wise, and his sister, Allie Wise Alexander, went into business together. Ford sold them a franchise and they began Wise Motor Company. They constructed a building in 1918 said to contain some of the lumber from the Wesson Mills, which closed in 1910. Around 1920, John let his brother and sister take over the company. Wise Motor Company stayed in the family for many years but is no longer in business. (Courtesy of George W. Covington Memorial Library.)

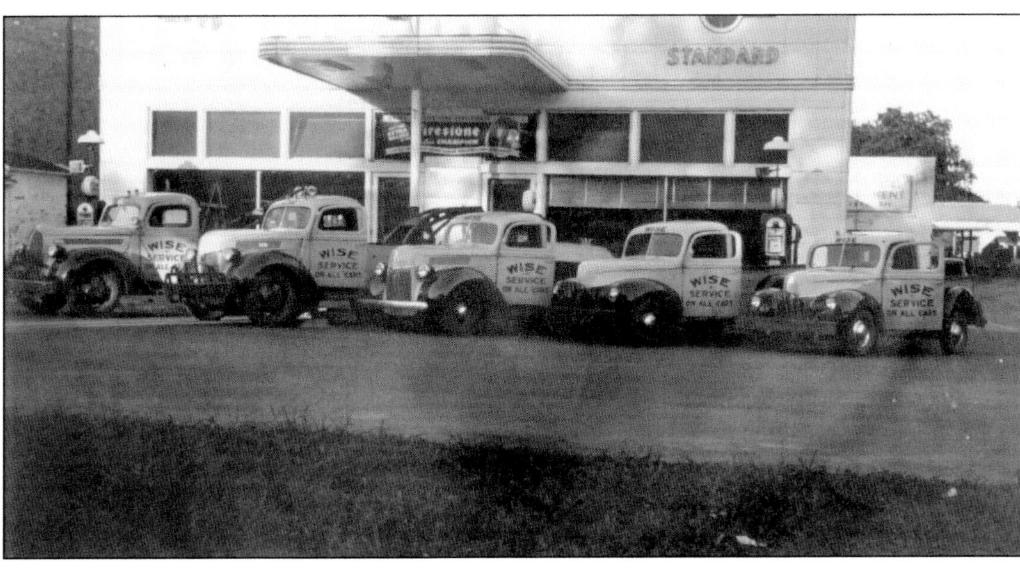

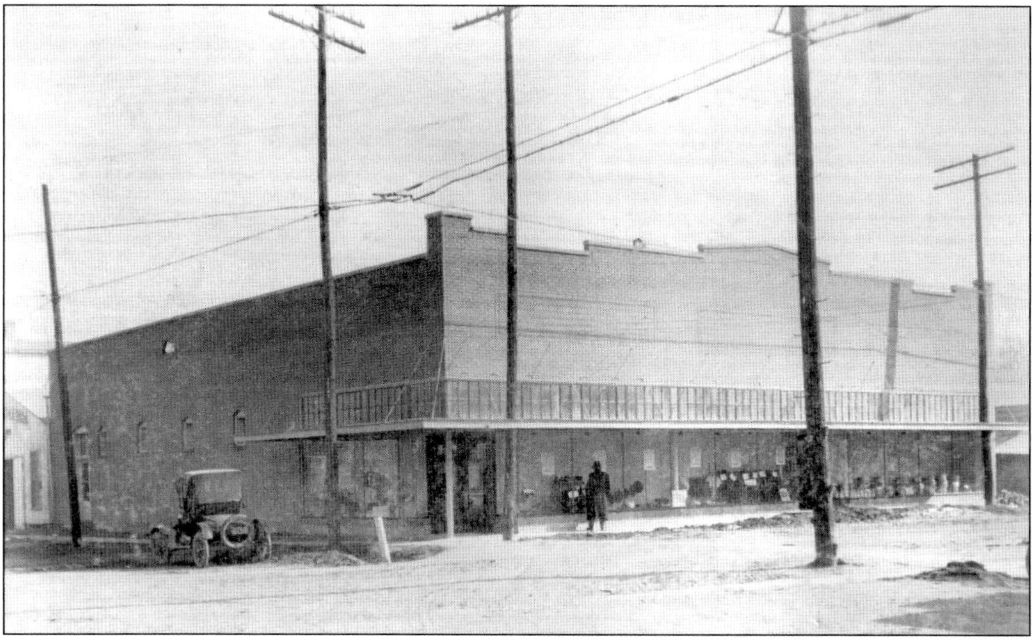

J. T. Biggs Sr. and his son J. T. Biggs Jr. owned several businesses in Crystal Springs. The two most remembered today are the drugstore and the hardware store. The Biggs family also had an ambulance and funeral service for Crystal Springs and Utica. Both the drugstore and hardware store still clearly display the family name on the building. This photograph is of the Biggs Hardware building before it was remodled. The current mural on the side of the building of an early truck reminds one of how long they have been in business. This photograph, taken in 1942 inside one of their stores, shows from left to right J. T. Biggs Jr. and wife Mary Scott Biggs, Rufus Myers, Shug McDonald, Ernest Farrar, "Smut" Bryant, Amy Biggs, Mrs. Terrell, and Martha Biggs. (Courtesy of Martha and Buddy McCoy and Tomato Museum.)

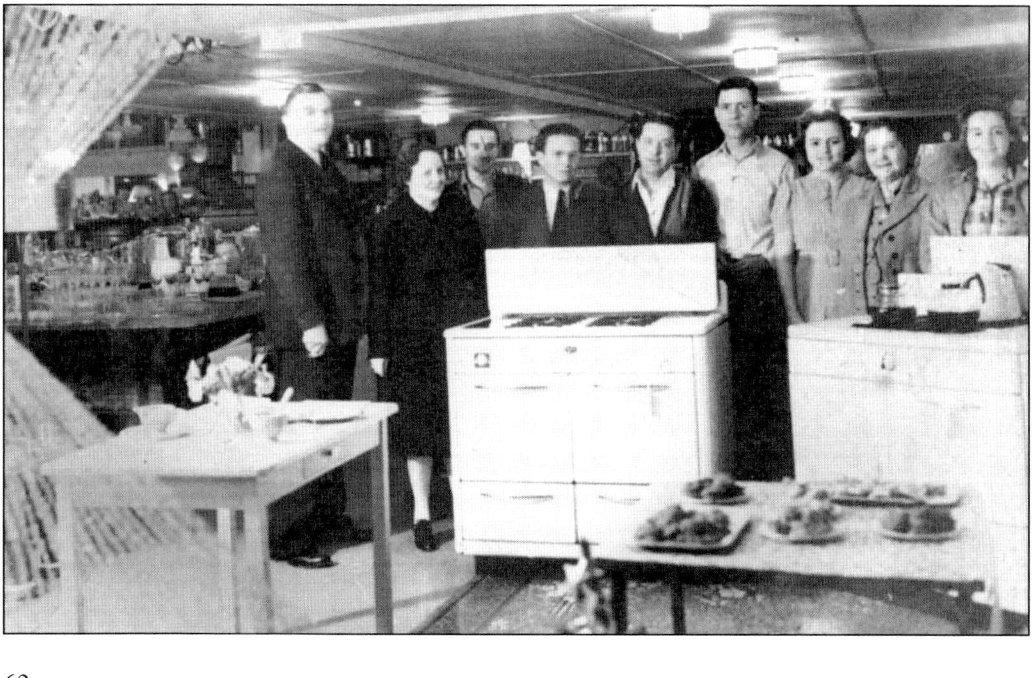

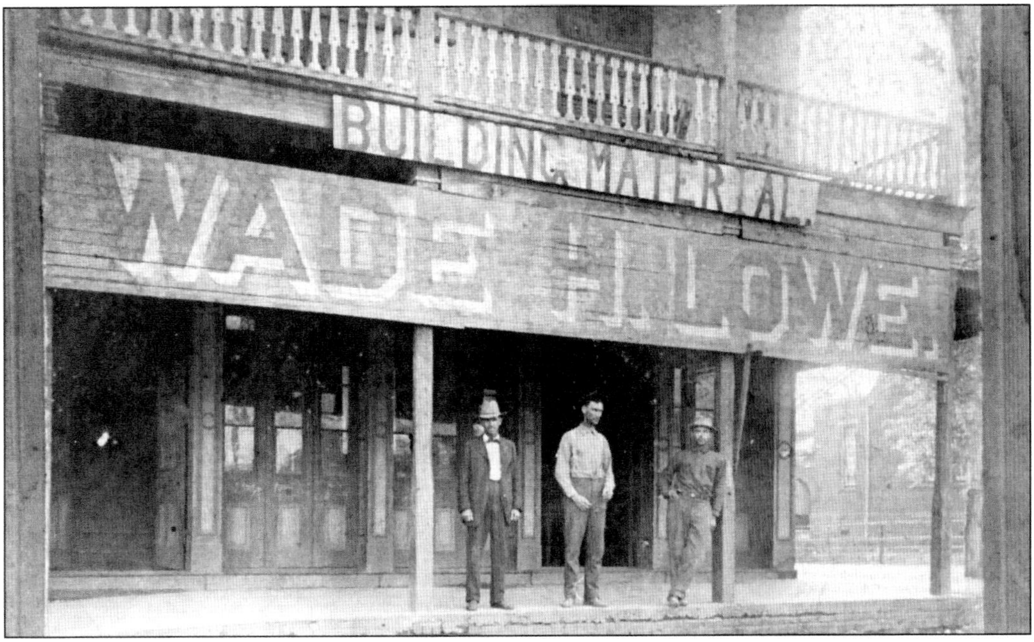

Wade H. Lowe opened this building materials business in February 1906. From left to right are ? Thigpen, Wade H. Lowe, and Johnny Massa. The First Baptist Church of Hazlehurst is barely visible on the right in this picture. (Courtesy of George W. Covington Memorial Library.)

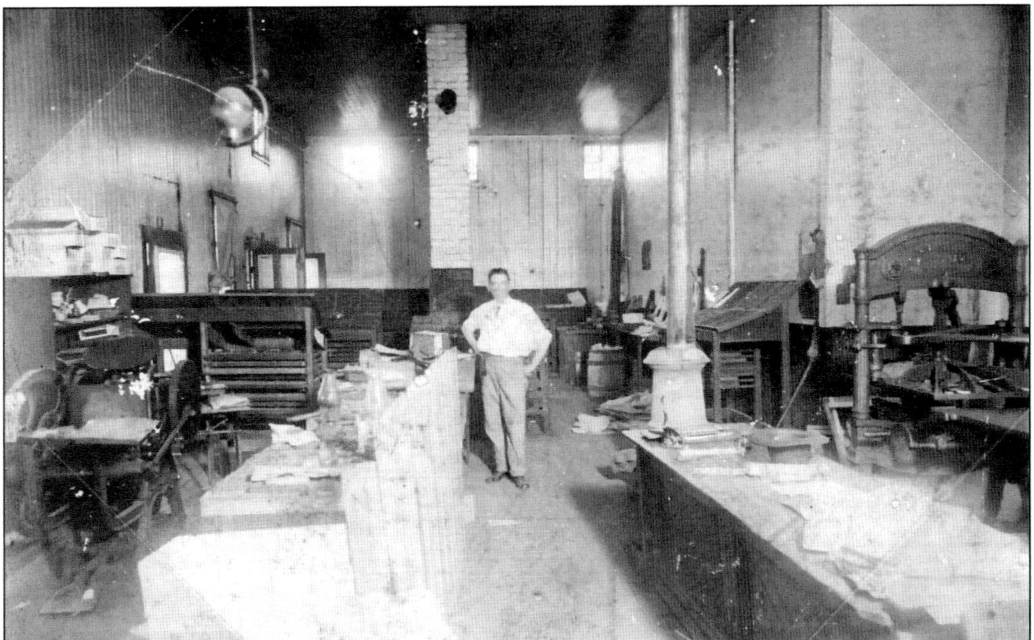

Walter W. Robertson established the *Wesson Enterprise* in May 1899, becoming the owner and editor until his death March 21, 1955. (Courtesy of MDAH.)

If I have made good, reward me with a second term.

LUTHER RAMSEY
Candidate for re-election
COUNTY ASSESSOR
Your Support Will Be Appreciated

THE METEOR

T. F. GODWIN, Publisher

Established in 1881

Large Circulation

Subscription Rate, in Copiah Co.......$1.50 year
Subscription Rate out of county......$2.00 year

Modern Equipped Job Printing Department

88

The first edition of the *Meteor*, edited by Sam H. Aby, appeared on May 16, 1883. Around 1885, it was turned over to Rev. H. J. Harris, who in turn gave it to W. N. Hurt to run. Aby returned in the fall of 1888. He remained the editor until August 11, 1922, when his building was destroyed by fire. He then sold the business to T. F. Godwin and continued to write articles. Aby used the pen name Silas Wegg for articles he submitted to the Hazlehurst *Courier*. T. F. retired in 1948 and sold it to his son, George Godwin. In 1950, George's sister, Eloise Godwin Carney, became both editor and business manager for her brother. The following year, Carney and her husband, John Carney Jr., purchased the business. Their son, Henry, is the current owner. (Courtesy of J. T. Biggs Jr. Memorial Library.)

Four

EDUCATIONAL INSTITUTIONS

Before the War Between the States, the education of children was left largely to private schools and academies. The schools were funded primarily from proceeds raised from 16th-section lands, private donations, and students' tuition. The schools and academies were designed primarily to educate the wealthy and privileged. Very few children, white or black, had access to a free public education prior to Reconstruction. The Mississippi Constitution of 1868 was the first piece of legislation that provided for free public education "for all children between the ages of five and twenty-one years." Enabling legislation passed in 1870 created county school districts under the supervision of an elected state superintendent of education and appointed county superintendents. Towns with at least 5,000 were permitted to establish separate school districts. The Constitution of 1890 maintained a free public education. Legislation passed in 1908 provided for the creation of agricultural high schools. By 1926, forty-nine agricultural high schools existed in Mississippi, including Copiah-Lincoln Agricultural High School, which formed in 1915. Most of the smaller schools eventually consolidated with Crystal Springs and Hazlehurst.

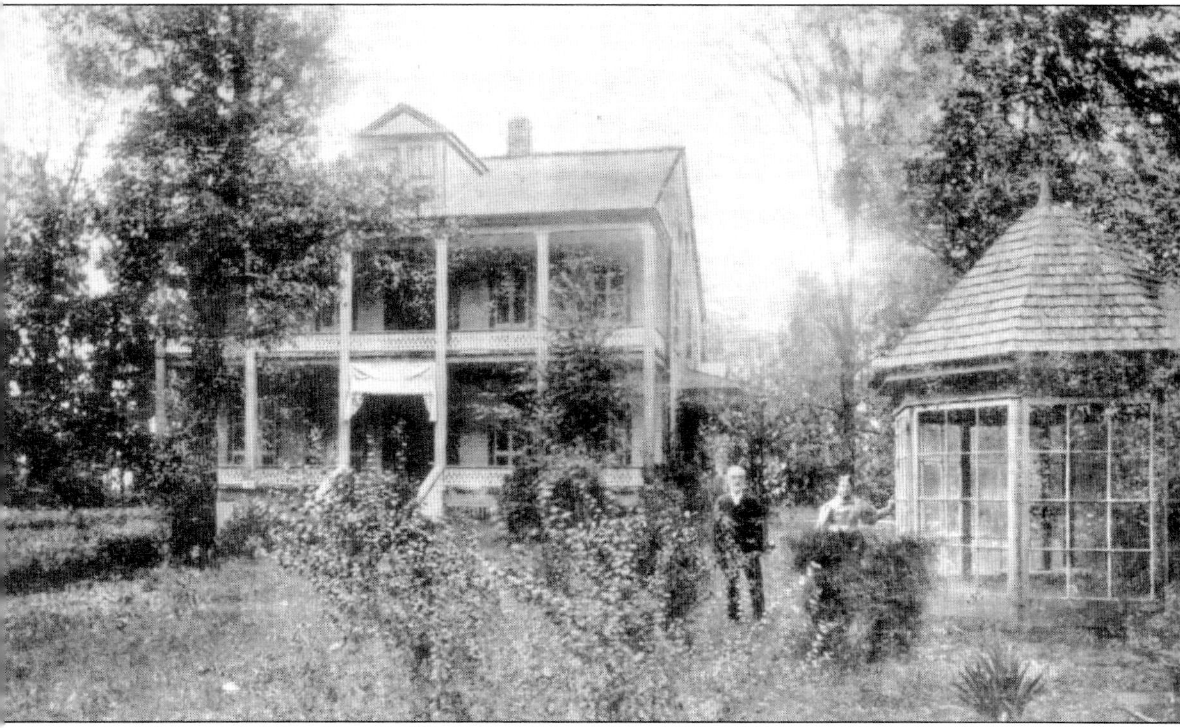

Pictured is the Newton Institute, originally the Young Ladies' Institute, which was founded by Rev. Oscar Newton and his wife, Maria Colton Newton, in 1860. The school stood on the present site of the Crystal Springs High School. It consisted of 20 acres bought from the Willing and Osborne estates. The young ladies boarded at the school, and it was said, in its upper grades, to be on the level of today's community colleges. In 1890, young men were admitted as day students. Reverend Newton's father, Dr. Alexander Newton, founded Hampstead Academy (now Mississippi College) in Clinton in 1842. The institute was destroyed by fire on Thanksgiving night, 1912. Another early school was the Peabody Institute, which stood at the corner of West Railroad Avenue and Cayuga Street. In 1860, the building was owned by the Osborne family. It was a public school from 1869 to 1875. In 1891, it became the Rhymes home, and in 1919, it became the Evans Hotel. (Courtesy of MDAH.)

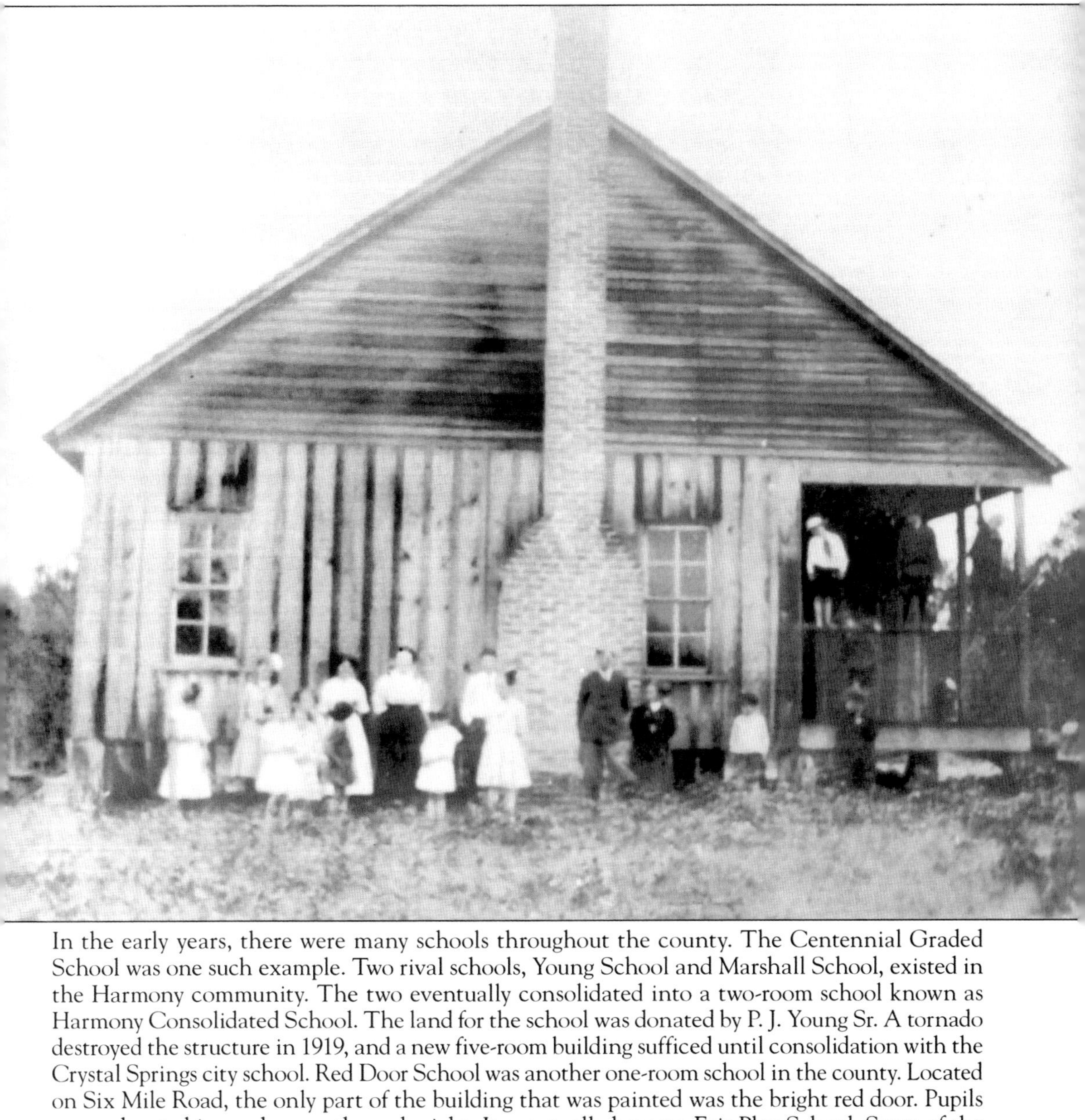

In the early years, there were many schools throughout the county. The Centennial Graded School was one such example. Two rival schools, Young School and Marshall School, existed in the Harmony community. The two eventually consolidated into a two-room school known as Harmony Consolidated School. The land for the school was donated by P. J. Young Sr. A tornado destroyed the structure in 1919, and a new five-room building sufficed until consolidation with the Crystal Springs city school. Red Door School was another one-room school in the county. Located on Six Mile Road, the only part of the building that was painted was the bright red door. Pupils were educated in grades one through eight. It eventually became Fair Play School. Some of the pupils included Enie (Rowene), Barney, Marvin, and John Funchess; Lessie and Betty Manning; and Ethel Hennington. Doris Funchess (Eady) chose Fair Play for her first teaching experience. In the last year of its existence, Mattie Brown Ashmore was its teacher. Among her pupils were Mary Jane and Lorena Palmer. (Courtesy of Tomato Museum.)

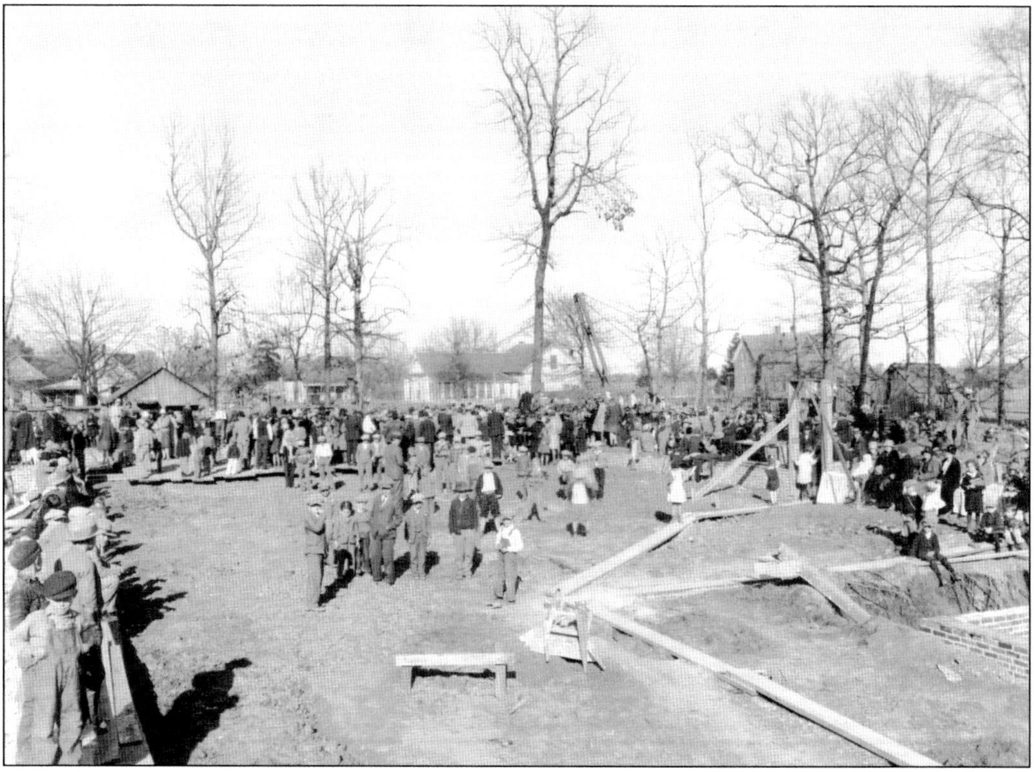

The original school in Crystal Springs was a two-story wood structure built in 1891 at the corner of North Jackson Street and Lee Avenue. In 1899, the senior class had 19 members, including Byron Pat Harrison, a future senator. By 1902, the school had over 400 students. Eventually, due to the growth of the town and students, a new building was needed. The three-story Crystal Springs Consolidated School was a celebration for everyone, as seen in the photograph. Constructed on a 25-acre campus where the Peabody Institute once stood, it consisted of 88 rooms and was, at one point, the largest consolidated school in the United States. Today it serves as the Crystal Springs High School. (Courtesy of MDAH.)

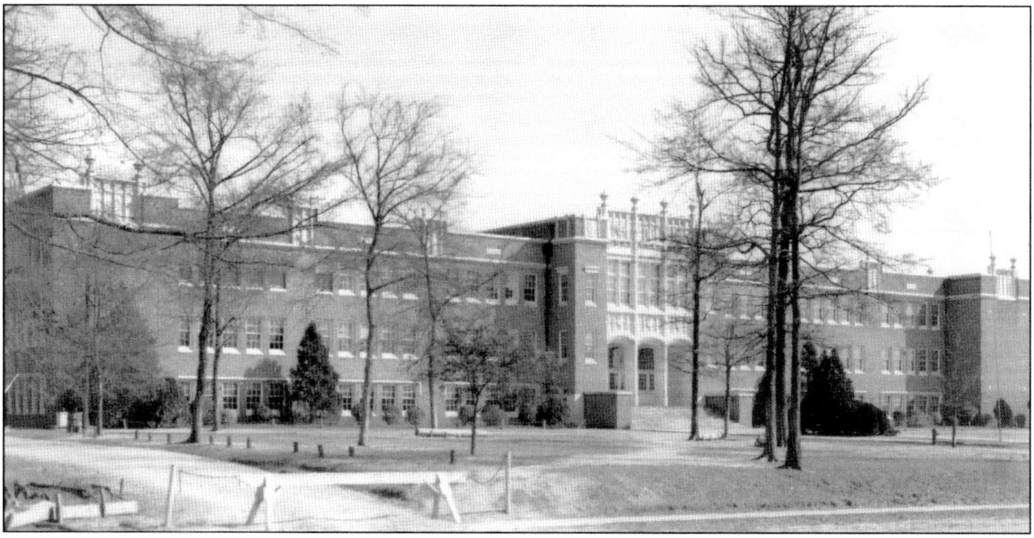

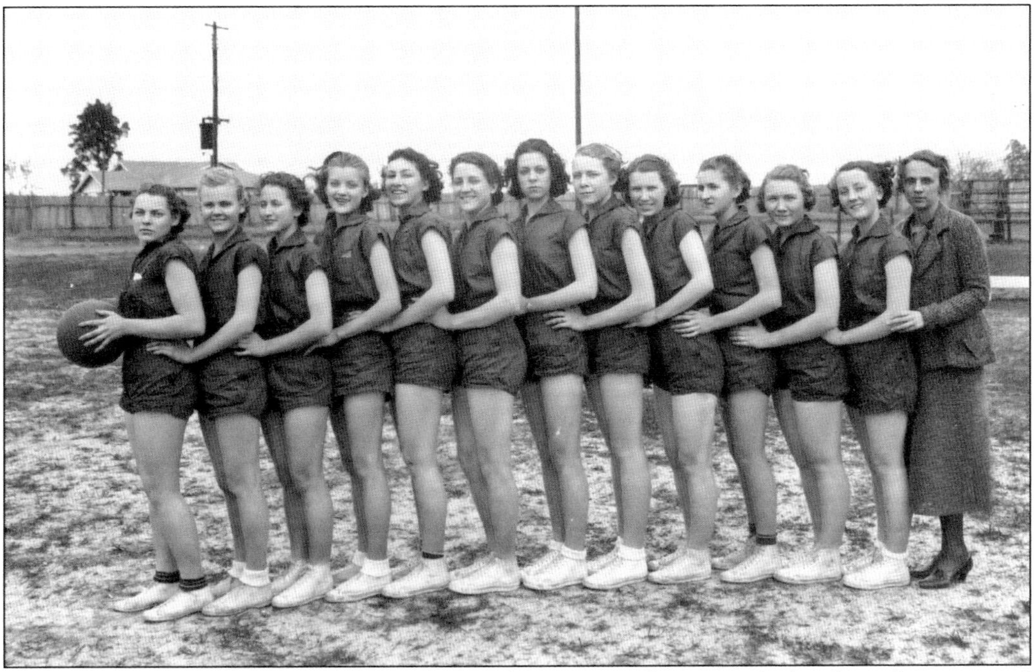

In 1846, Gov. A. G. Brown successfully pushed for a general system of schools in the state, and by 1870, a uniform system was adopted. Education was making strides, but it was not until the consolidation of smaller schools that pupils could become well rounded, both academically and socially. Now there were enough students of the same age that separate classrooms could be used for separate grades. With consolidation came a larger school, more teachers, more students, and more choices in extracurricular activities. For example, Crystal Spring Consolidated School had a girls basketball team and a band. (Courtesy of MDAH.)

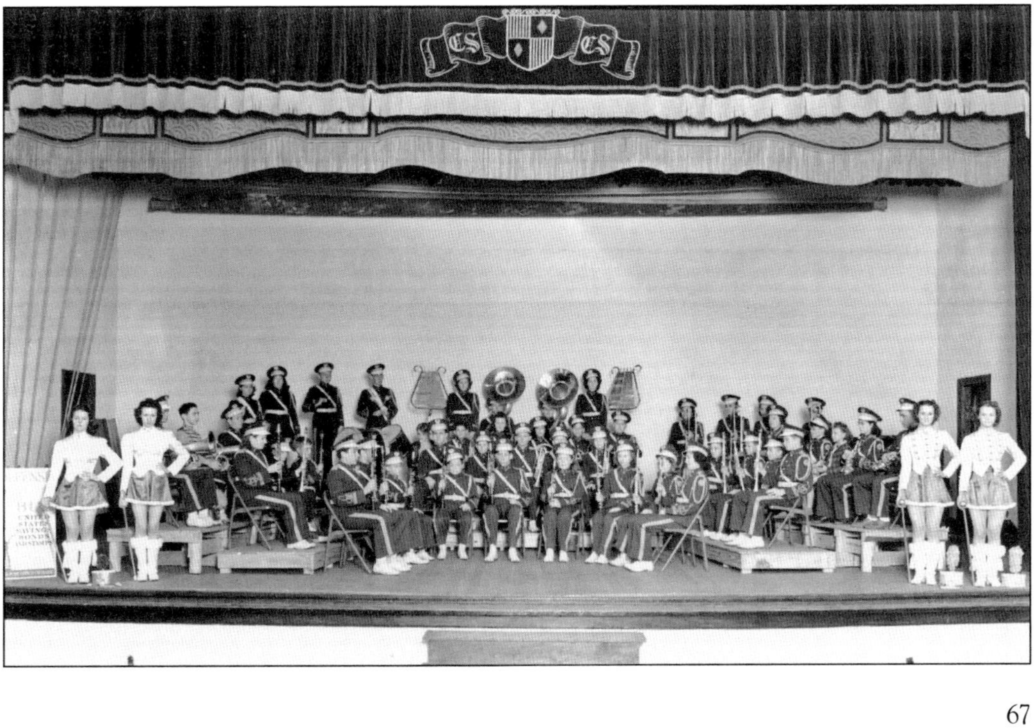

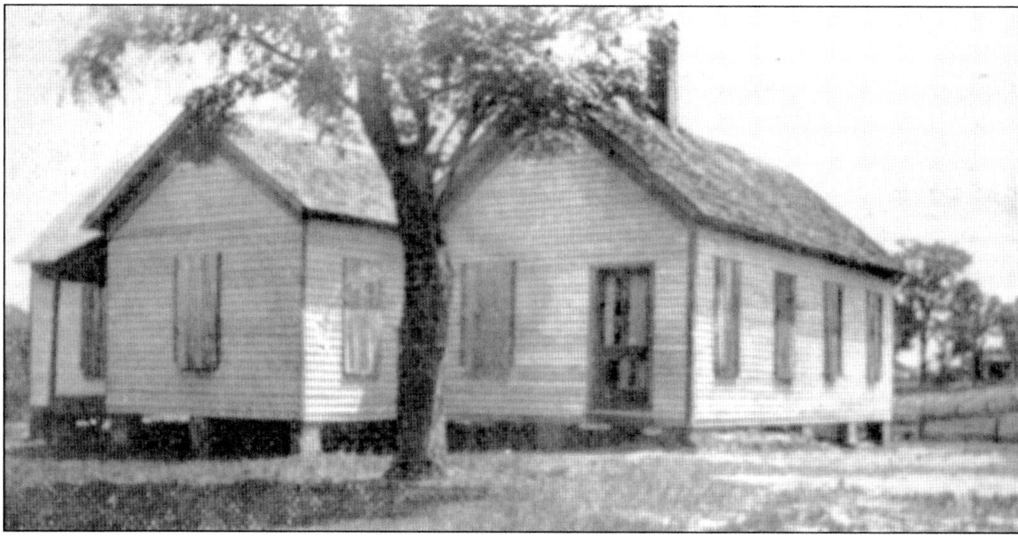

The first school organized in Hazlehurst was the Hazlehurst Male and Female Institute on Georgetown Street. L. Campbell was the first principal. The school was erected and operated by the town of Hazlehurst, assisted by the Peabody Educational Fund. This was the Hazlehurst High School in its infancy. (Courtesy of George W. Covington Memorial Library.)

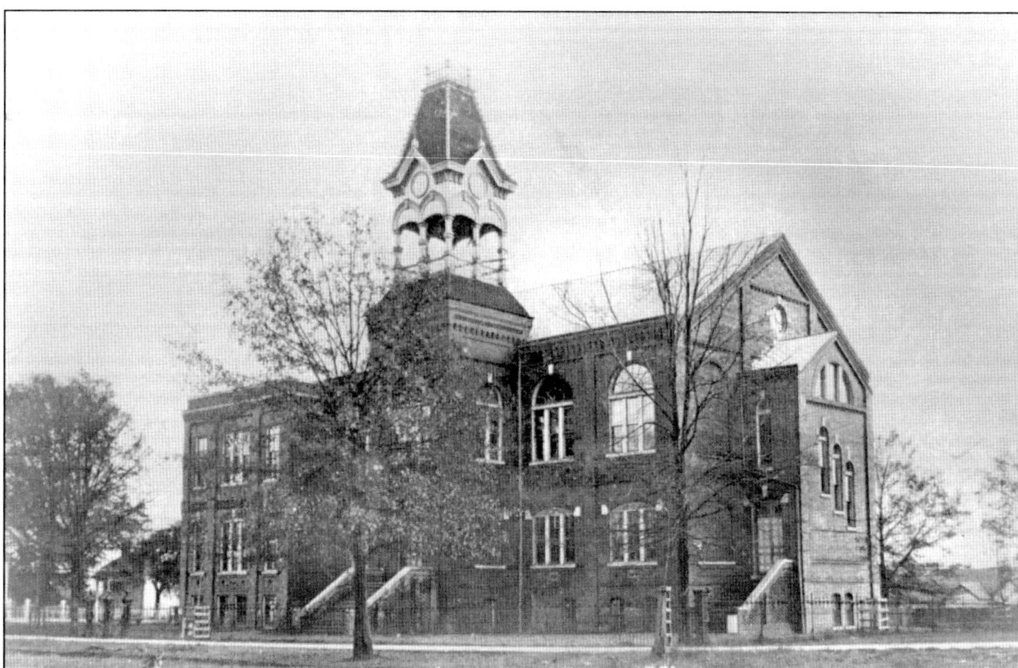

There were quite a number of private schools in town. Some who ran private schools were Mrs. R. W. Millsaps, Mrs. McKinnell, Mrs. E. E. Inslee, Mittie Jones, Mrs. McNeil, Mattie Miller, Miss Curtiss, Lou Jones and Inzy Wise, Mr. Burch, Maude Hawkins, and Dr. Douglas. This is the new Hazlehurst High School, not long after it was built. (Courtesy of George W. Covington Memorial Library.)

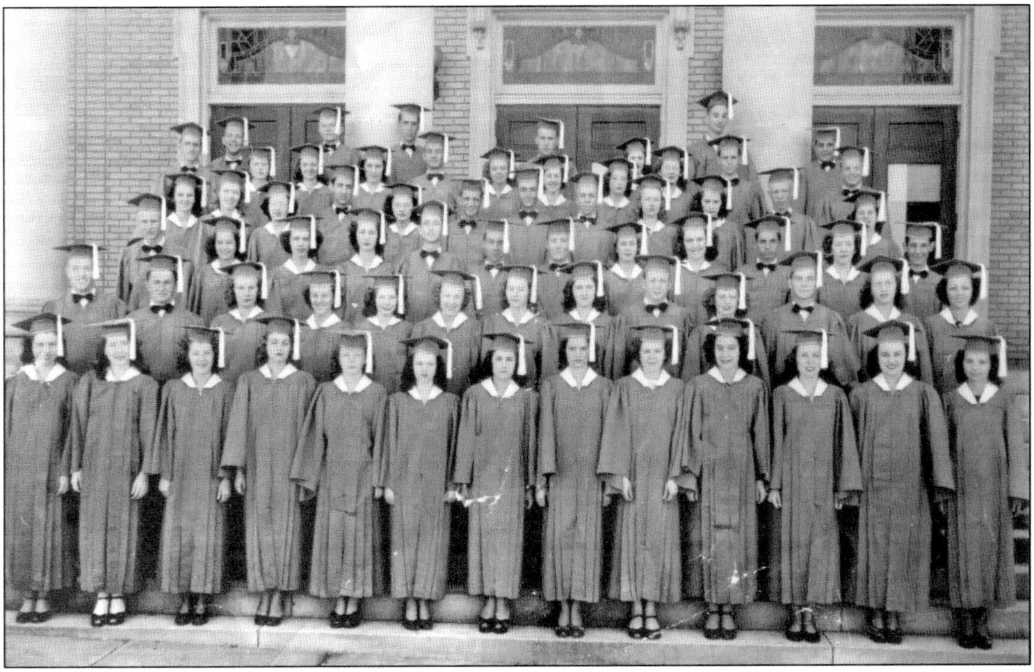

The Hazlehurst Separate School District was organized in 1886. The central section of Hazlehurst High was erected in 1888 and opened with eight grades. By 1906, there were 10 grades, and by 1911, there were 12 grades. One of the teachers at that time was Rea Ard. Pictured is the graduating class of 1948. (Courtesy of Patrick Roper.)

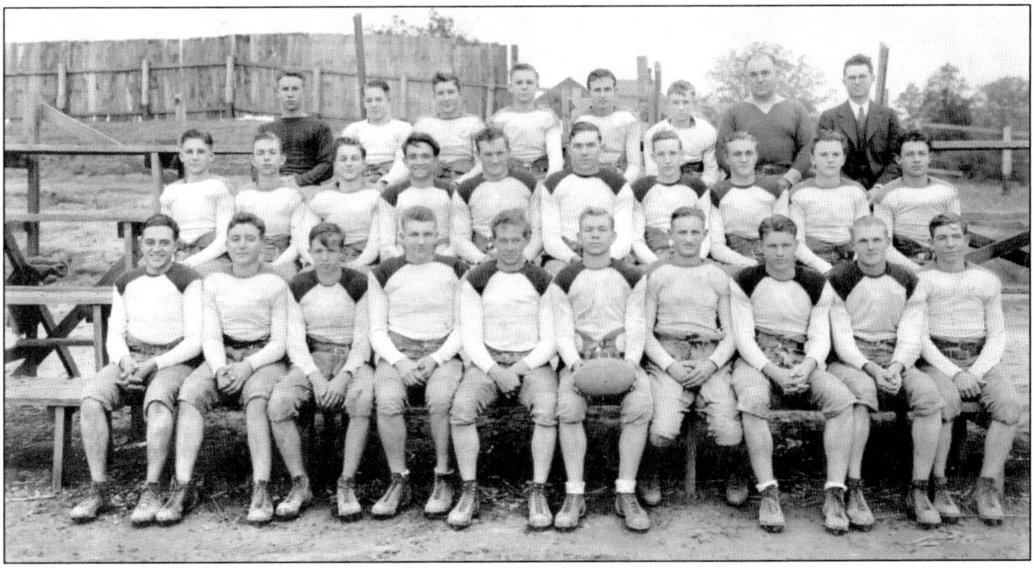

In 1910, a wing was added, and the first PTA meeting took place in 1913. On April 10, 1939, school time was rescheduled to 8:00 a.m.–1:00 p.m. to allow the boys time to work in the shipping sheds and help with the crops. The first football game was played in Hazlehurst against Brookhaven. Pictured is the Hazlehurst football team of 1935–1936. (Courtesy of Shirley Fitzgerald.)

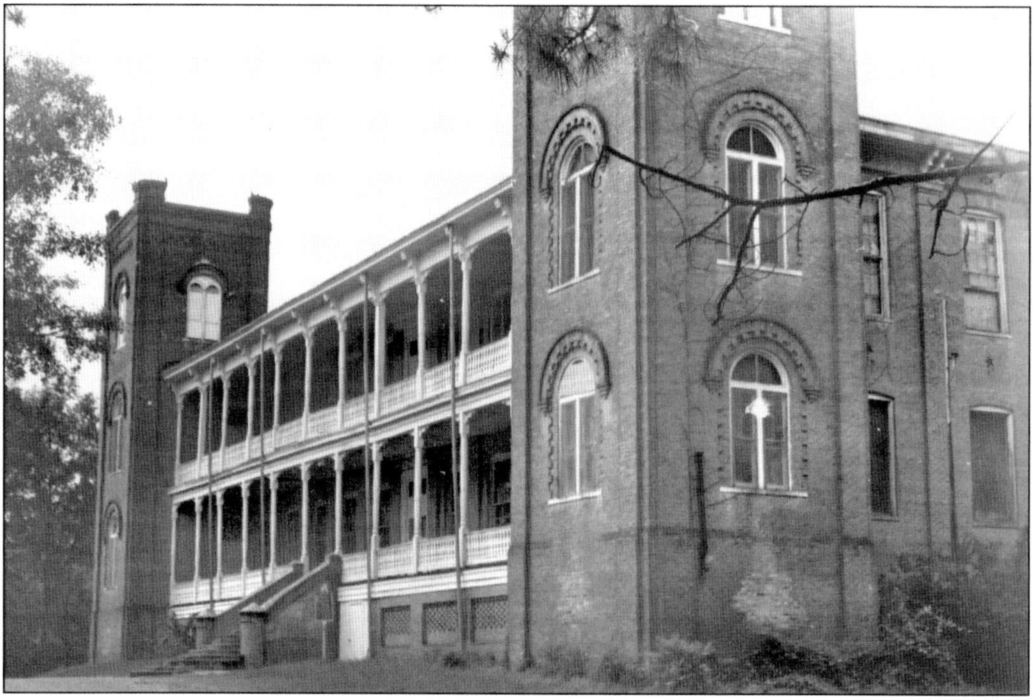

The Old Wesson Public School on Eighth Street was financed in 1889 by the owners of the Wesson Mills. The structure burned in 1890 and was rebuilt in 1893 in the Romanesque style with twin towers flanking each side of the front of the building. It was used as a school until 1960, when a new school was built across town. It was then named the Oswalt Community Center in honor of Mr. and Mrs. Frank Oswalt. Frank Oswalt was the principal for many years. It is listed on the National Register of Historic Places. Pictured are all the students in May 1920. (Courtesy of Longie Dale Hamilton Memorial Library.)

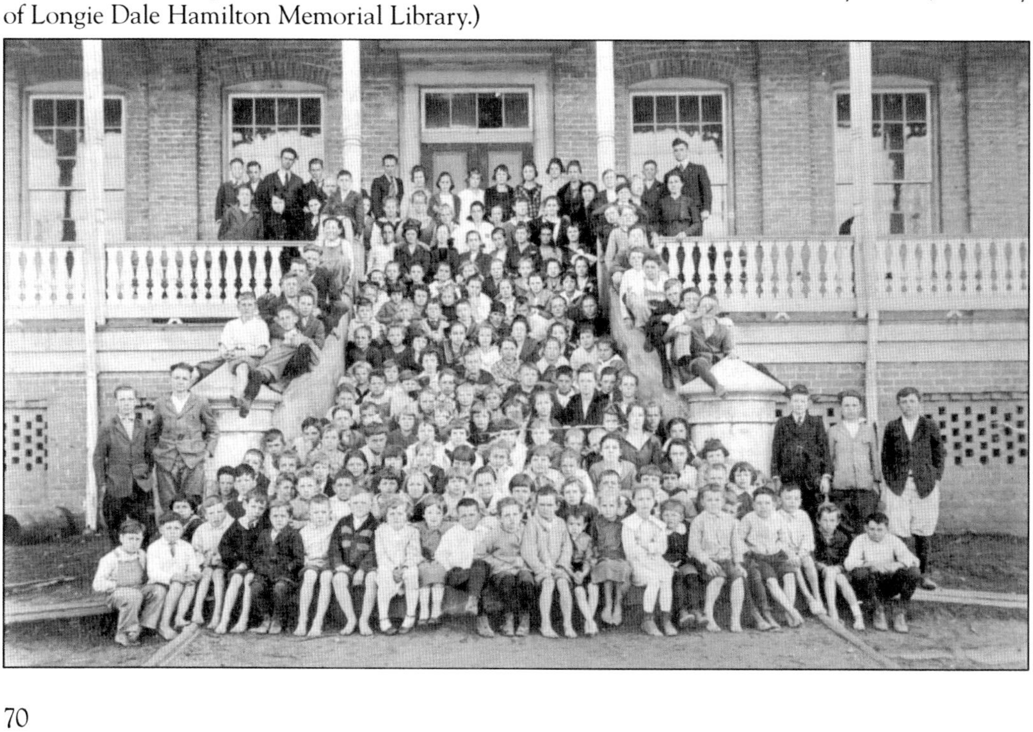

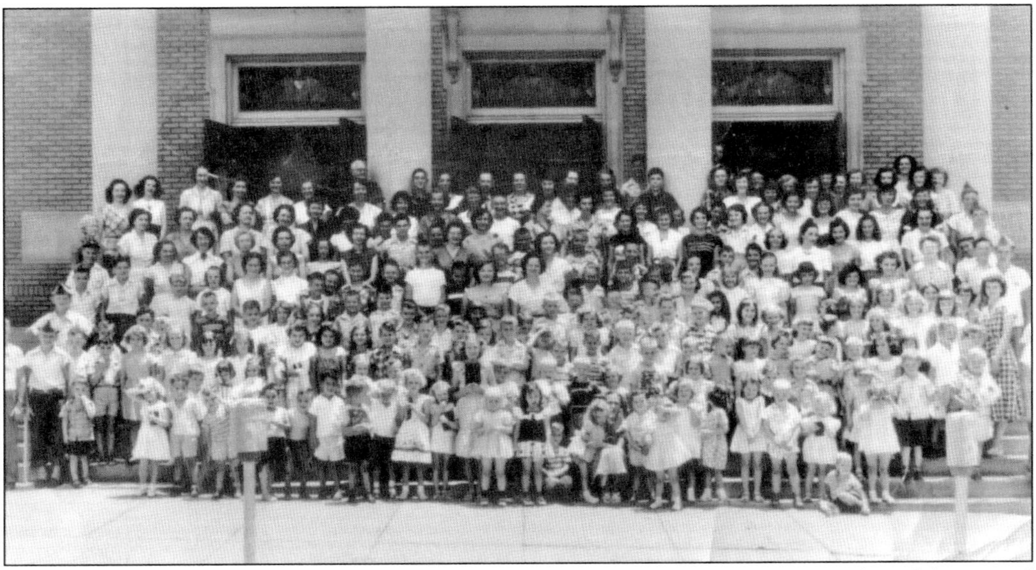

Gallman was incorporated on November 27, 1896, between Crystal Springs and Hazlehurst and was named for one of its first settlers, W. B. Gallman. The town had a consolidated school in which high school students remained until 1946, when they transferred to Hazlehurst. Grades one through eight remained until 1954, when the school closed. A big reunion was held on September 4, 1982, and 300 attended. (Courtesy of Patrick Roper.)

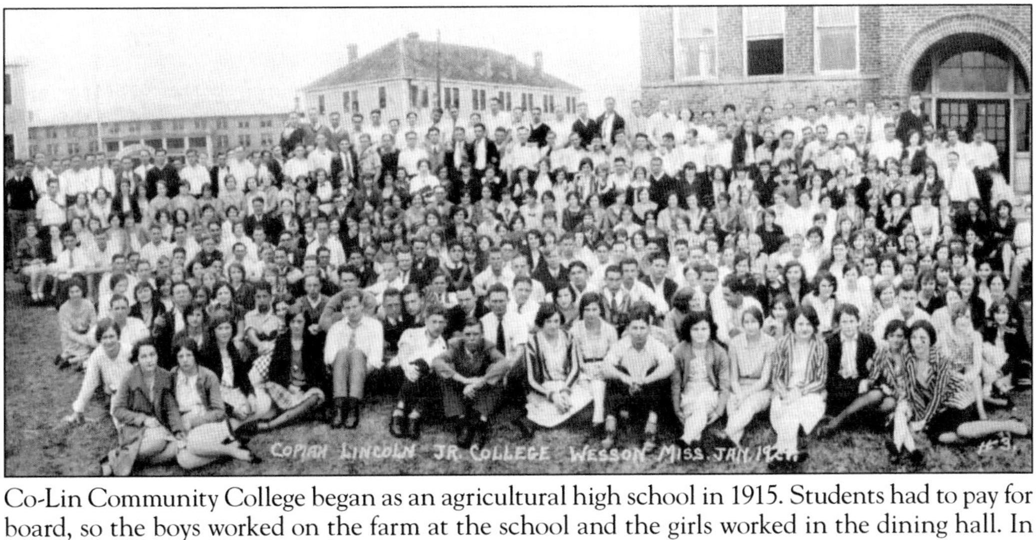

Co-Lin Community College began as an agricultural high school in 1915. Students had to pay for board, so the boys worked on the farm at the school and the girls worked in the dining hall. In 1928, it became a two-year junior college in addition to a high school. Pictured are the students of the college in January 1929. (Courtesy of Evelyn W. Oswalt Library.)

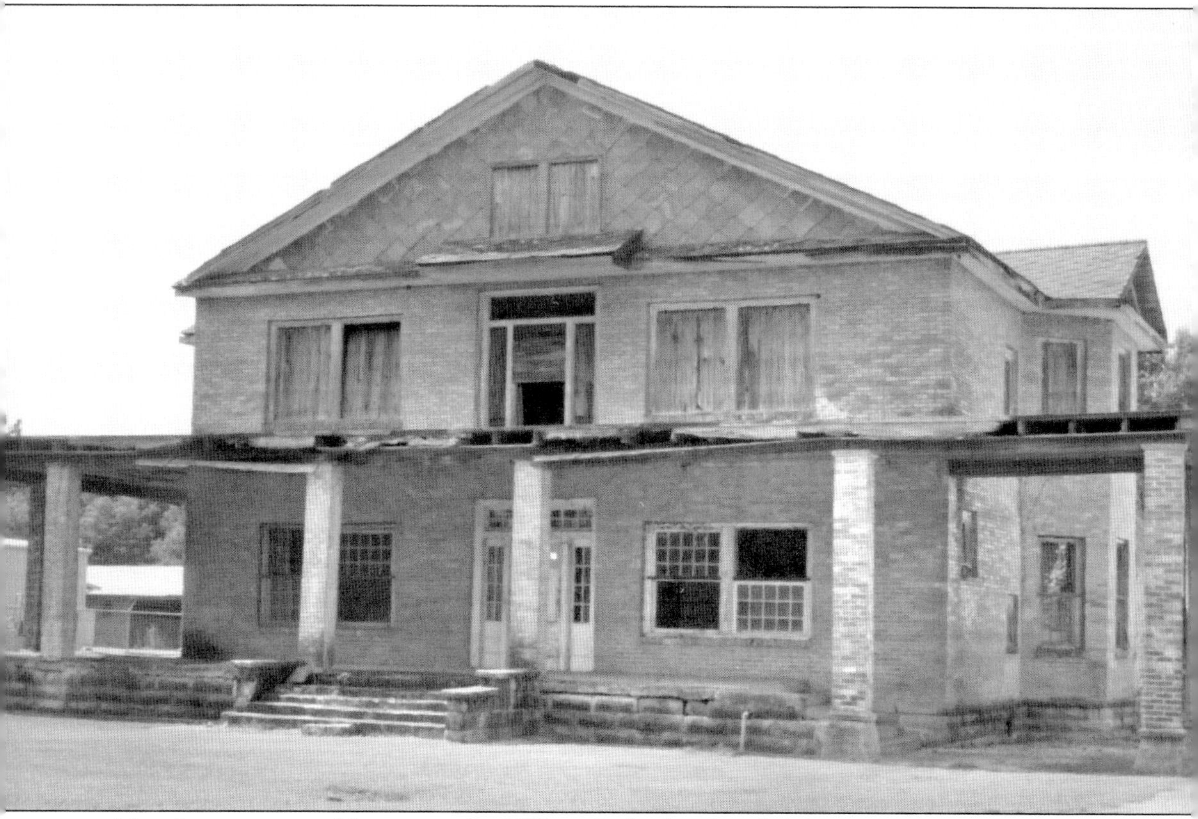

After three unsuccessful attempts, Dr. William Holtzclaw founded the Utica Normal and Industrial Institute for the Training of Colored Young Men and Women. From 1903 to 1910, the school was in Utica, Hinds County. Around 1907, he sought property farther away from distractions and ended up with several acres in Copiah County on the Hinds County line. Holtzclaw wrote *The Black Man's Burden*, which chronicles the struggles he overcame in order to provide an education to those who would otherwise do without. When he passed away in 1943, the school had 22 teachers, 1,600 acres of land, 14 buildings, and over 400 students. His son continued the school for about four years, and then the family decided to donate it to Hinds County. The board decided to change it to Hinds County Agricultural High School, Colored. This eventually became the Utica campus of Hinds Community College. The Holtzclaw Mansion, now in poor condition, is all that remains of the original buildings. (Courtesy of CCHGS.)

Five

Houses of Worship

Copiah County is deeply rooted in religion, just as Mississippi and the South are. Some churches were organized before Copiah was even a county. Church buildings symbolize a commitment by their congregations to the community and a certain level of permanence within the development of the town. Few original churches exist in their original state. Many have been modernized with brick exteriors and additions to accommodate the growing congregations. Sundays were a day of worship and rest. No business whatsoever was conducted on Sunday, not even cooking. Meals were prepared the day before so women would not have to work on the Sabbath day.

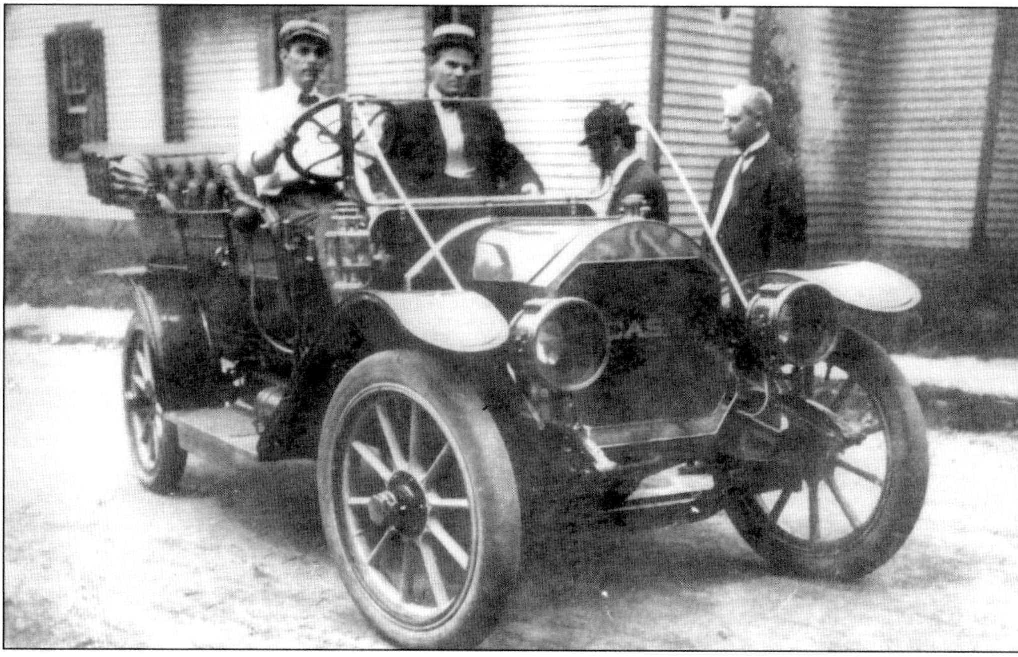

Lake Chautauqua is in Crystal Springs on the old Hennington Campgrounds. In 1872, several leading Methodist ministers of the Brookhaven district decided to establish a camp meeting and build a tabernacle where people might come and peacefully worship. The Hennington family donated the land for the campground. At the self-supporting campground, meals were 50¢ and beds were another 50¢. In 1873, there were 28 cottages. The congregations grew enormous. People would arrive on the train, which made multiple stops each day. They were carried by buggies, wagons, and hacks that charged 10¢ for the short drive to the campgrounds through where Camp Street is today. These are the types of taxis they used. Rufus Lawless drove the bus. (J. T. Biggs Jr. Memorial Library and Mary Taylor Guy.)

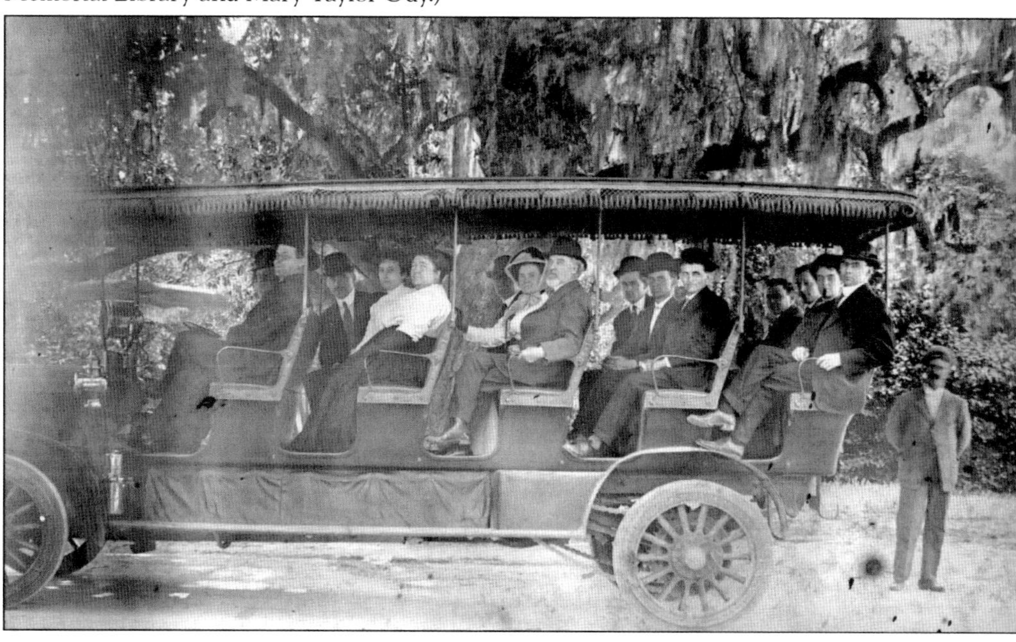

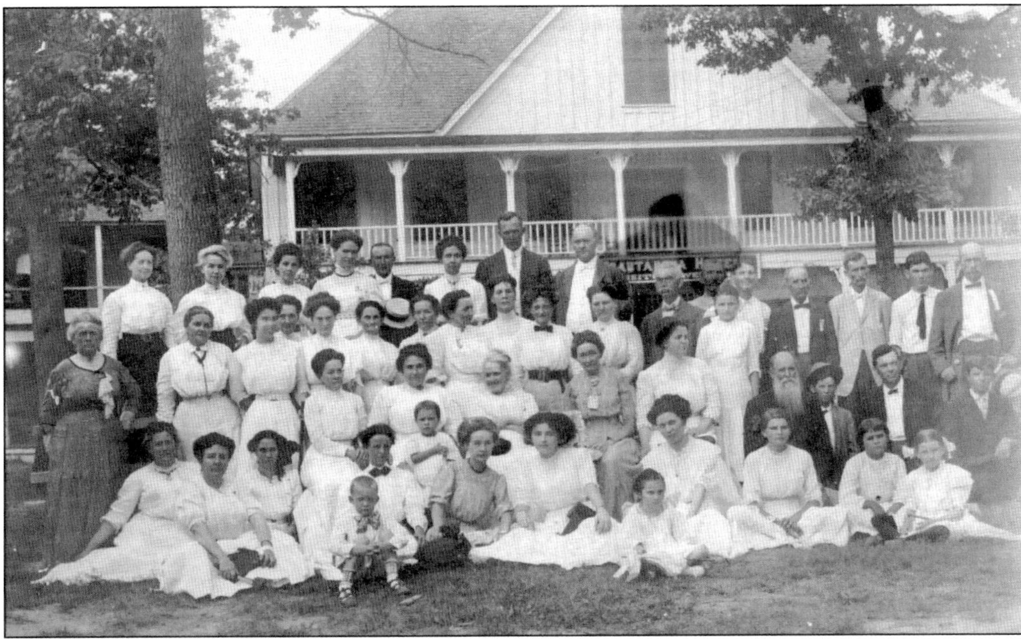

The first Chautauqua Assembly was founded in New York in 1874. The Crystal Springs Chautauqua organized at the Hennington Campgrounds and became one of the most notable of the assemblies in the United States. It was active from 1892 to 1917. The Chautauqua Institution was initially a summer training program for Sunday school teachers. It eventually evolved into a scientifically, politically, and culturally stimulating experience. (Courtesy of J. T. Biggs Jr. Memorial Library.)

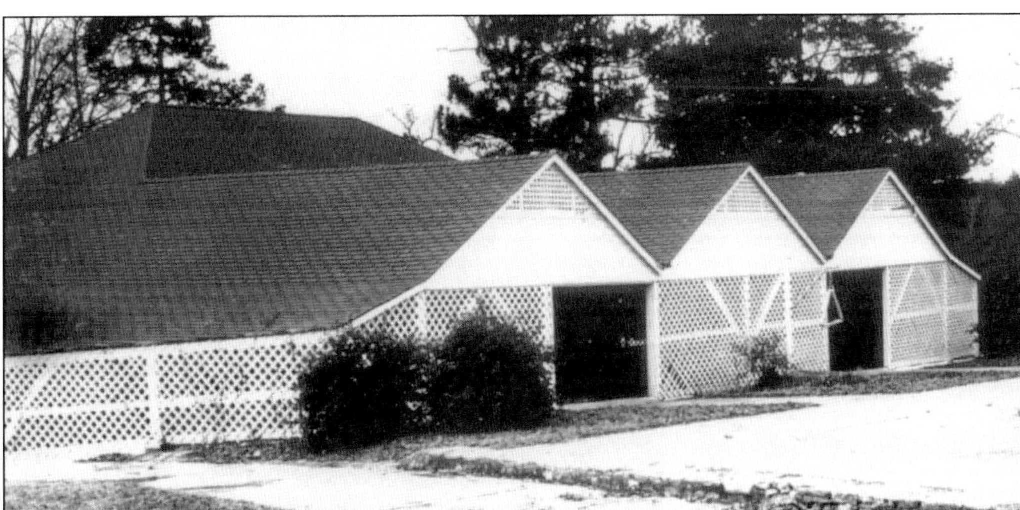

Soon a tabernacle was built. By 1916, the park had 88 cottages, a 40-room hotel, a restaurant, and a grocery store. The tabernacle could seat 1,000 people. The structure is no longer standing, but the triangle used to call attention was saved by two Crystal Springs city employees, Tally Jackson and Robert Sims. The triangle hangs in the Tomato Museum at Chautauqua Park. (Courtesy of Tomato Museum.)

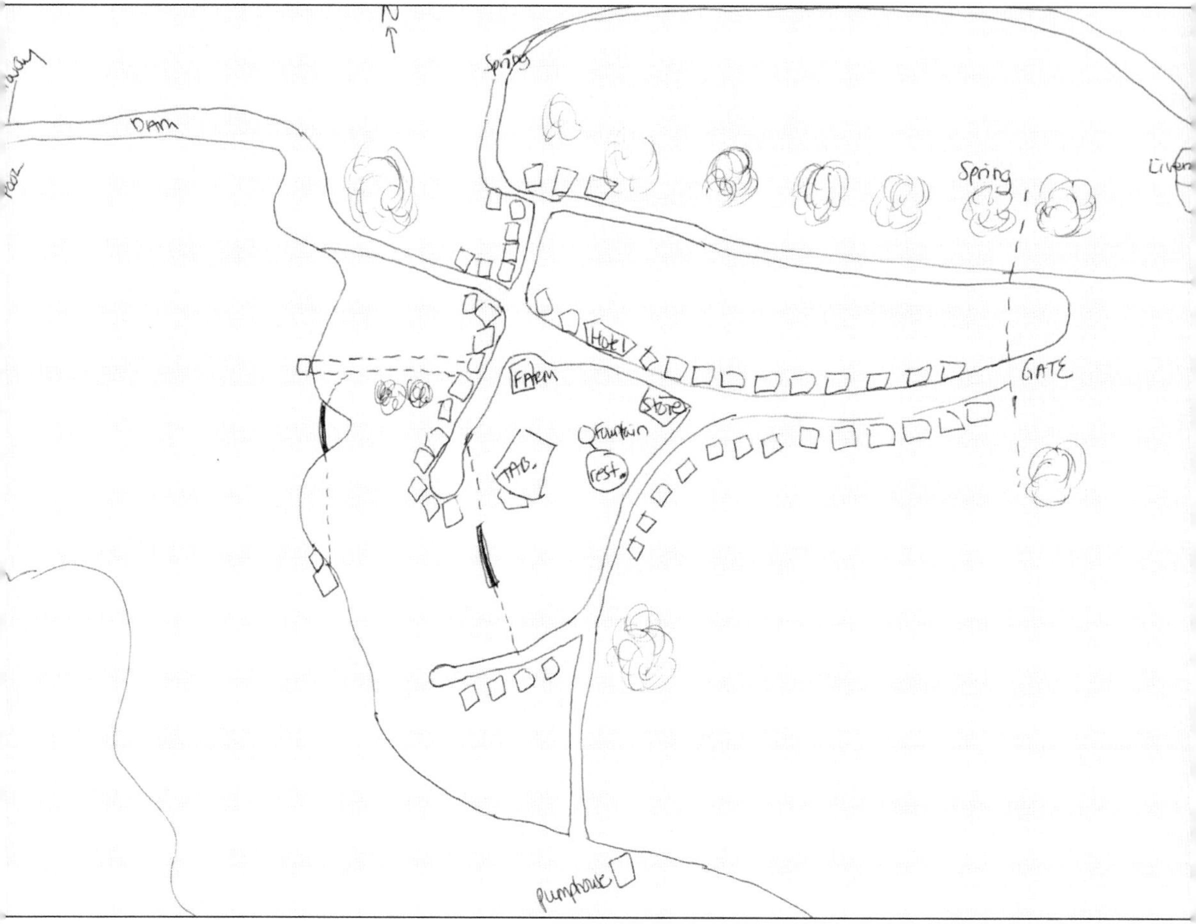

According to a map originally drawn by Robert Cook Jones, a livery stable was on the outside of the gate. Just inside the gate, on the right, was a spring. Cottages lined the main road on the left and right. There were also cottages along the remainder of the roads throughout the campgrounds. The hotel was farther down on the right. There was a store on the left, with a restaurant behind it and a fountain in front of it. The tabernacle was farther down on the left. The pump house was on the lake, since it pumped water to the railroad in town. Across the dam there was a swimming area. With the coming of World War I, the Chautauqua movement died nationally as well as in Crystal Springs. During the 1930s, the WPA provided native stone walks and abutments in the park. A pavilion and a springhouse were constructed of the same material. Today Chautauqua Park is operated by the City of Crystal Springs as a municipal park. (Courtesy of J. T. Biggs Jr. Memorial Library.)

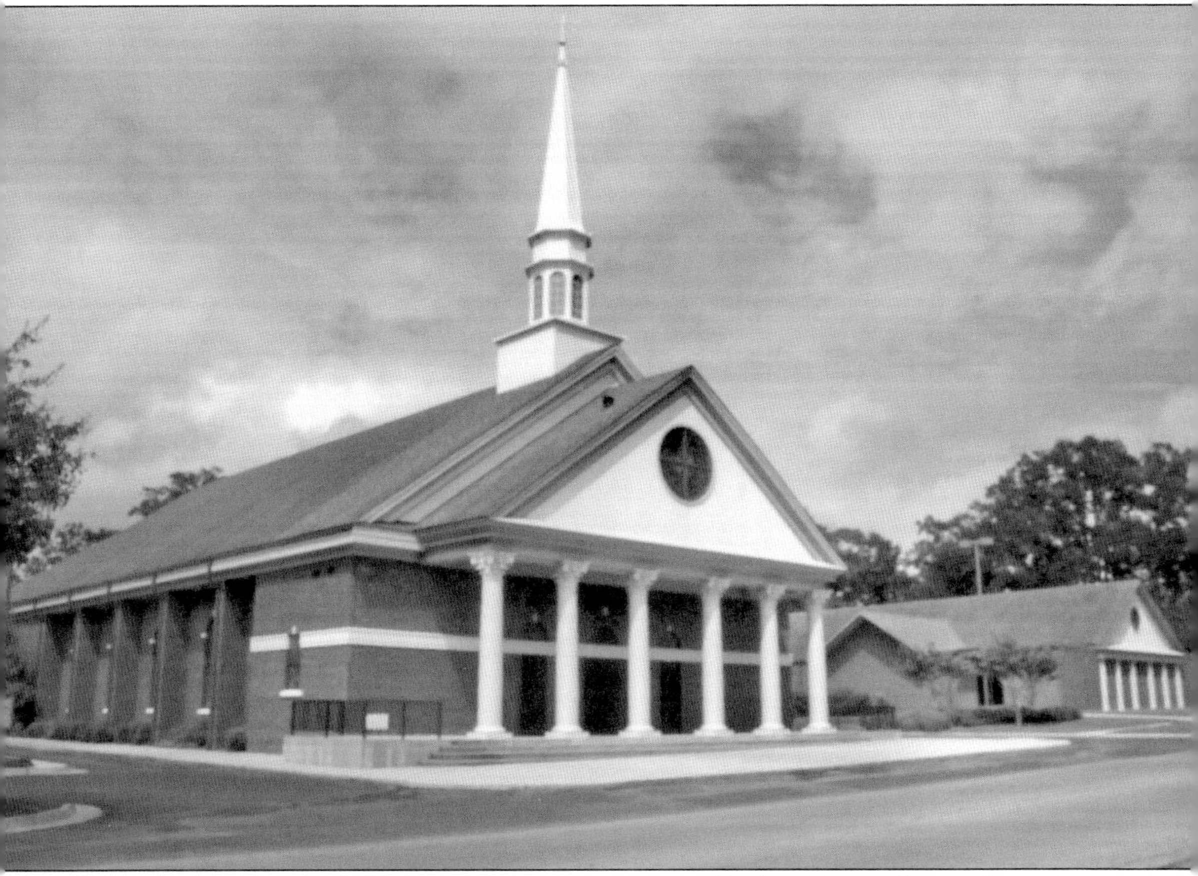

The Methodist Church of old Crystal Springs was organized before Copiah County formed in 1823. There was a church on the Bayou Pierre Circuit called Crystal Spring (singular) as early as 1826. This church existed for over 100 years and also had camp meetings. The buildings were on a lot of five acres that had been donated by Pleasant Moore and were adjacent to the Old Crystal Springs Cemetery. A new Methodist church was built when the town moved east to the site of the new railroad. Located on the same site as the present church, it hosted the Mississippi Conference in 1864, 1870, 1882, and 1889. A new church was built in 1919 at a cost of $40,000 and was said to be the first in the county to have separate classrooms, a recreation room, and a parlor. In 1963, two lots, including the lot on which the A. Lotterhos home stood, were purchased, making the church one continuous block. Pictured is the current church building. (Courtesy of CCHGS.)

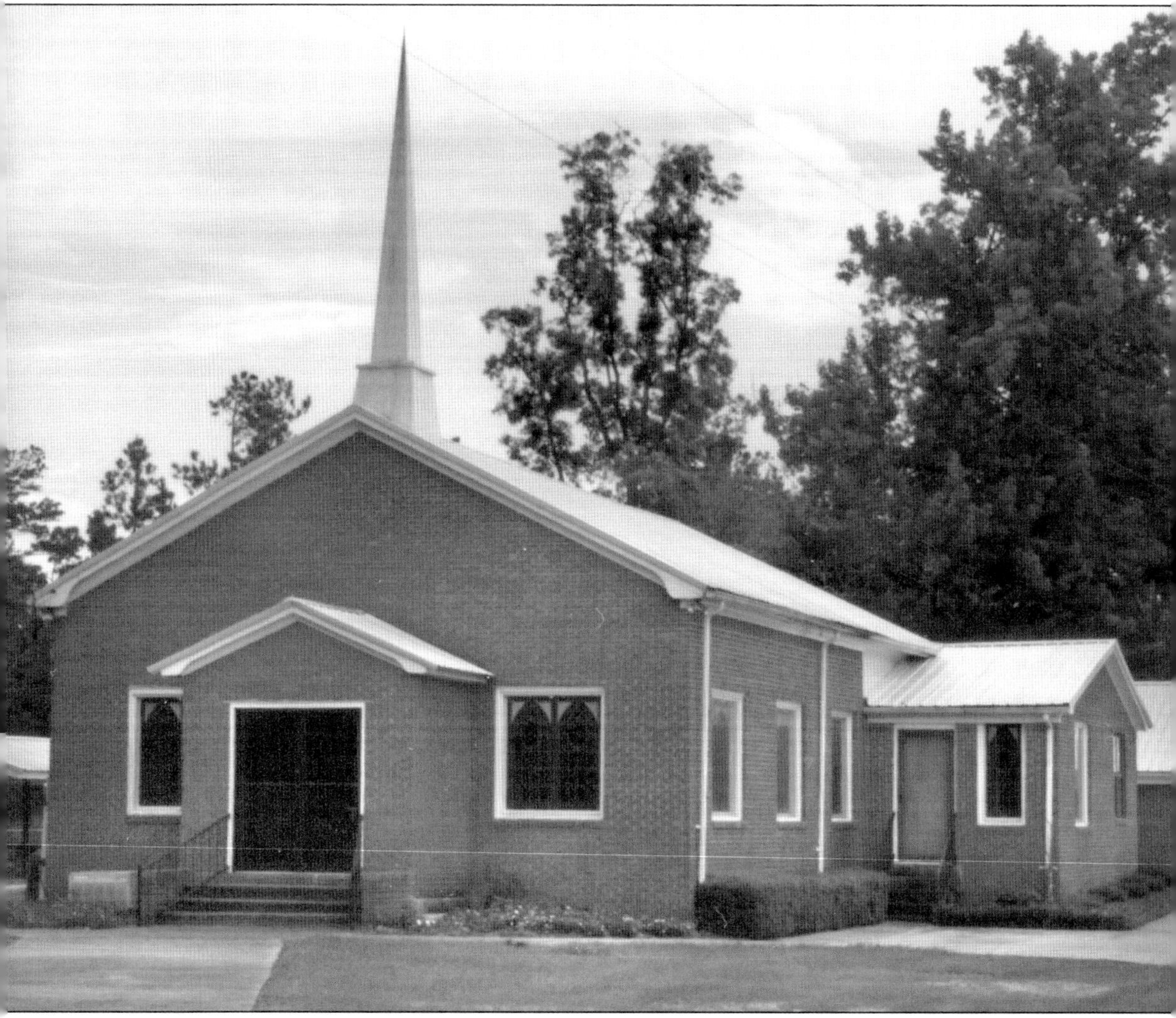

Antioch Baptist Church was organized in July 1824 by a group of families from South Carolina. They met on the land of Benjamin Bufkin and built a crude log cabin for use when the weather got colder. The seats were made of split logs with peg legs. It had a dirt floor, one door at the side, shuttered windows, and a clay mud chimney. Between 1827 and 1840, a larger log cabin was built with a slave gallery. It had puncheon floors and walls, shuttered windows, and a big dirt chimney. The earliest recorded pastor is William Mullens in 1827. The biggest membership, 221, was recorded in 1865. In 1874, the land was deeded to the church trustees by David Bufkin, a son of Benjamin. A larger framed building was built in 1890 and was replaced with a better structure in 1946. Many improvements have been made to the building since that time. The church was dedicated on May 11, 1947. (Courtesy of CCHGS.)

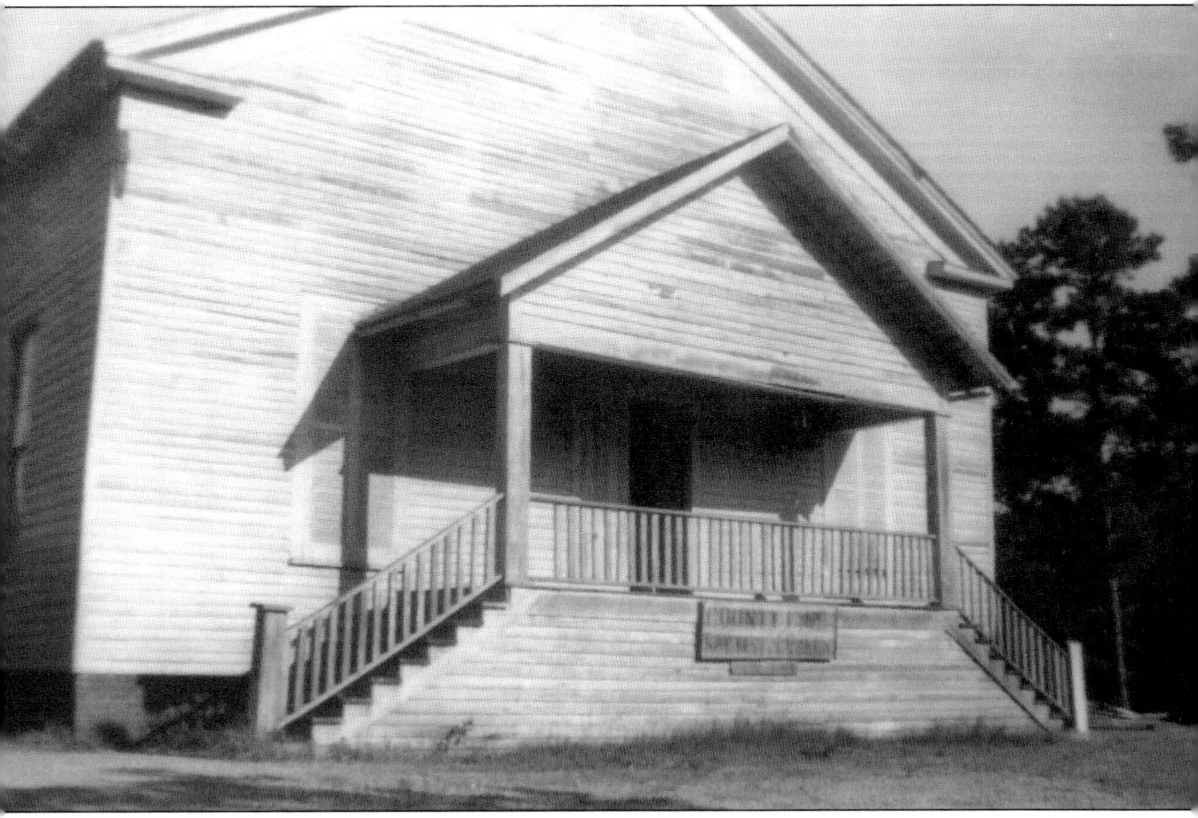

Five miles north of Crystal Springs, County Line Baptist Church was organized on January 4, 1828, with the following charter members: H. Tillman, I. Hollingsworth, J. Rice, R. Tillman, and E. Wroten. The first pastor was Nathan Morris. The land was purchased from Joseph A. and Elizabeth Ferguson for $37.75. In 1855, a new building was erected, and for almost a century, this is where services were conducted. Reverend Holloway came every fourth Saturday and Sunday, and music was provided by the Slays and Clements, noted singers. Many prominent families attended, such as the Terry, Haley, Cox, Smith, Moore, Reid, Ailles, Tillman, Beard, Didlake, Mims, and Goodes families. In 1927, some Sunday school rooms were built, and in 1935, more land was given to the church by Delia Davis's daughters, Mrs. Robertson and Mrs. Kayhee. In 1944, the old frame building was razed, and a new building was completed in 1945. In 1949, an educational annex was built. They have since built a new sanctuary and parsonage. (Courtesy of MDAH.)

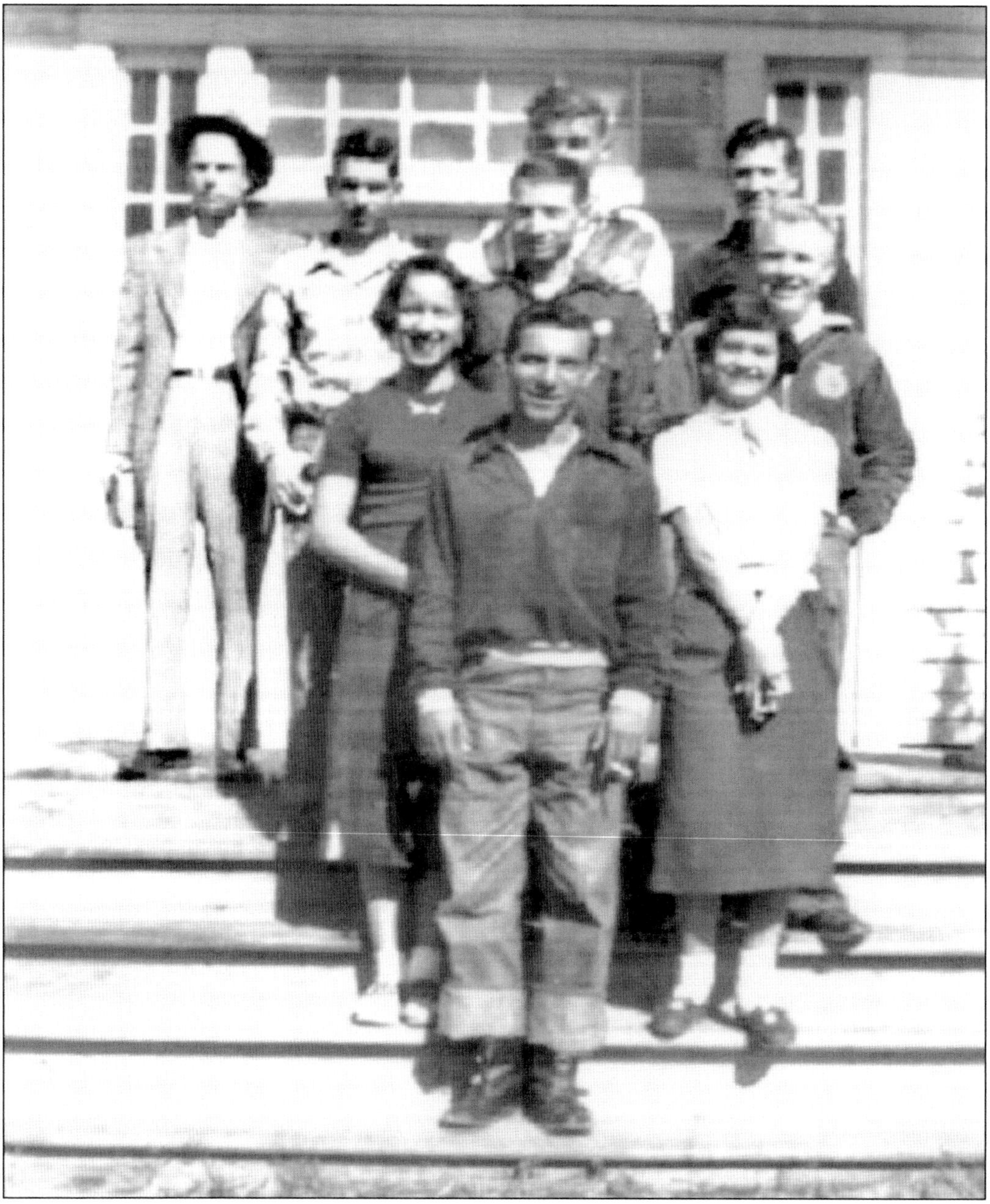

On November 3, 1847, John and Charlotte Hickman deeded one acre of land near Gatesville to Henry Hennington, John Sistrunk, Jesse Holman, Richard Hutson, Georgia Sistrunk, and W. J. Sistrunk. This was the first site of Mount Pleasant Baptist Church. Since then, the church has occupied three other sites. At one point, the old Evans schoolhouse was used by the church. Pictured is a Sunday school class on the steps of the building. Some of those pictured include Nadine Bevill (Johnson), Jimmie Ruth King (Noto), Otho Lee Roberts, Ernest Johnson, and Ellzy Johnson. In 1955, three acres were purchased from the Bob Evans estate. Rev. Decatur Butler was the pastor from 1954 to 1956 and was instrumental in building the new church. Currently the member with the longest tenure is John Harding Johnson, representing the fifth generation of the Johnson family to attend Mount Pleasant. (Courtesy of Dan H. Johnson.)

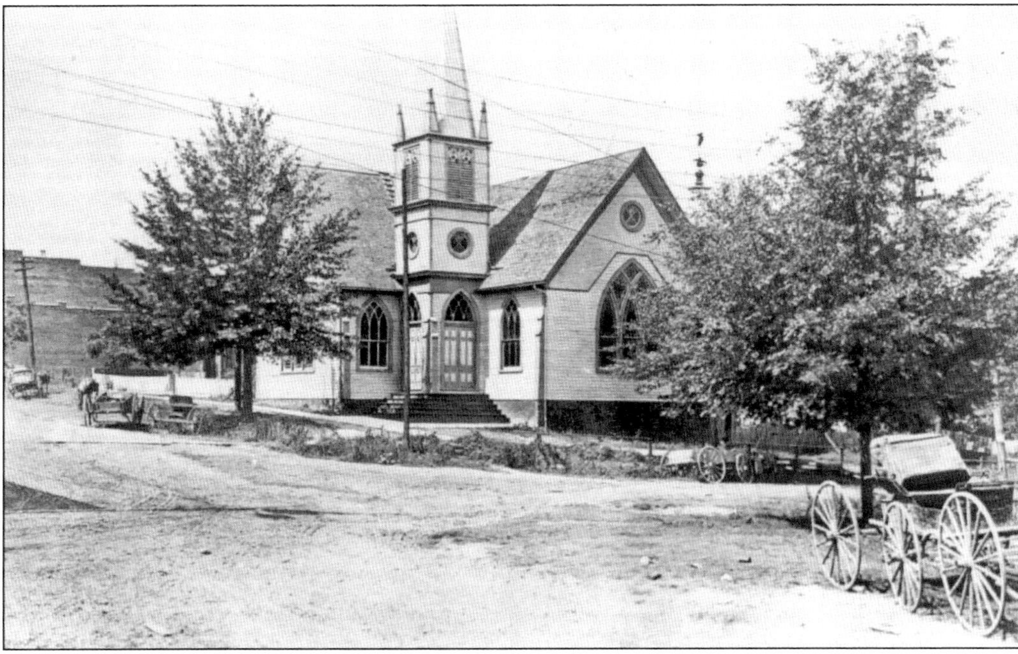

When the railroad came through Hazlehurst in 1858, the Methodists wanted a church in town. On June 20, 1850, a site near the old Peabody School on Georgetown Street was secured and a small building was erected. Andrew J. Wheat was the first pastor of Hazlehurst Methodist Church. In 1869, the old building was moved to a new lot purchased on the corner of Croker and Green Streets. A man named Rector, from Vicksburg, took a month to move it using mules. During the move, the congregation held services outside. A new building was built between 1891 and 1893 on the present site. This church was torn down on September 6, 1927, and a new one was built in 1928. Pictured are the second and the third (present) church buildings. (Courtesy of George W. Covington Memorial Library.)

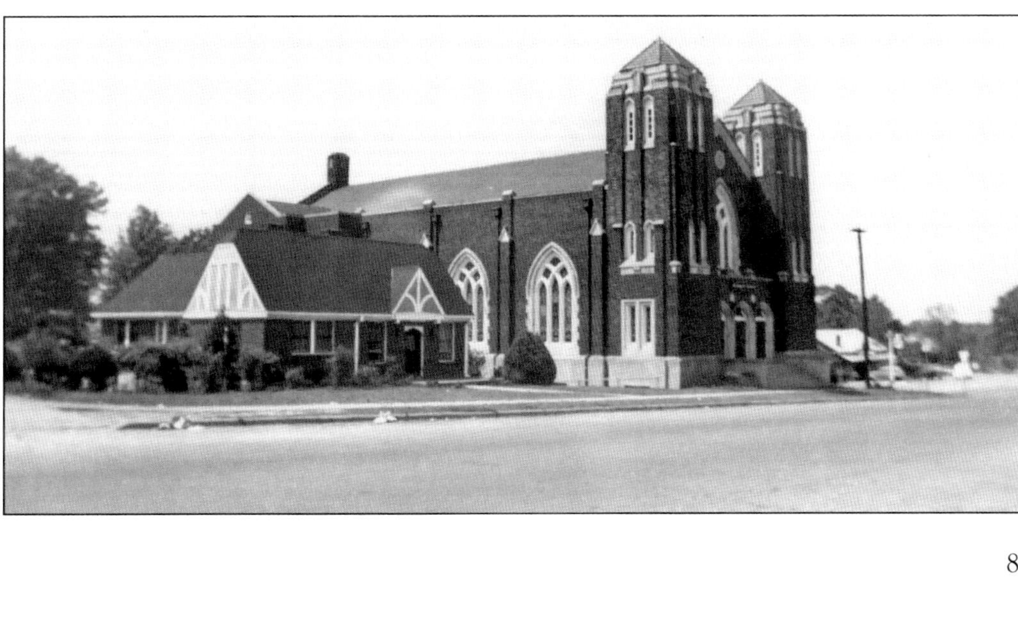

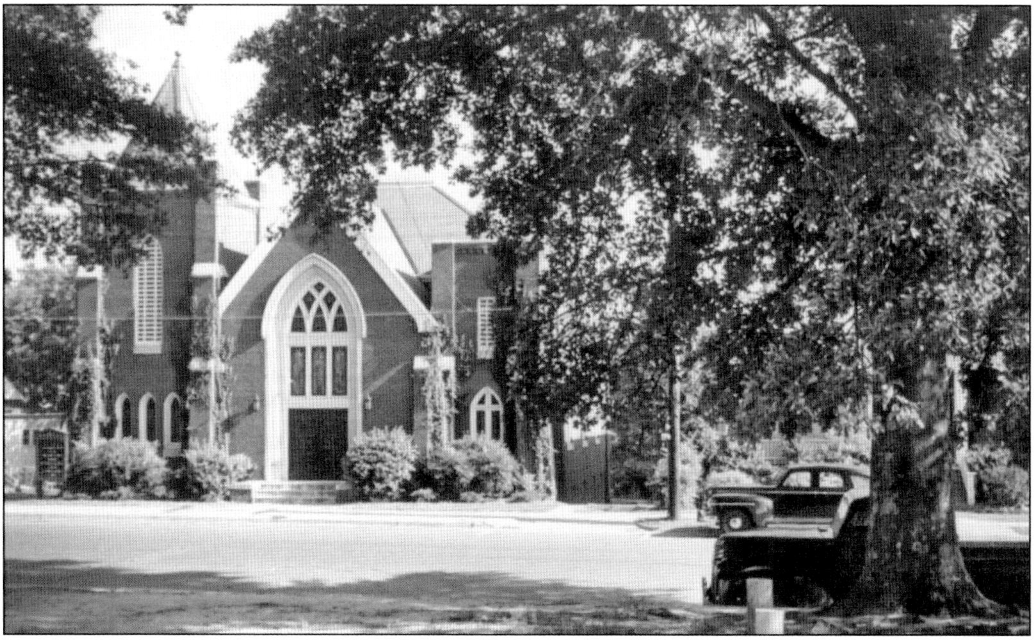

In 1832, a Presbyterian church was organized in Gallatin. The church prospered until 1858, when the railroad missed Gallatin. On July 29, 1860, Rev. D. A. Campbell founded the Hazlehurst Presbyterian Church. A congregation of 25 adults joined the Hazlehurst church, and Martin W. Trawick became the first pastor. The church building was completed in 1867. (Courtesy of George W. Covington Memorial Library.)

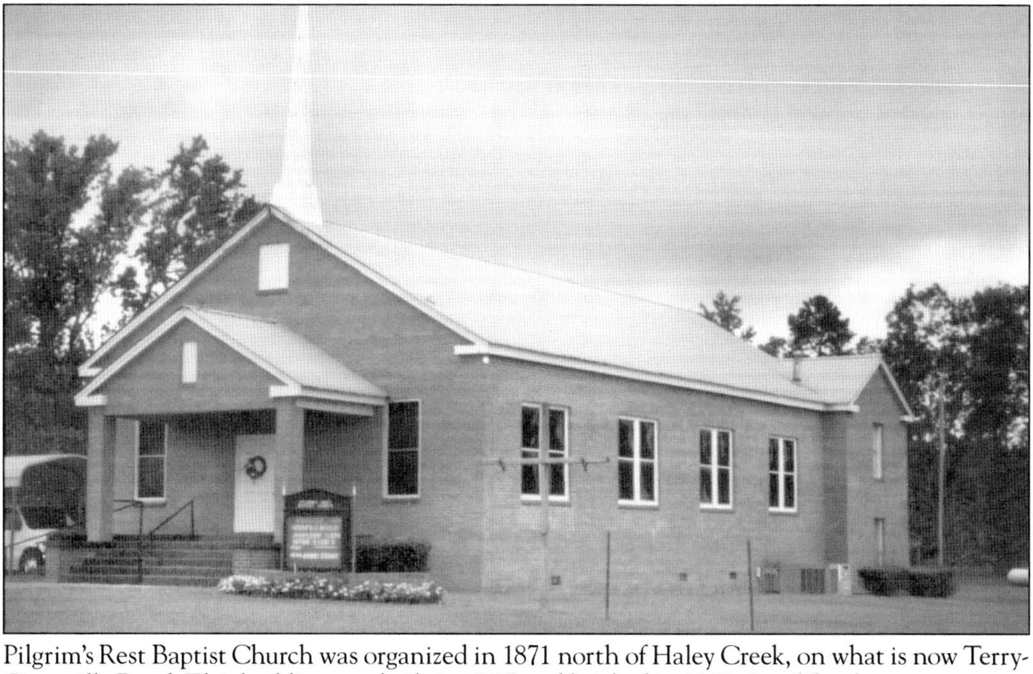

Pilgrim's Rest Baptist Church was organized in 1871 north of Haley Creek, on what is now Terry-Gatesville Road. This building was built in 1905 and bricked in 1982. Land for the cemetery was purchased from the Evans estate in 1955. Dr. George Pat Bufkin was the pastor for many years before becoming the director of the Copiah County Baptist Association. (Courtesy of CCHGS.)

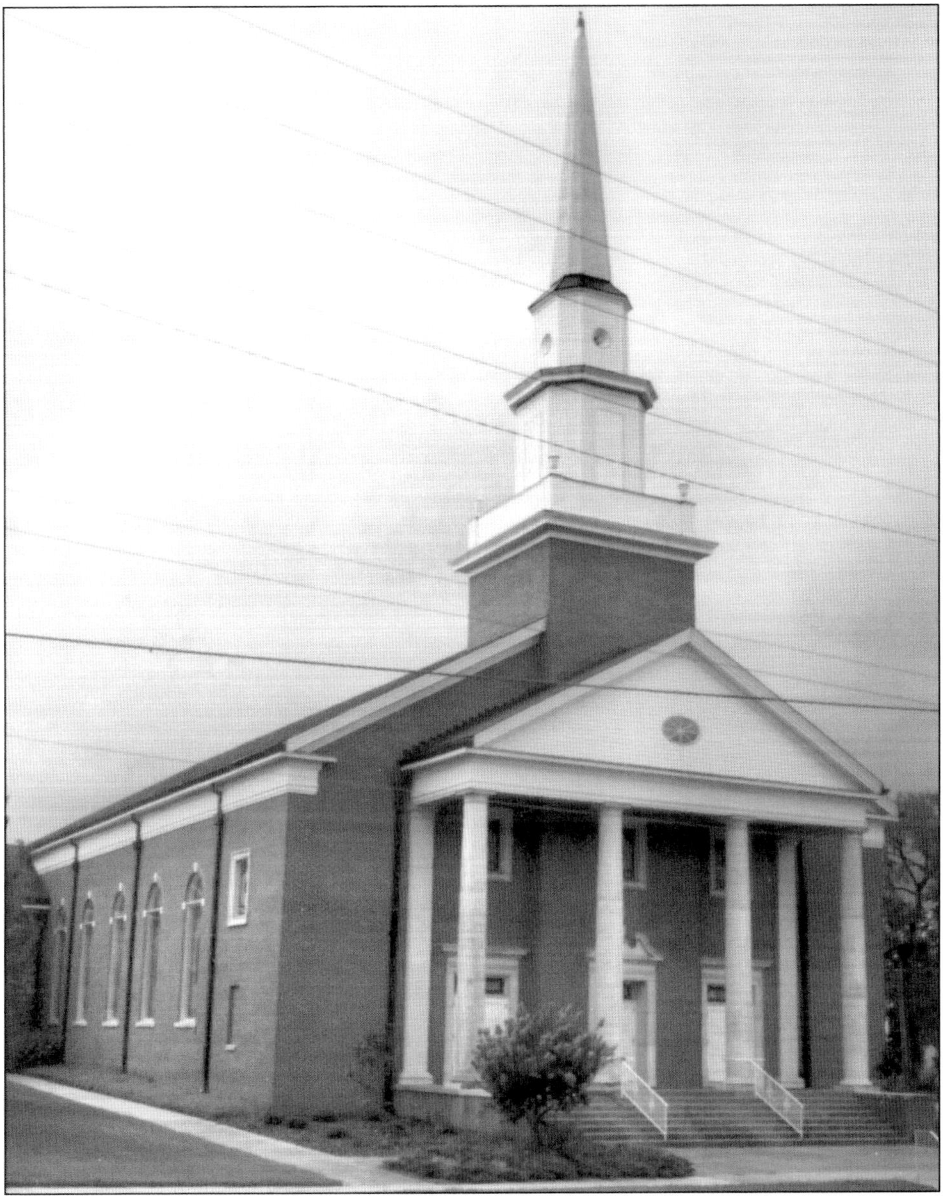

On January 20, 1861, Crystal Springs Baptist Church was formed with Rev. L. B. Holloway as the first pastor. The nine charter members were James A. Sturgis, A. J. Sturgis, Joel Davis, E. C. Linder, Joel F. Evans, James A. Tillman, Sarah E. Sturgis, Mary Gillaspy, and Mary F. Mayfield. By 1883, the two-story wood building was too small, so a brick building facing west was begun. Once again, in 1915, it became necessary to expand, so a third church building was constructed. The preschool building was constructed in 1946. Known as the "Baby Building" when constructed, it was one of the first in the state. An educational building was added in 1949, and the present sanctuary was built and the old sanctuary renovated for an educational space in 1956. In 1965, the educational wing was added, and in 1978 the pastorium was completed. In 2006–2007, the sanctuary was renovated again. The chimes were donated in memory of Rev. Estus Mason's son-in-law, Bob Evans, who was fatally injured while training for Vietnam. (Courtesy of First Baptist Church.)

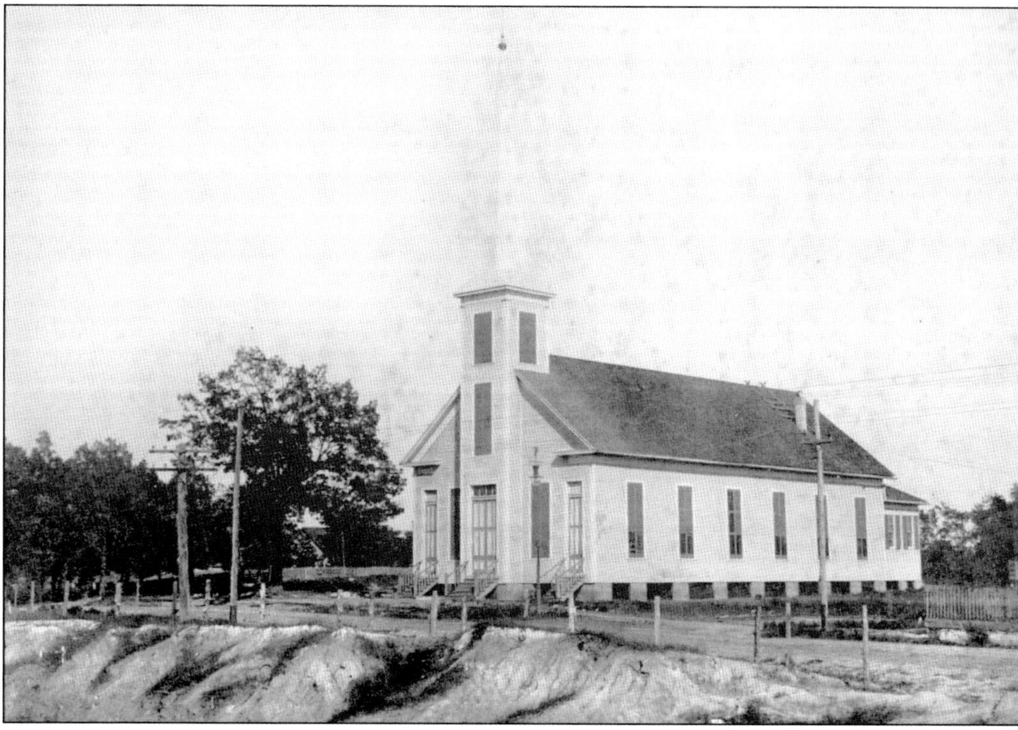

In 1869, the New Bahalia Baptist Church changed its name to the Baptist Church of Christ in Wesson. It faced Main Street and was built from lumber donated by the Mississippi Mills. By 1880, Wesson had grown so much that a new church was needed. The new Wesson Baptist Church was located one block north of the old one. As seen here, the building was frame construction with a steeple 60 feet above the cone of the roof, or 90 feet from the tip to the ground. At the base of the steps was a large bell used to call the membership to worship. This building was used until 1949, when the new building, seen here, was constructed. (Courtesy of MDAH.)

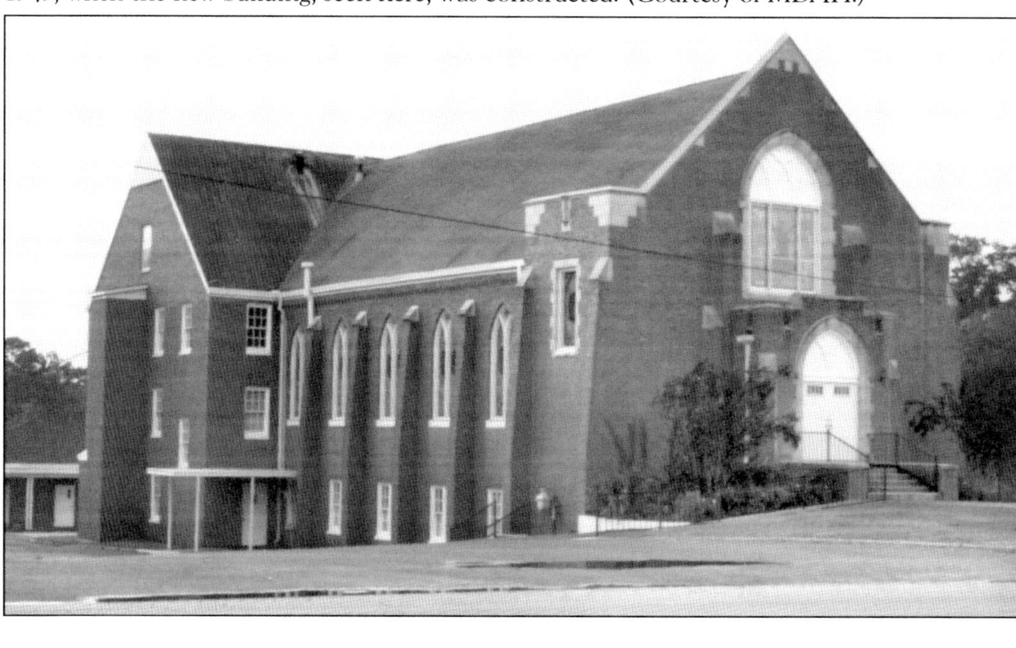

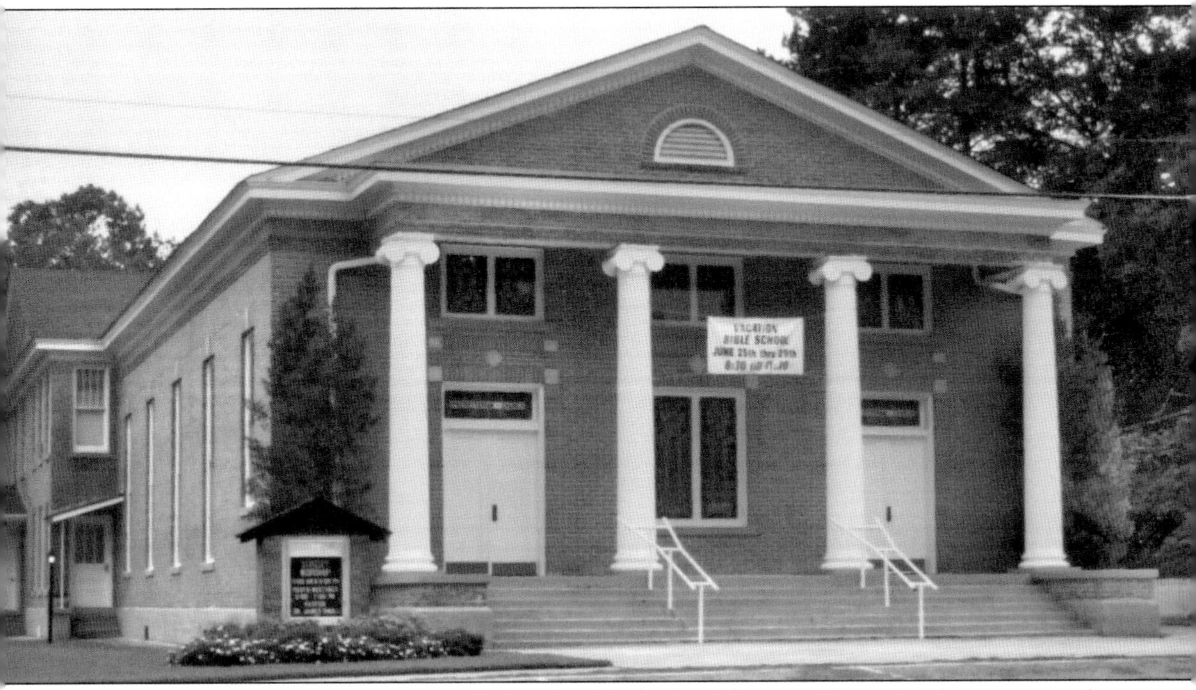

On April 28, 1865, a meeting was called at the Methodist Meeting House for the purpose of organizing the First Presbyterian Church of Crystal Springs. Credited with forming the church is Rev. Oscar Newton, Rev. Martin W. Trawick, Julius C. Alford, and A. W. Griffing. Reverend Trawick, who also ministered at the Hazlehurst Presbyterian Church from 1865 to 1873, was the first preacher. Since the Presbyterians had a congregation but no building in which to hold services, the Crystal Springs Baptist church lent its building. On October 19, 1868, Mr. and Mrs. Ozias Osborne sold the small congregation a desirable plot on East Marion Avenue for $100 in order to build a church. On May 15, 1870, the new building was dedicated, and later on, A. Lotterhos and C. M. Huber deeded the church an adjacent lot for $1 that would later be used for a new manse. On November 8, 1924, the original church burned during a morning service. The present church was completed May 26, 1926. (Courtesy of CCHGS.)

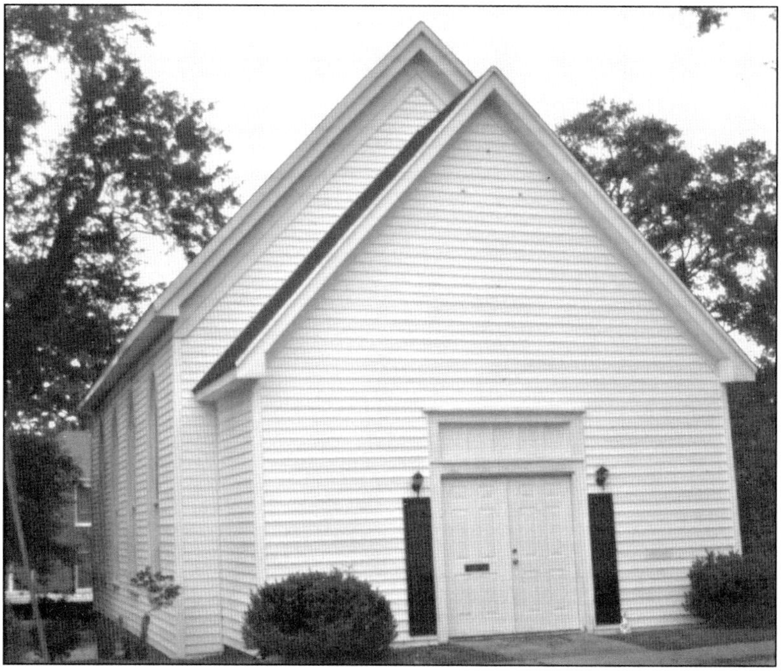

The Mission Church of St. Stephen was established on May 6, 1868. The present church building was constructed by David Lowe. In June 1872, St. Stephens was admitted into union with the diocese. The first priest in charge was Rev. William Carnahan. Between 1880 and 1885, the priest Dr. William K. Douglas had a private school in the building during the week. (Courtesy of CCHGS.)

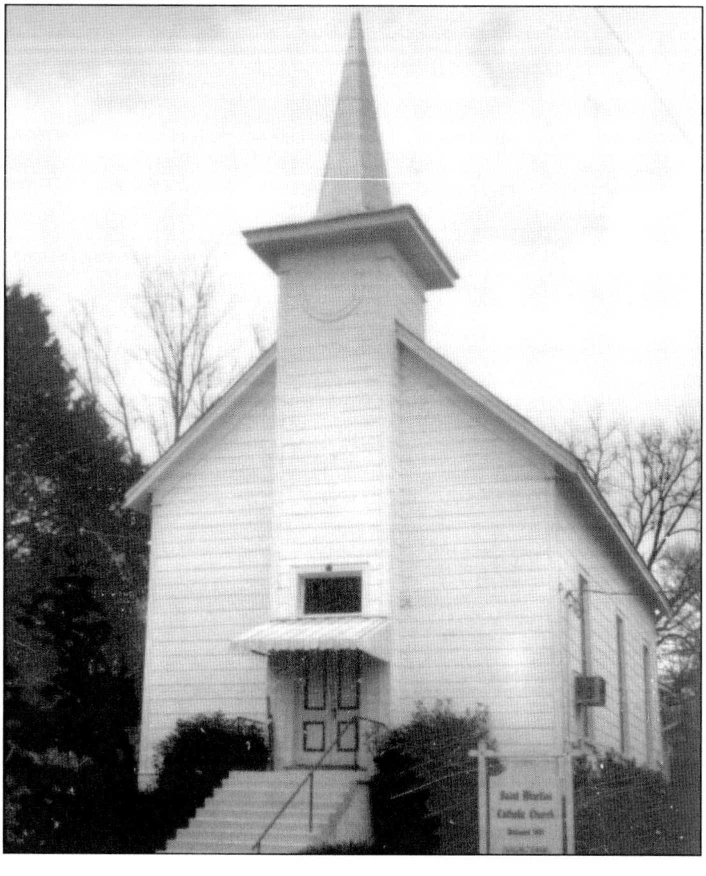

St. Martin's Catholic Church was built and dedicated by Reverend Father Bally on May 7, 1882. The Catholic population at the time was 27. Copiah County was largely Protestant, and the church struggled for many years to maintain a congregation. For several years, the bishop paid the insurance for the church because the members were too poor to pay it. (Courtesy of George W. Covington Memorial Library.)

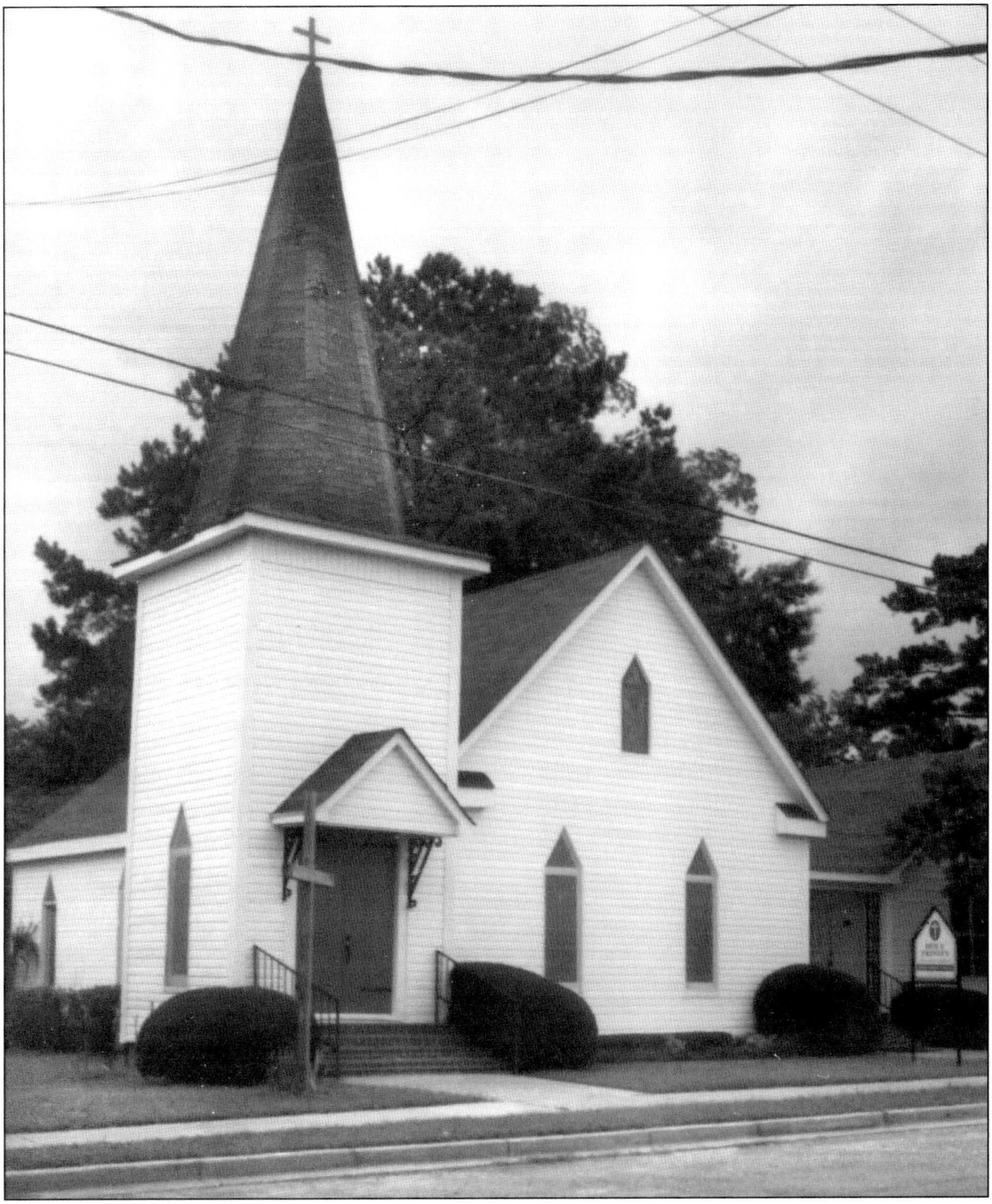

In 1868, Rev. William Mercer Green, first bishop of Mississippi, visited Brookhaven, Hazlehurst, and Crystal Springs. From this visit, the Brookhaven Field Protestant Episcopal Diocese of Mississippi was formed. Two years later, the Holy Trinity Episcopal Church was built on the south side of West Marion Avenue, but in the early 1880s, the church was badly damaged by a severe storm. In 1886, the present church was completed on West Railroad Avenue with the land having been donated by Kenneth Donald Nicolson. Surnames of early members of the church include Blanchard, Towne, Gillmore, Rhymes, Dabney, Mortmer, and Didlake. The first rectory was built in 1905. An annex was added in 1956 and was named Johnston Hall as a memorial to Clarence Johnston's mother. He contributed generously to the annexation fund. The centennial of the church was celebrated on November 10, 1968. (Courtesy CCHGS.)

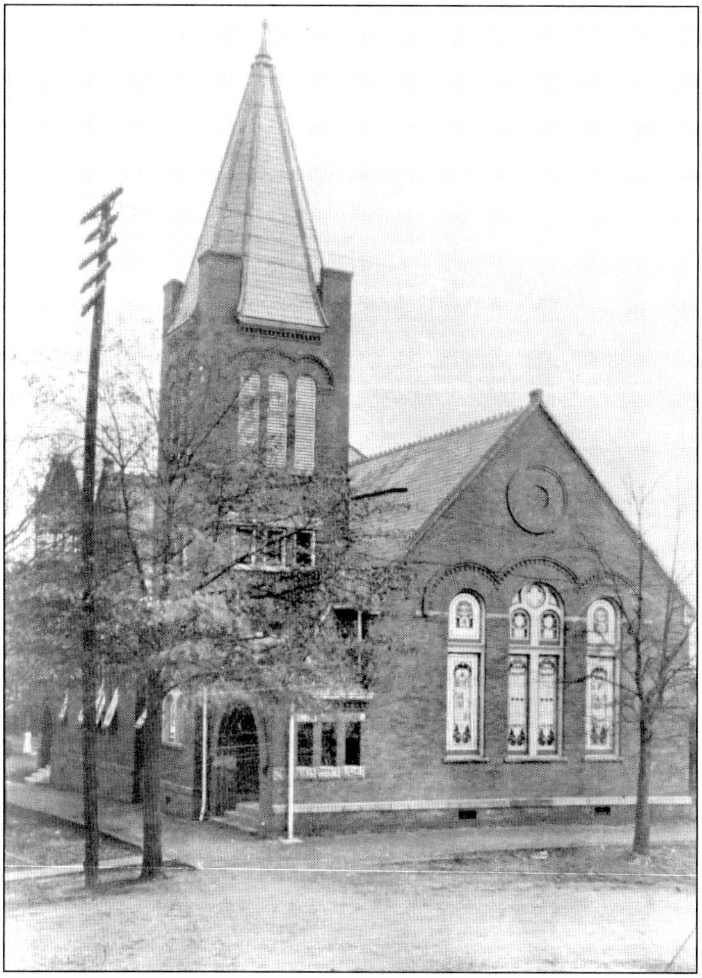

On February 27, 1870, Hazlehurst Baptist Church was formed, and J. R. Farish was elected pastor. Soon thereafter, the church was built on a lot owned by L. F. Birdsong that was deeded to the church in 1871. On June 29, 1872, when the citizens of the county voted to move the county seat from Gallatin to Hazlehurst, the board of supervisors ordered the record books of the chancery and circuit clerks be placed in the basement of the Hazlehurst Baptist Church for safekeeping. This building served the congregation until 1892. Services began in the new building on May 18, 1893. In May 1923, I. N. Ellis donated land for a new church building. The new church was dedicated on April 3, 1927. Pictured are the second and third (latest) church buildings. (Courtesy of George W. Covington Memorial Library.)

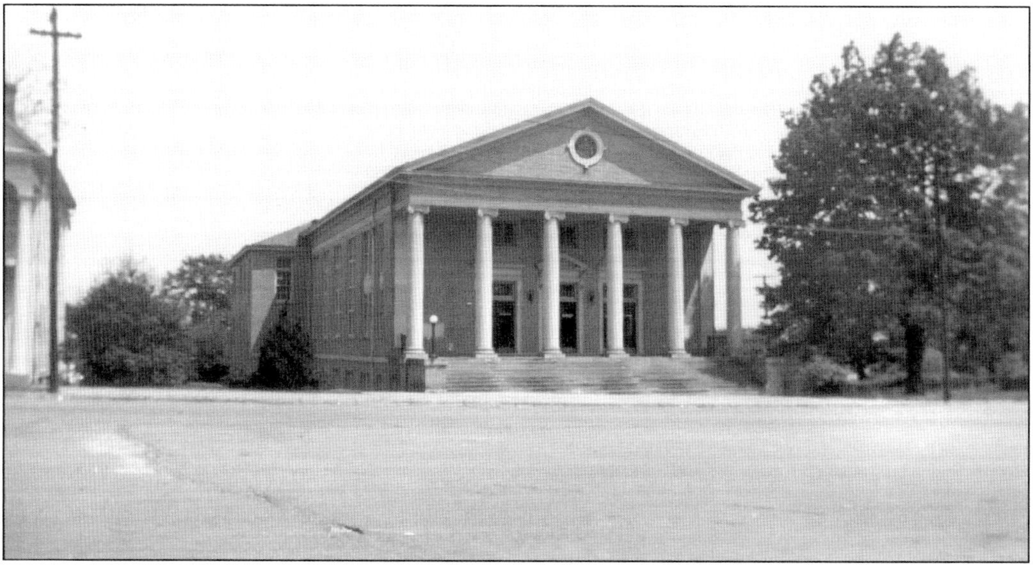

Capt. William Oliver pushed for the creation of a Presbyterian church in Wesson. The Wesson Presbyterian Church was organized on December 31, 1871. The members delayed building a church until the mills, which had been destroyed by fire in 1873, were rebuilt. Col. James Wesson donated the land, and on March 24, 1878, the first service took place. (Courtesy of Longie Dale Hamilton Memorial Library.)

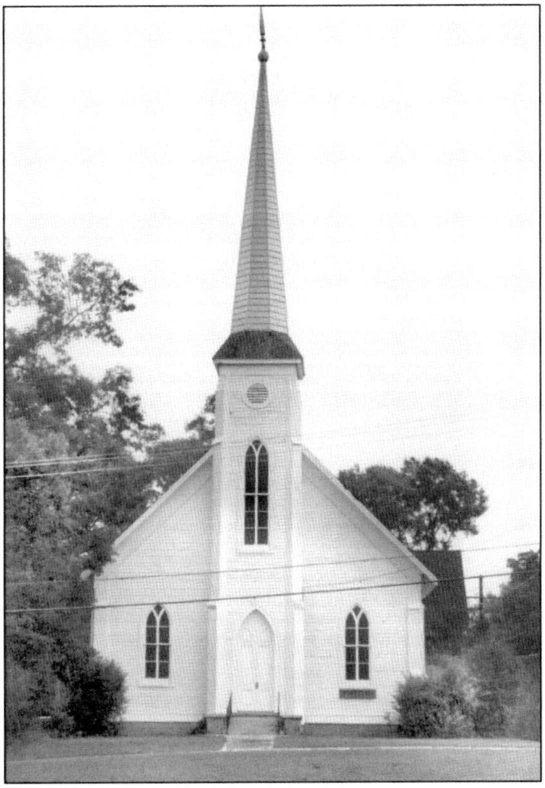

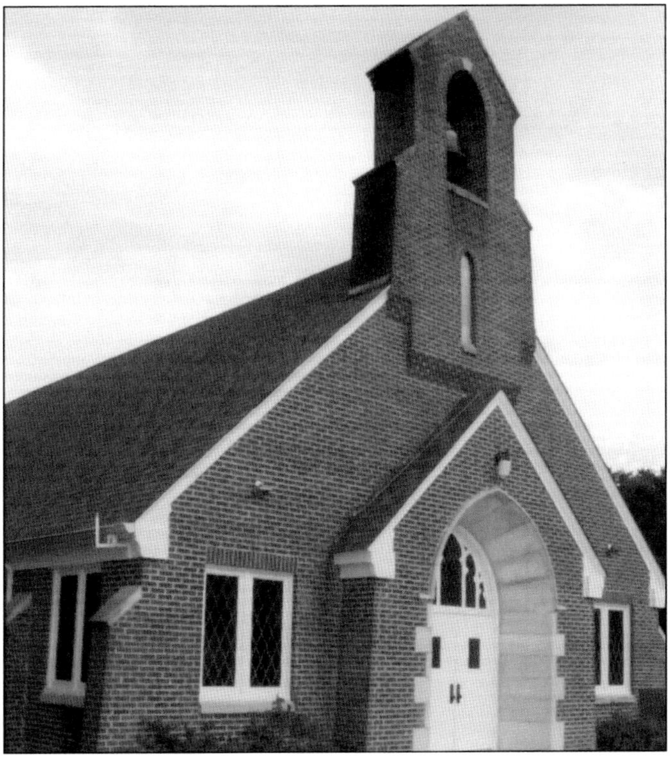

The Methodist church in Wesson was encouraged by Colonel Wesson in 1867. The first building was on the corner of Main and Church Streets. In May 1885, the church burned, and a lot was purchased from the Wesson Mills. The second church building was dismantled in 1944. The new church was named in honor of Bishop Decell, a life-long friend of the community. (Courtesy of CCHGS.)

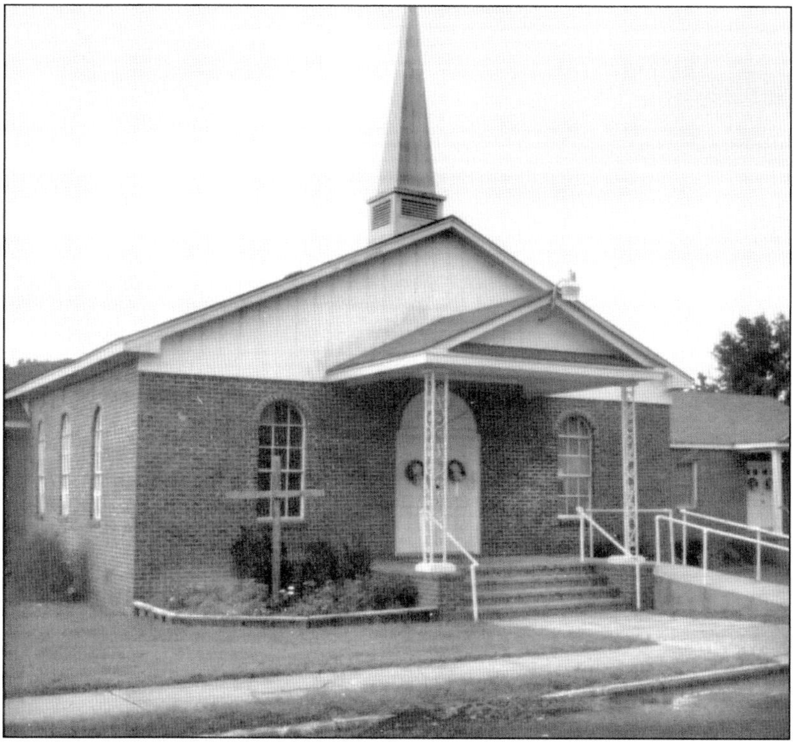

The Gallman Baptist Church was organized in 1879 by J. N. Tucker, a pastor on the Terry Circuit. The land was donated by Dorcas Mariah Hennington Welch. A parsonage was secured as well. The church building was destroyed by a storm in 1934. The church was rebuilt during the year. (Courtesy of CCHGS.)

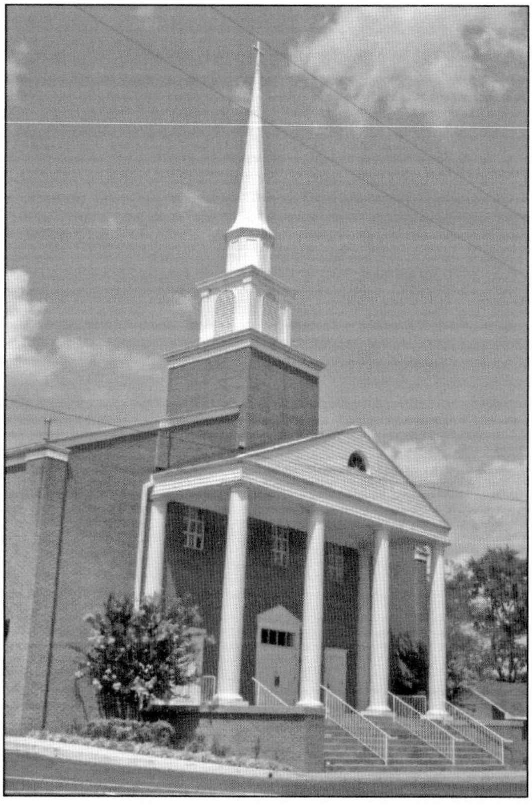

In 1887, 20 members, including A. D. and Norval Slay, Rev. R. D. Middleton, E. T. Bailey, and L. B. Sojourner, formed a church. Reverend Middleton met with the group on March 8, 1887, and the Harmony Baptist Church was organized. There were 34 charter members. On September 10, 1950, the church voted to go into a fulltime program. Since then, two new sanctuaries have been built. (Courtesy of CCHGS.)

Six

Communities and People

Even before the county was formed in 1823, people came together to participate in activities. This chapter takes a look at some of the businesses and groups that existed in early Copiah County that made it a better place to live. This includes some of the libraries, post offices, and civic organizations that were organized, for the most part, before World War II. Most of the civic clubs are still in existence today. There are many individuals who helped shaped the history of Copiah County.

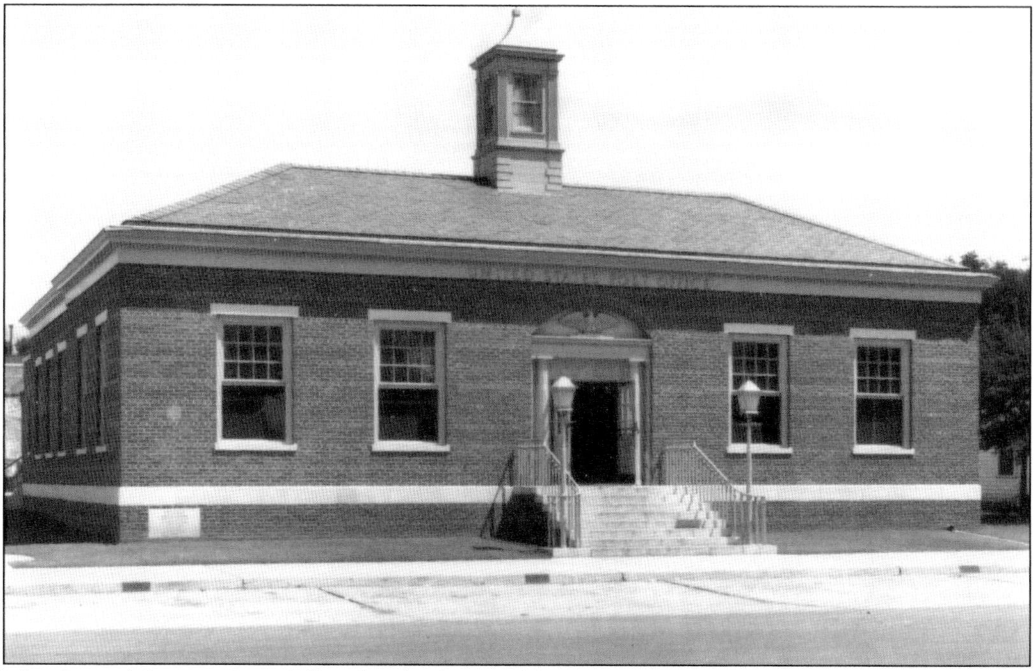

The Crystal Springs Post Office has had several locations since its inception on July 14, 1857. Orren F. White was the postmaster in 1901. The ceremony of breaking ground for the current building was one of the highlights of the Tomato Festival on June 6, 1940. Inside a beautiful mural depicts a time when tomatoes were king. (Courtesy of MDAH.)

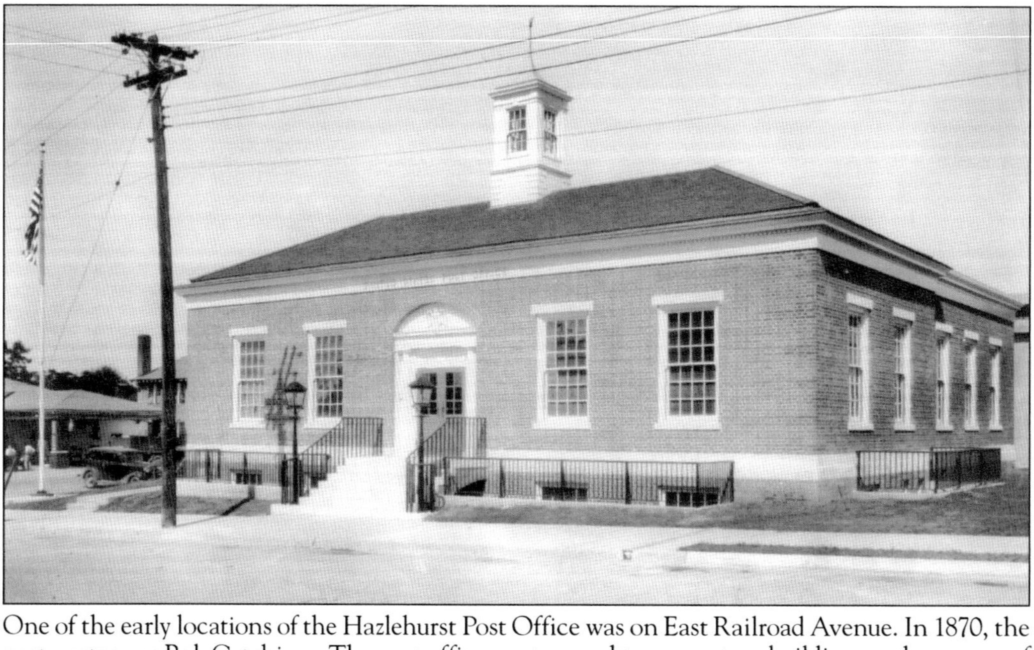

One of the early locations of the Hazlehurst Post Office was on East Railroad Avenue. In 1870, the postmaster was Bob Catchings. The post office next moved to a one-story building on the corner of West Railroad Avenue and Green Street. Next the post office moved farther down West Railroad Avenue to the central block. The first postmistress was Cora Matthews. (Courtesy of MDAH.)

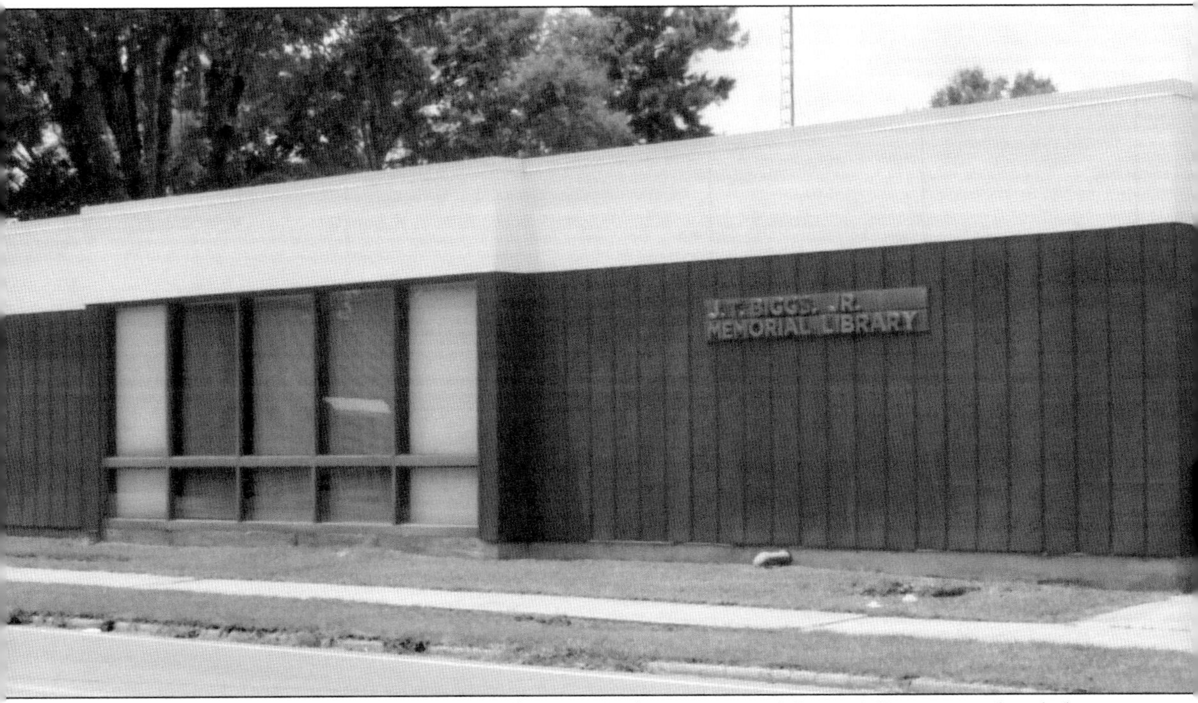

When the WPA library was discontinued in 1943, the citizens of Crystal Springs realized the great need for a public library. At first, the library was funded by clubs and a part-time librarian was paid for by the city. In 1945, Mrs. J. Cliff Thomas, president of the Floral Club, appointed a committee of members to help the library. They raised $1,000 through the donations of the men of the city. In 1949, a group comprised of citizens from several towns in the county approached the board of supervisors. The board agreed that it would benefit the county and levied a one-mill tax; thus, the Copiah Library was begun. The Copiah Library assisted the Crystal Springs Library in many ways. In 1958, during the Centennial Celebration of Crystal Springs, the city opened the J. T. Biggs Jr. Memorial Library. J. T. Biggs Jr. was a prominent businessman in Crystal Springs. (Courtesy of CCHGS.)

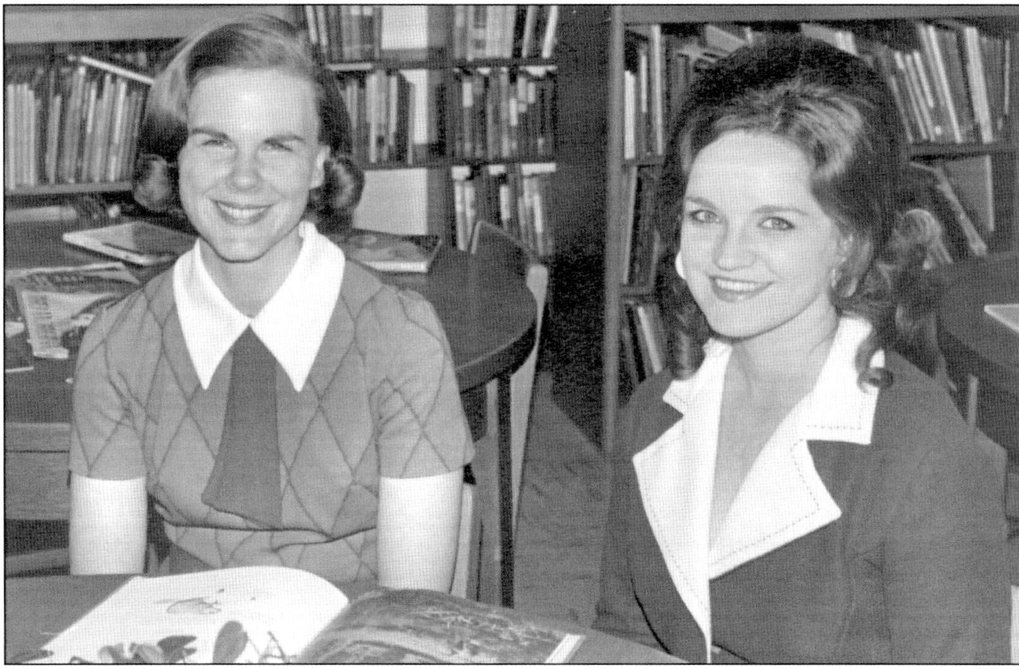

The library in Hazlehurst opened to the public on July 1, 1904, in the Bass Building, and in January 1905, it was moved to a room above the Bank of Hazlehurst. For economic reasons, it was later moved to the home of Mrs. S. Sokoloski, the first librarian. In 1919, it was moved to city hall. This continued until 1948, when Mrs. James H. Williams, president of the city library board, asked for support in building a library. A few months before this meeting, George W. Covington had died and willed $5,000 to be used for civic work. The executors agreed to help the library. When the Covingtons lost their daughter, Carolyn, they donated a fountain to Hazlehurst High School in her memory. The fountain was eventually moved to the library. (Courtesy of George W. Covington Memorial Library.)

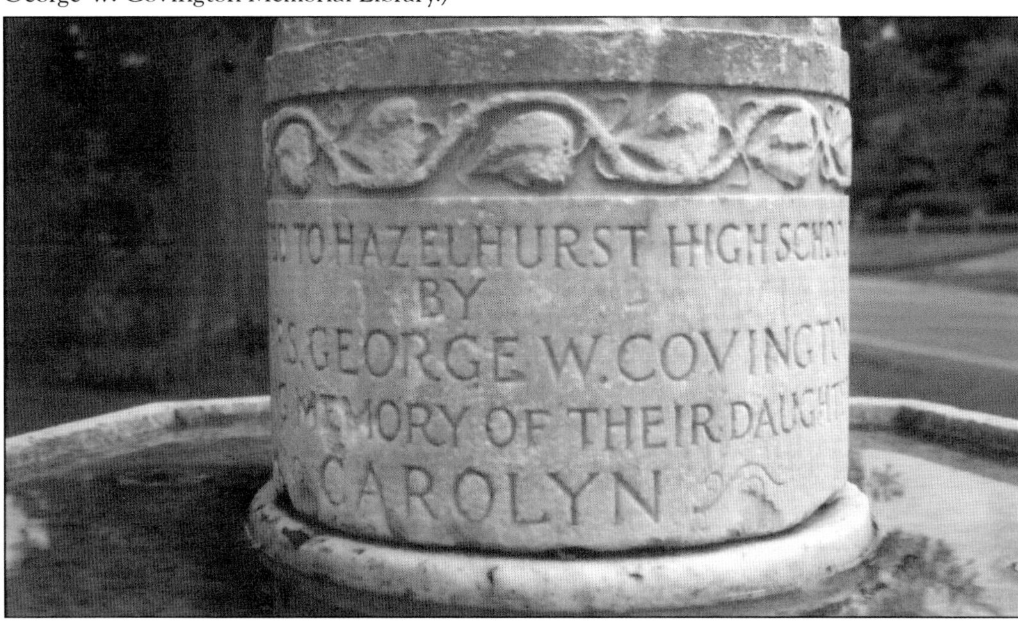

The Crystal Springs Floral Club was organized in 1894 by Elizabeth A. M. Jones and 20 charter members. The dues were 10¢ per year. The objective was to "promote the growth of flowers, especially the chrysanthemum, and to encourage sociability among members." The chrysanthemum is the club flower; club colors are lavender and white. The club held brilliant chrysanthemum exhibits for several years. (Courtesy of CCHGS.)

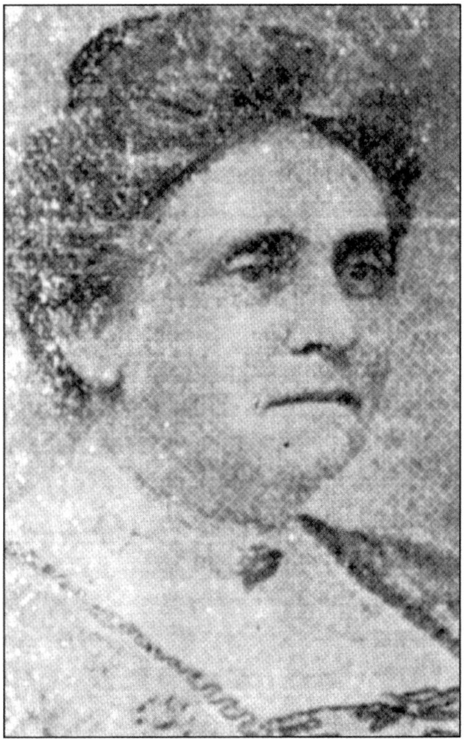

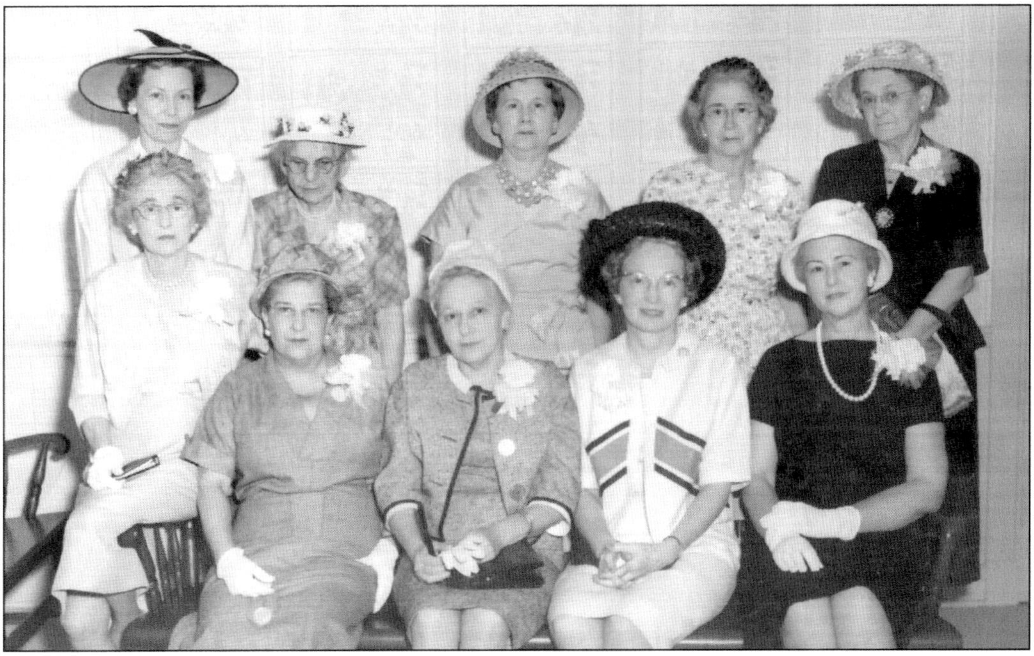

The Hazlehurst Garden Club met on May 10, 1939, at the home of Mrs. Fred Ellis. Mrs. Middleton and Mrs. VanDevender, both from the Wesson Garden Club, explained how to start a garden club in Hazlehurst. They presided over the election of officers, and Mrs. Robert Wise was elected president. This picture is from one of the club's scrapbooks. (Courtesy of George W. Covington Memorial Library.)

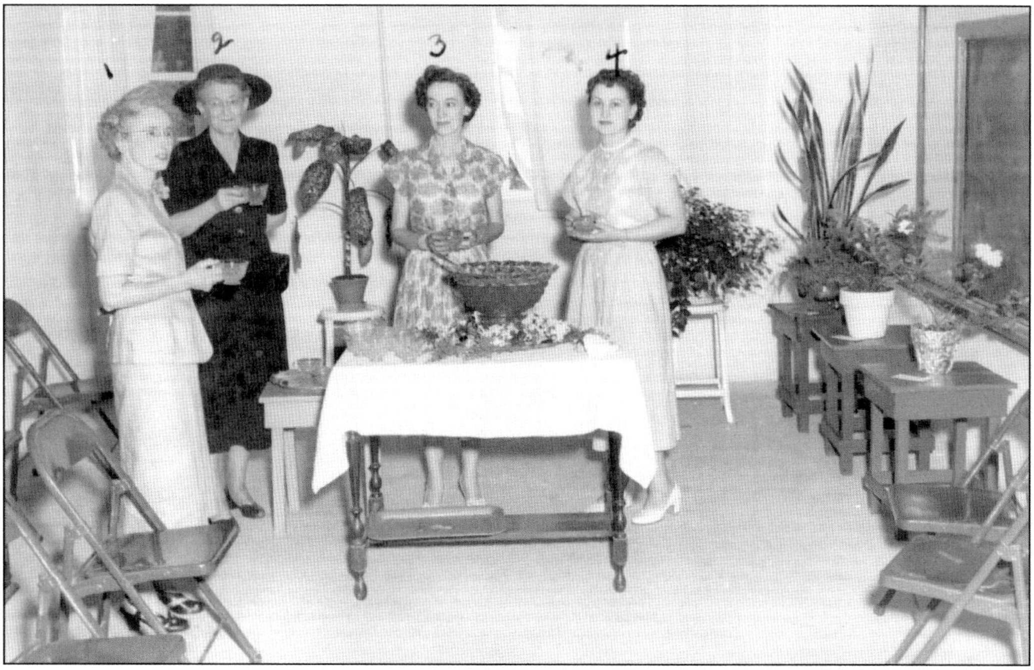

The Wesson Garden Club was organized in 1934 with 16 charter members. The club flower is the crepe myrtle. This picture is of a judged floral arrangement competition. From left to right are Mrs. Roper, unidentified, and two judges Elizabeth Rea and Katie Furr. This picture is from one of the club's scrapbooks. (Courtesy of Longie Dale Hamilton Memorial Library.)

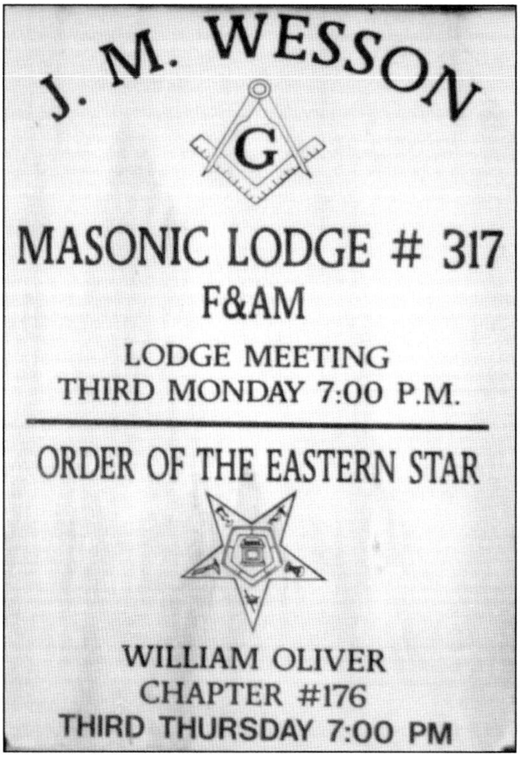

The Crystal Springs Lions Club, sponsored by the Jackson Lions Club, organized on February 27, 1936 with 26 charter members. The first officers were William Carmichael, president; Sollie M. Crain, secretary; and James H. Thomas, treasurer. The J. M. Wesson Lodge 317 of the Masons was established in April 1869. P. A. Strohecker was the first grand master. (Courtesy of CCHGS.)

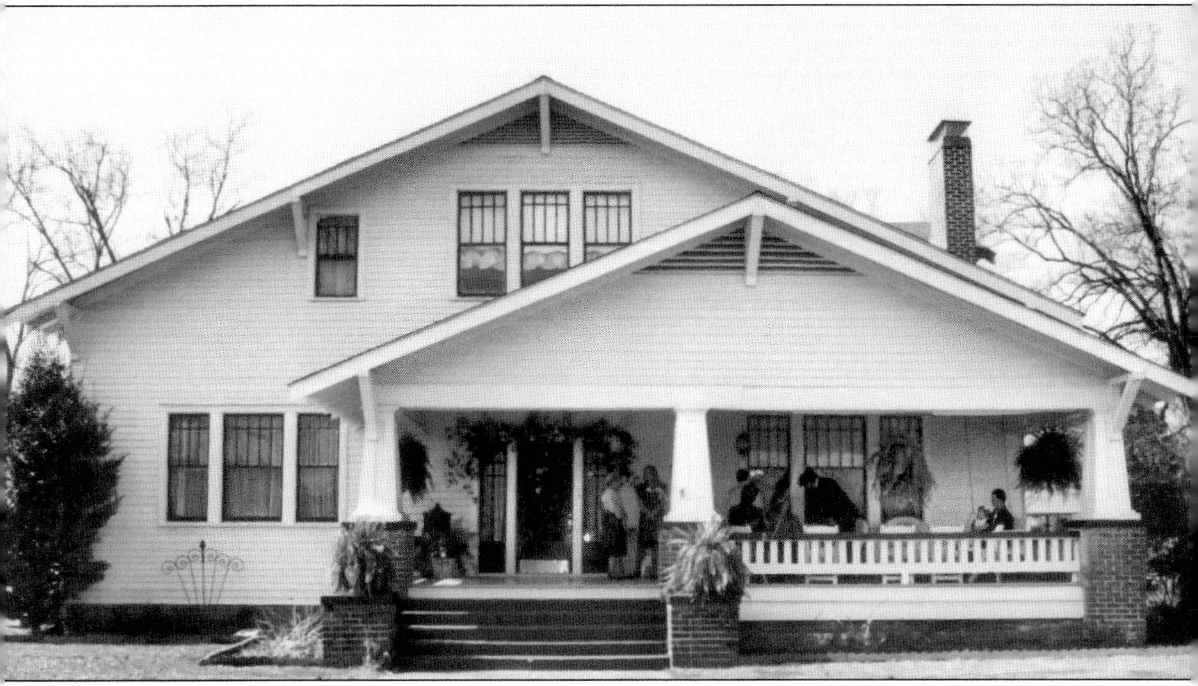

The MacDowell Music Club of Crystal Springs was organized in March 1936 at the home of Mrs. Glen Roll. Charter members were Sarah Alford, Mrs. L. O. Baldwin, Mrs. J. T. Biggs, Mrs. T. H. Cook, Mrs. W. B. Dickson, Mrs. O. G. Eubanks, Annie Taite Jenkins, Mrs. J. E. Lawrence, Jesse Leach, Mrs. Glen Roll, and Weneva Sumner. The objective was to bring musicians and music lovers into closer fellowship and harmony, hereby stimulating the desire for study and appreciation of music among its members and into the community. Clubs such as this would rotate the location of meetings. Ladies loved to host gatherings in their homes. Mrs. J. T. Biggs, whose husband was a successful businessman in town, was no exception. Many nice gatherings were hosted in their home on West Railroad Avenue. (Courtesy of LaTricia Nelson-Easley.)

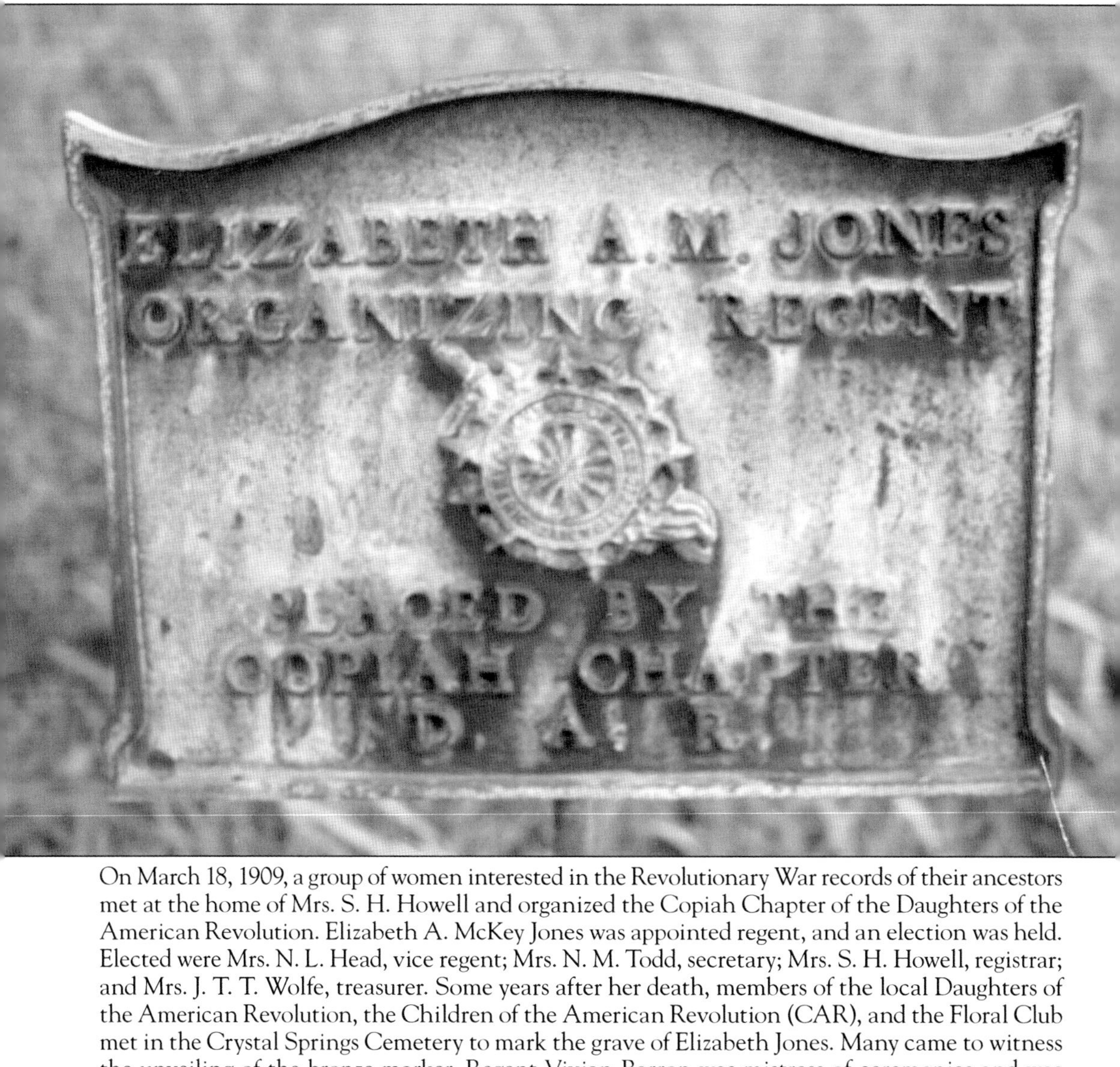

On March 18, 1909, a group of women interested in the Revolutionary War records of their ancestors met at the home of Mrs. S. H. Howell and organized the Copiah Chapter of the Daughters of the American Revolution. Elizabeth A. McKey Jones was appointed regent, and an election was held. Elected were Mrs. N. L. Head, vice regent; Mrs. N. M. Todd, secretary; Mrs. S. H. Howell, registrar; and Mrs. J. T. T. Wolfe, treasurer. Some years after her death, members of the local Daughters of the American Revolution, the Children of the American Revolution (CAR), and the Floral Club met in the Crystal Springs Cemetery to mark the grave of Elizabeth Jones. Many came to witness the unveiling of the bronze marker. Regent Vivian Barron was mistress of ceremonies and was assisted by Evelyn Williams. Mrs. C. M. Huber, representing the Floral Club, gave some remarks, for Jones was also the organizer of the Floral Club. Rena Jean Whittington of Natchez, great-granddaughter of Jones, unveiled the marker. Ann McCluney, Jones's granddaughter, accepted it on behalf of the daughters, granddaughter, and great-granddaughter. (Courtesy of CCHGS.)

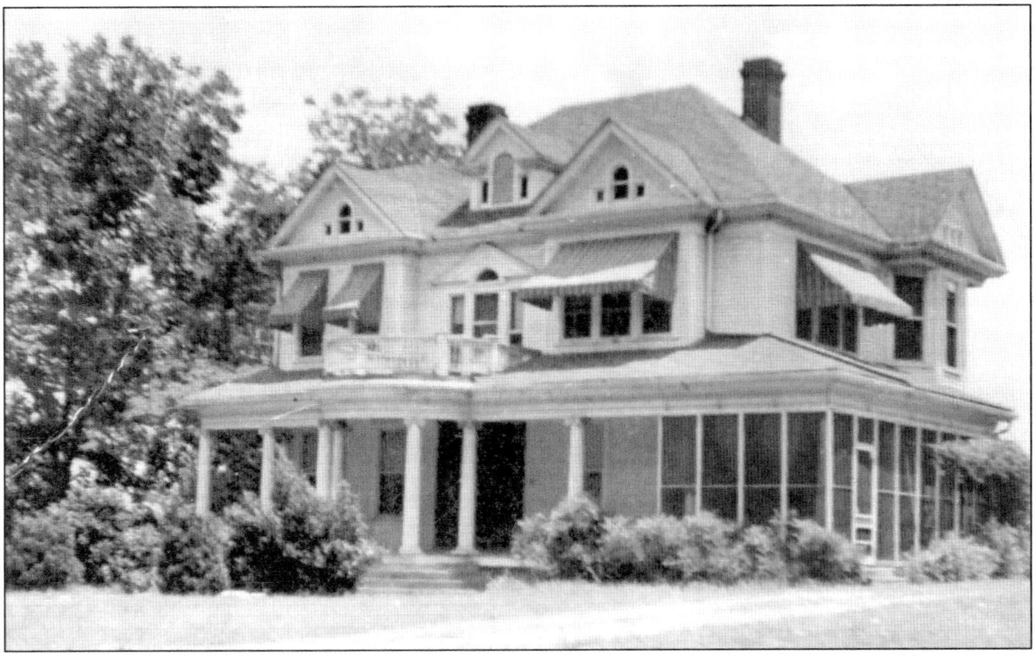

The Daughters of the American Revolution, Cherokee Rose Chapter, was organized here, at the home of Colie Covington, on April 27, 1949. Covington was designated the organizing regent, and there were 22 organizing members. The following officers were elected: Mrs. James Williams, vice-regent; Mrs. W. W. Murphey, recording secretary; Mrs. C. D. Wilson, treasurer; Mrs. U. G. Brunston, corresponding secretary; Mrs. R. B. Zeller, historian; Mrs. J. A. Wilson, registrar; and Mrs. F. M. Smith, librarian. The Cherokee Rose Chapter of the Daughters of the American Revolution marked this grave of John Strong, an American Revolutionary soldier, on October 18, 1970. (Courtesy of George W. Covington Library.)

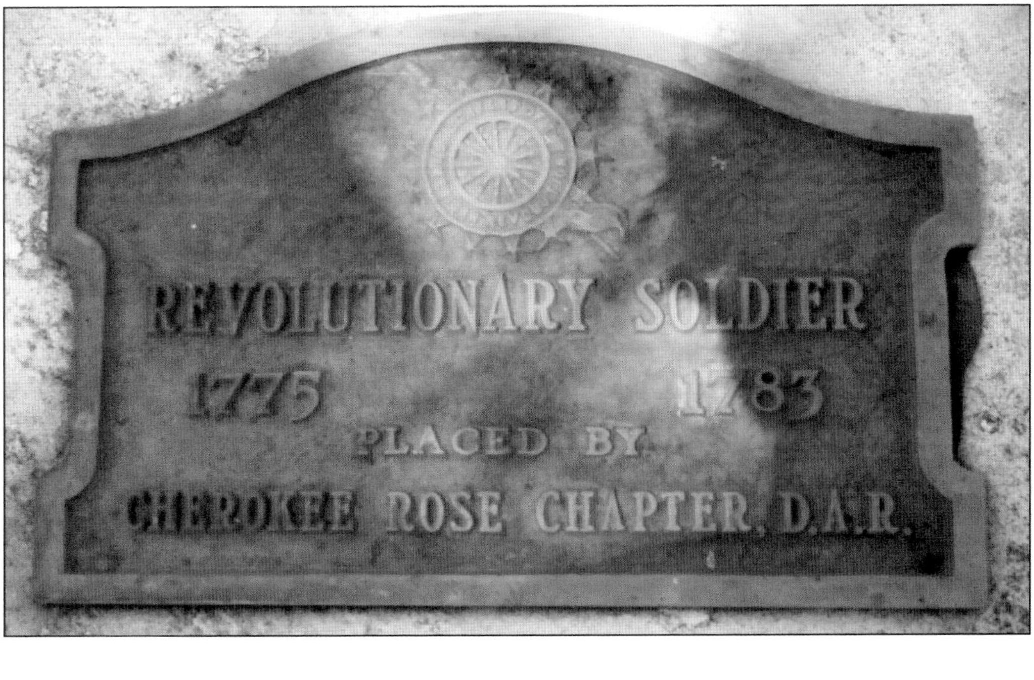

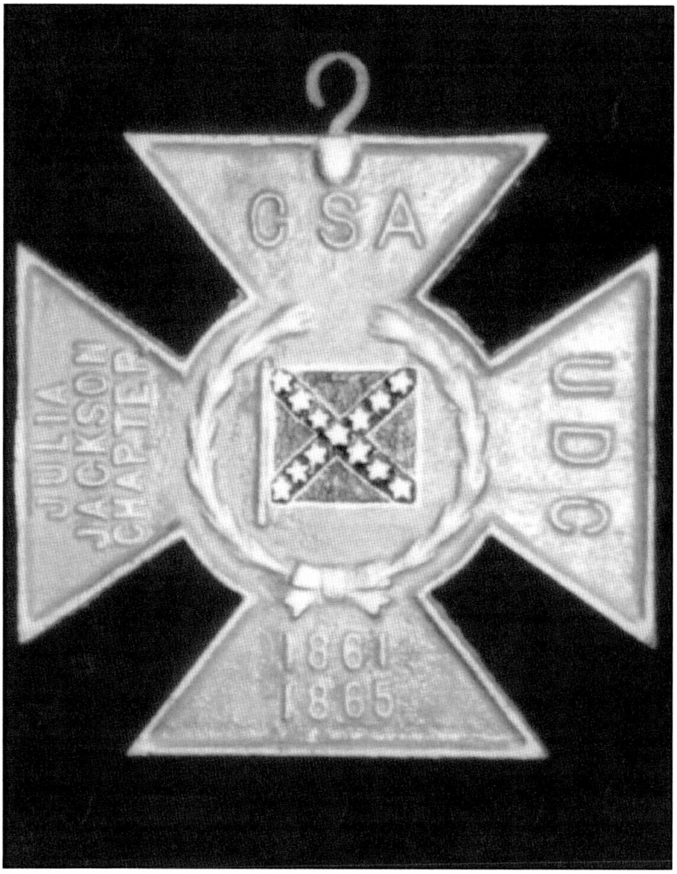

The United Daughters of the Confederacy, Julia Jackson Chapter, was organized on October 13, 1899. There were 21 charter members. The Julia Jackson Chapter placed this marker on Clark M. Johnson's gravesite. Pictured are Clark Mann Johnson and his wife, Sarah Elizabeth Nesom. The parents of six sons and two daughters, the couple endured the difficult times during and after the War Between the States. His grandfather, Daniel Johnson, fought for American independence in the Revolutionary War, and Clark enlisted in Crystal Springs in Mississippi 36th Infantry Company B, "Zollicoffer's Avengers," to fight for Southern independence. He was one of the fortunate soldiers who survived the hostilities. Clark died in 1895 and is buried in the Johnson Cemetery. (Courtesy of Dan H. Johnson.)

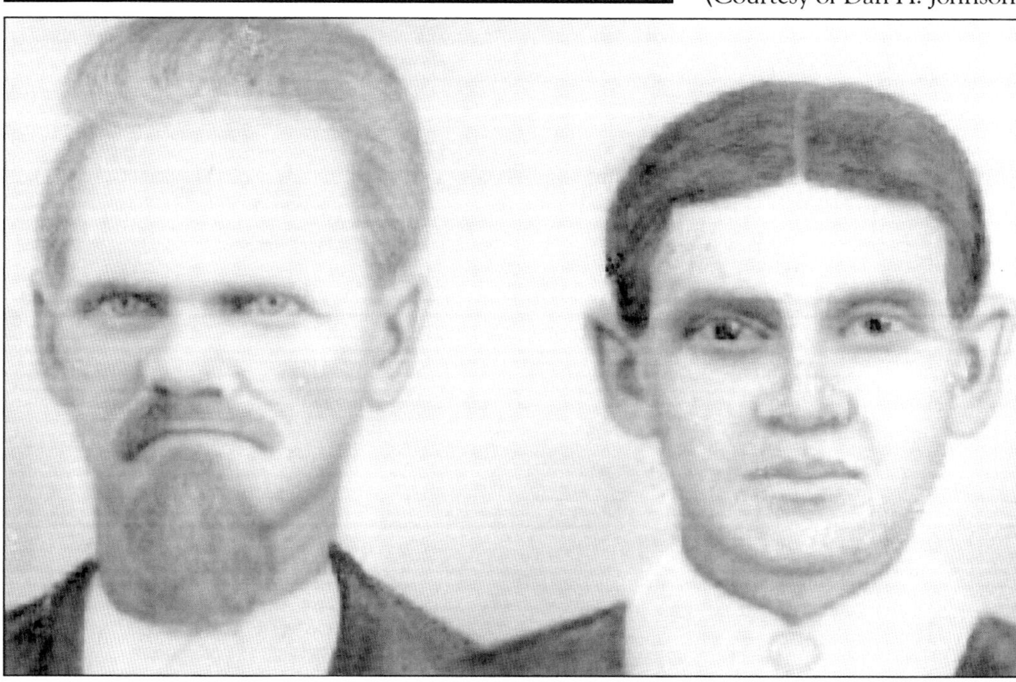

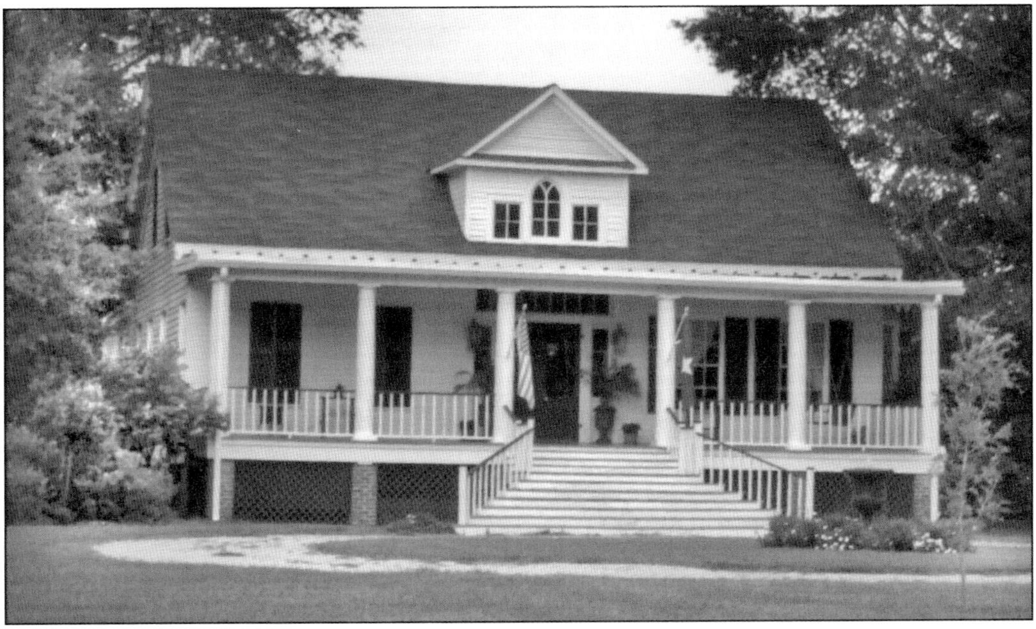

This was the home of Col. William J. Willing, who was born in Maryland in 1810. He moved to Gallatin and married Martha Patton, daughter of Francis Patton of Claiborne County. He later moved to Crystal Springs and built the first house in there in 1835. He served in many capacities, including being one of the early mayors of Crystal Springs. His home was known for its hospitality, and he entertained such notables as Jefferson Davis and Gov. Albert Gallatin Brown. In 1855, he built a large office next door to his house that is currently used as a home. (Courtesy of CCHGS.)

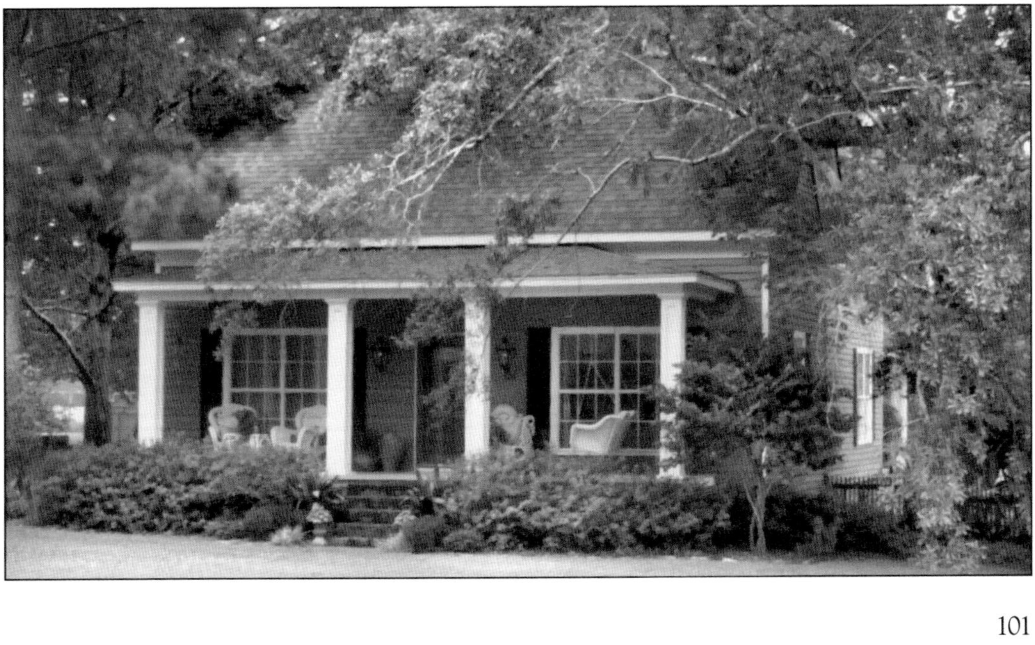

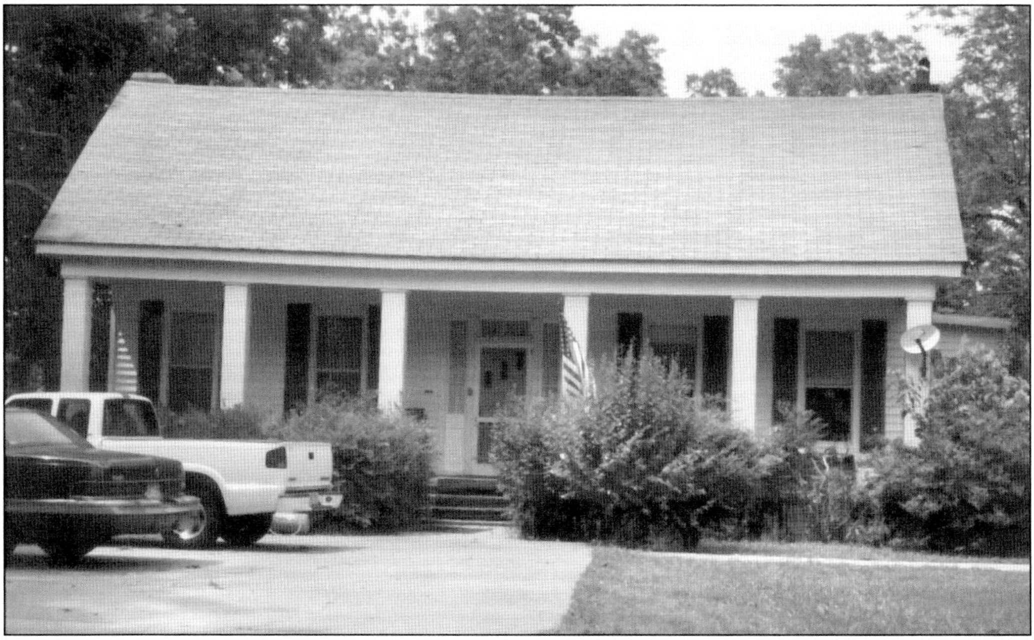

The Willing family also owned a large tract of land around Dentville named Willing. In 1913, Mrs. R. P. Willing sold the land to John Kamper of Lauderdale County. This home on Dentville Road was part of the purchase and was for one of his daughters, Katie, who married R. E. Dear in 1897. The property still remains in the family. (Courtesy of Bertie Mae and Bobby Young.)

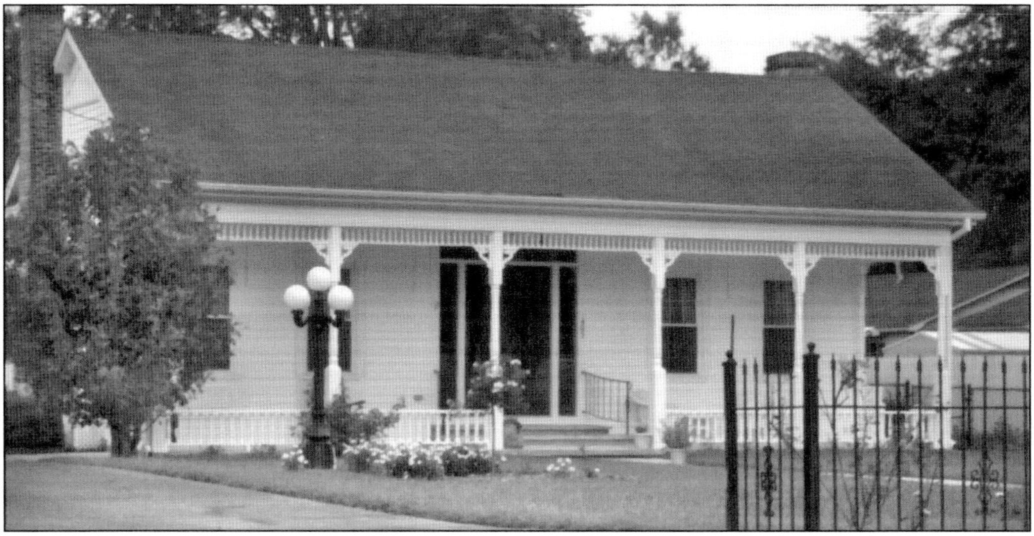

On the same street as the Willing house is the second oldest house in Crystal Springs, built in 1835 by Ozias Osborne and his family, originally from the state of New York. In 1859, the Newton Institute purchased part of Osborne's land and part of Colonel Willing's land on which to build a school. Nine years later, Osborne sold part of his land for the Crystal Springs Presbyterian Church. (Courtesy of CCHGS.)

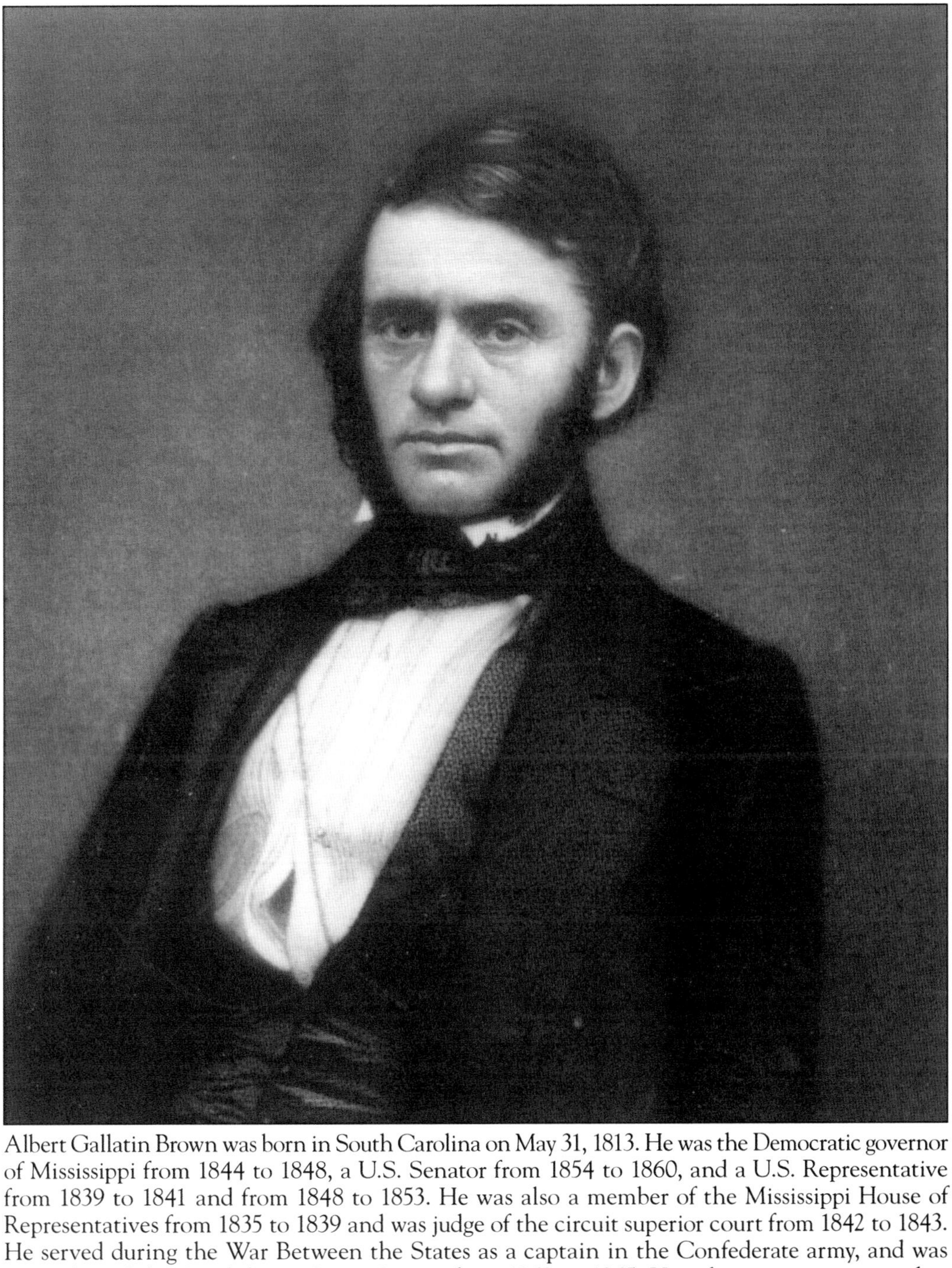

Albert Gallatin Brown was born in South Carolina on May 31, 1813. He was the Democratic governor of Mississippi from 1844 to 1848, a U.S. Senator from 1854 to 1860, and a U.S. Representative from 1839 to 1841 and from 1848 to 1853. He was also a member of the Mississippi House of Representatives from 1835 to 1839 and was judge of the circuit superior court from 1842 to 1843. He served during the War Between the States as a captain in the Confederate army, and was a member of the Confederate States Senate from 1862 to 1865. His education was attained at Mississippi College and at Jefferson College, both in Mississippi. He studied law and was admitted into practice in 1834, establishing his practice in Gallatin. In 1846, he succeeded in passing an act to have a general system of schools in the state. During his tenure as governor, a state university at Oxford (University of Mississippi) was authorized. He passed away on June 12, 1880, and is buried in Greenwood Cemetery in Jackson, Mississippi. (Courtesy of MDAH.)

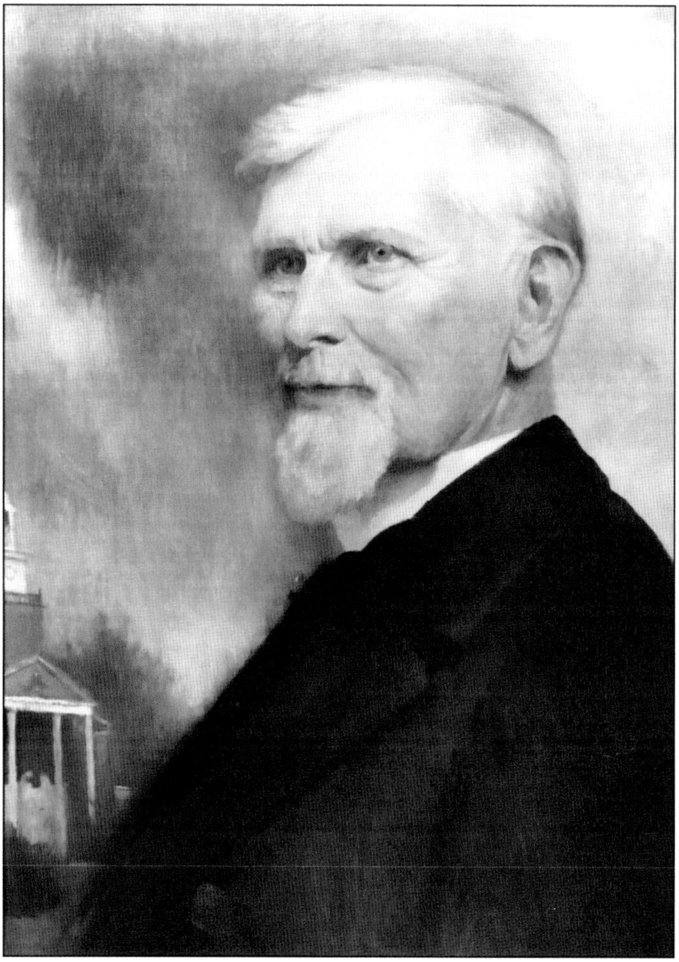

Born in 1833 in Copiah County, Reuben Webster Millsaps obtained a law degree from Harvard Law School and practiced in Pine Bluff, Arkansas, until the beginning of the War Between the States. After several years of service, he moved back to Mississippi, where he began a business buying and transporting cotton. He also had a merchandising business in Brookhaven. In 1880, he sold his business and moved to St. Louis, Missouri, where he established yet another business. He moved back to Mississippi, settled in Hazlehurst, and established the Merchants and Planters Bank. He then moved to Jackson in 1887 and became the president of the Capitol State Bank. He laid the foundation for Millsaps College, pictured below, by providing an initial gift of $50,000 in 1889 and subsequent gifts thereafter. (Courtesy of MDAH.)

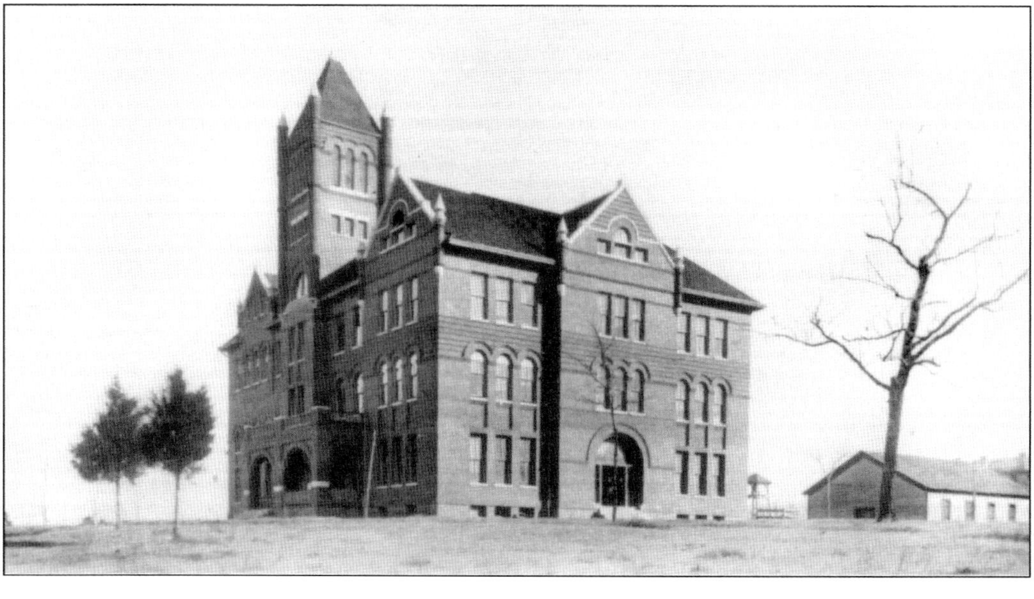

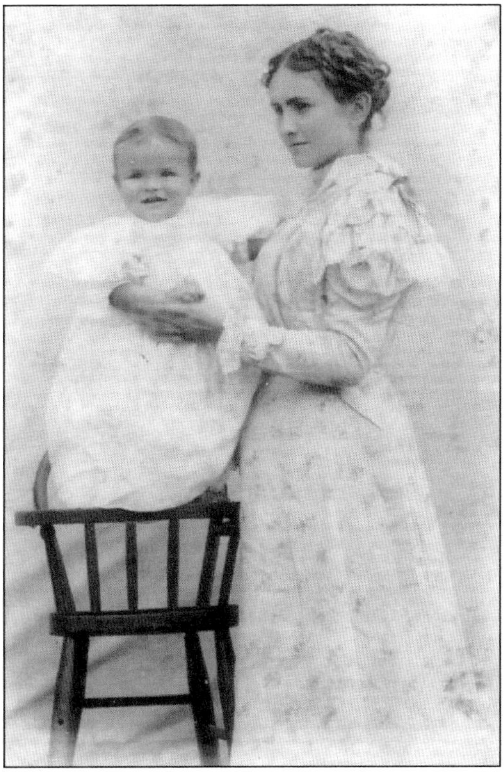

Maj. R. W. Millsaps's aunt, Charity Millsaps, married Henry Barlow of the Barlow community. They had two daughters who married sons of Benjamin and Celia Bufkin of Copiah County. Bufkin's brother, B. F. Bufkin, married Maryanne Singletary and had a beautiful daughter, Katherine (Kate), born in 1883. Kate married William Jack Thompson on February 6, 1897, but the marriage was short-lived, as William Jack died on November 23, 1900, from a kick to the head by a mule. This photograph was taken around 1899 with William Jack Jr. Kate then married John McKee. She died at age 40 and is buried in McGee Cemetery. A lot of the Millsaps, Bufkin, and Thompson family members stayed in Copiah County. Pictured is Ike Thompson of Hazlehurst, who owned Thompson's Grocery with Garland Pitts on Highway 28. (Courtesy of Janice Brown and Cheryl Rabalais.)

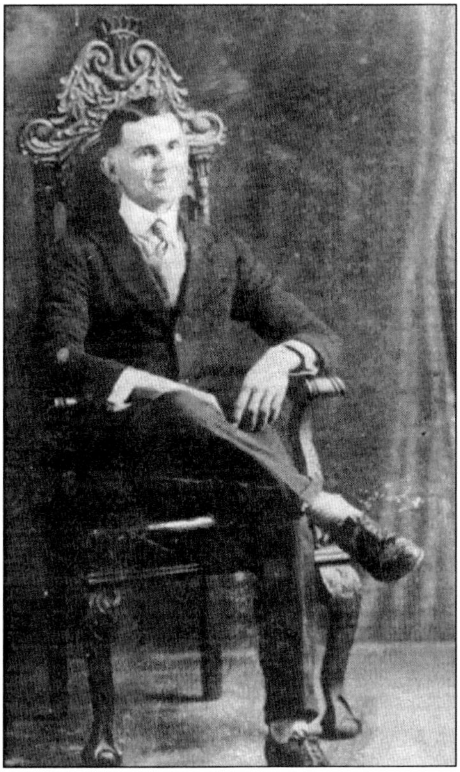

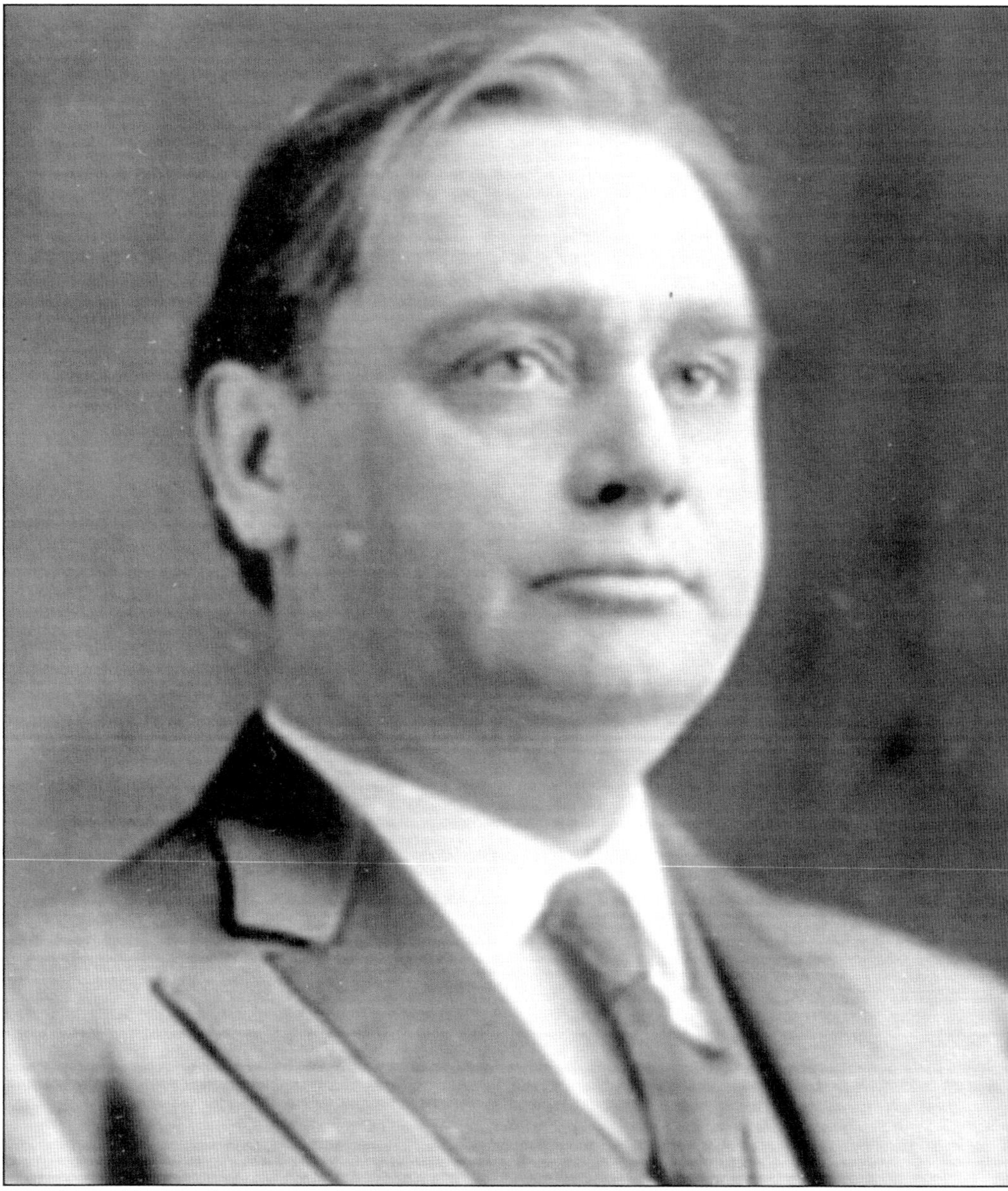

Joseph Weldon Bailey Sr. was born near Crystal Springs in October 6, 1862. Born as Joseph Edgar Bailey, he replaced his middle name with the family name Weldon. After finishing school in Crystal Springs, he attended Mississippi College before obtaining a law degree in 1883 and establishing a practice in Hazlehurst. He was an avid Democrat. He moved to Gainesville, Tennessee, in 1885 to practice law. He was elected to the 52nd and to the four succeeding Congresses (March 4, 1891–March 3, 1901). He was elected to the U.S. Senate in 1901 and reelected in 1907. Facing a heavy challenge in 1912 and disillusioned by the progressive movement within the Democratic Party, he resigned from the Senate in 1911. He resumed a lucrative law practice in Washington, D.C., and subsequently moved to Texas in 1921, where he continued the practice of law. He was unsuccessful as a candidate for governor of Texas in 1920. He died in a courtroom in Sherman, Texas, on April 13, 1929. He is interred in Gainesville Cemetery, Gainesville, Texas. (Courtesy of Library of Congress.)

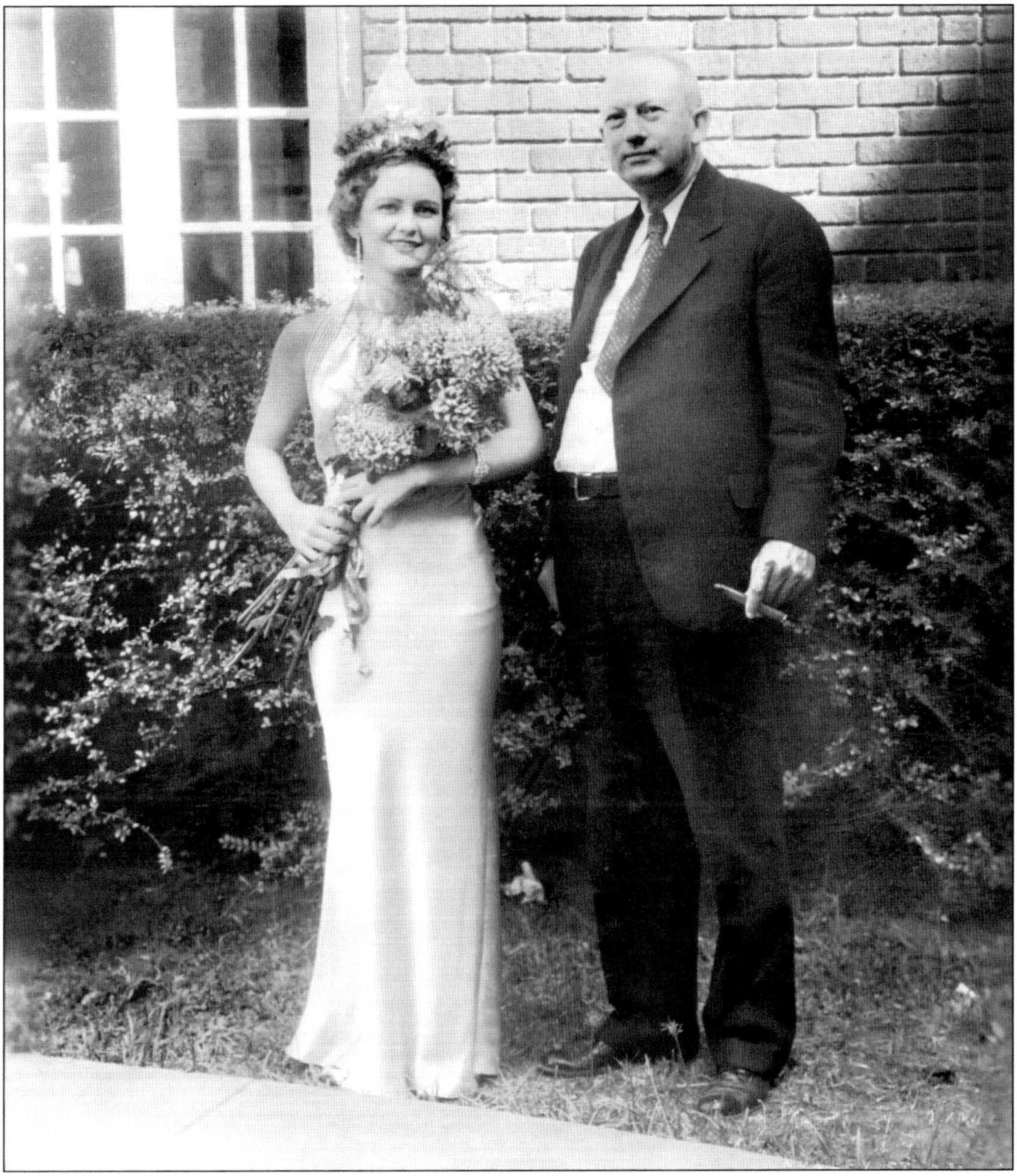

Byron Patton "Pat" Harrison was born August 29, 1881, in Crystal Springs. After graduating from Louisiana State University, he taught school in Leakesville and married Mary Edwina McInnis, and they had three children. He became an attorney and practiced in Leakesville. At the age of 23, he became district attorney for the Second District of Mississippi. Four years later, in 1908, he became one of Mississippi's representatives to the national convention of the Democratic Party. In 1920, he had this same distinction. In 1911, he became a member of the U.S. House of Representatives, where he remained until 1918, when he defeated Sen. James K. Vardaman to become a U.S. Senator. At the time of his death in June 1941, he was president pro tempore of the Senate. Three thousand Crystal Springs residents attended a memorial service for him held at the tabernacle at Lake Chautauqua. Today a road winding through Crystal Springs is named Pat Harrison Drive in his honor. Here he is standing with Miss Mississippi Rachel Smith of Booneville. (Courtesy of MDAH.)

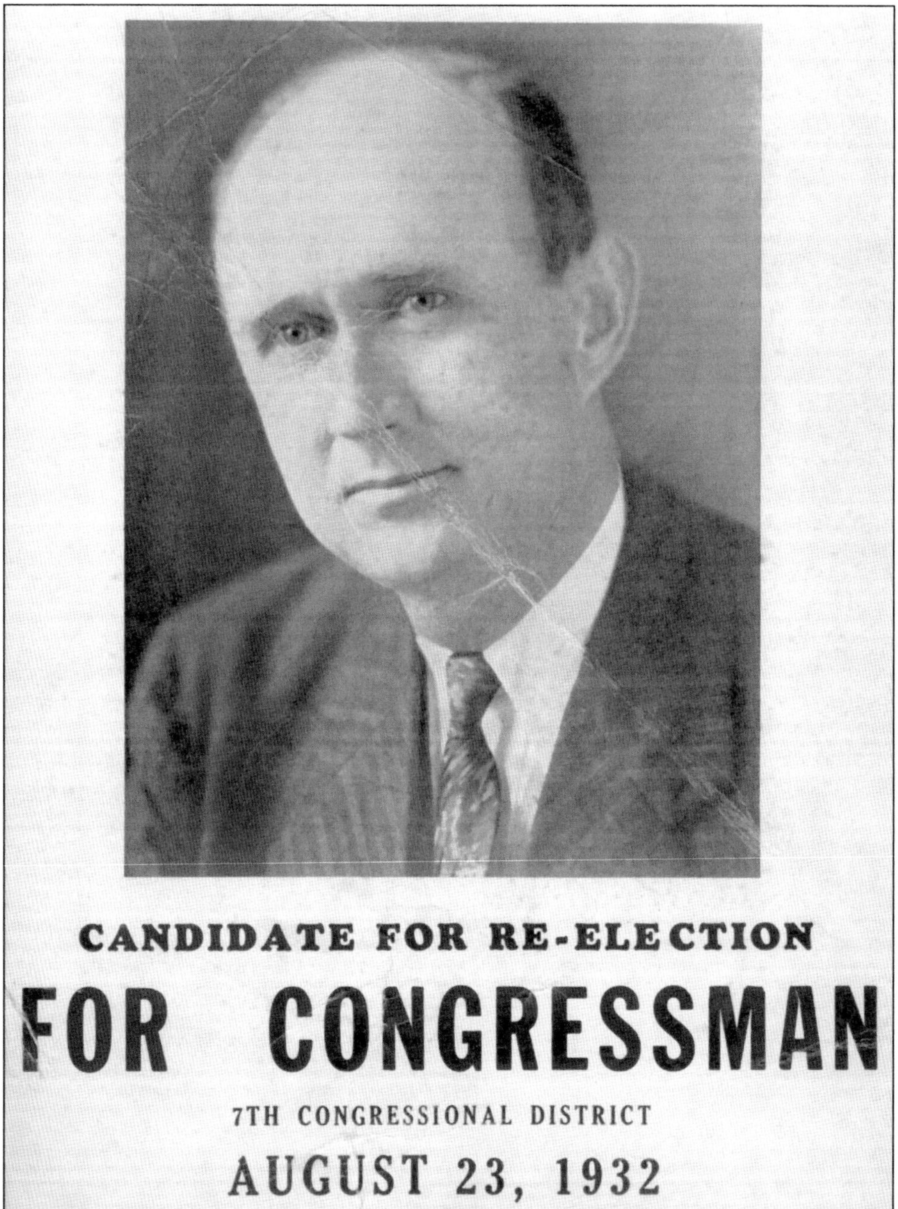

Lawrence Russell Ellzey was a U.S. Representative from Mississippi born near Wesson on March 20, 1891. He graduated from Mississippi College and was a teacher in the consolidated county schools from 1912 to 1917. His served a brief time in the military and then served as superintendent of education of Lincoln County from 1920 to 1922. He must have enjoyed teaching, for he returned to the profession, teaching at the agricultural high school in Wesson from 1922 to 1928. He was the president of Copiah-Lincoln Community College in Wesson from 1928 to 1932. He left the college when he was appointed to Congress by special election to fill the vacancy caused by the death of Percy E. Quin. He was reelected, serving from 1932 to 1935. He was an unsuccessful candidate for nomination in 1934. Residing in Jackson, he died December 7, 1977, and is interred in Wesson Cemetery. (Courtesy of Susan Alsbury and Longie Dale Hamilton Memorial Library.)

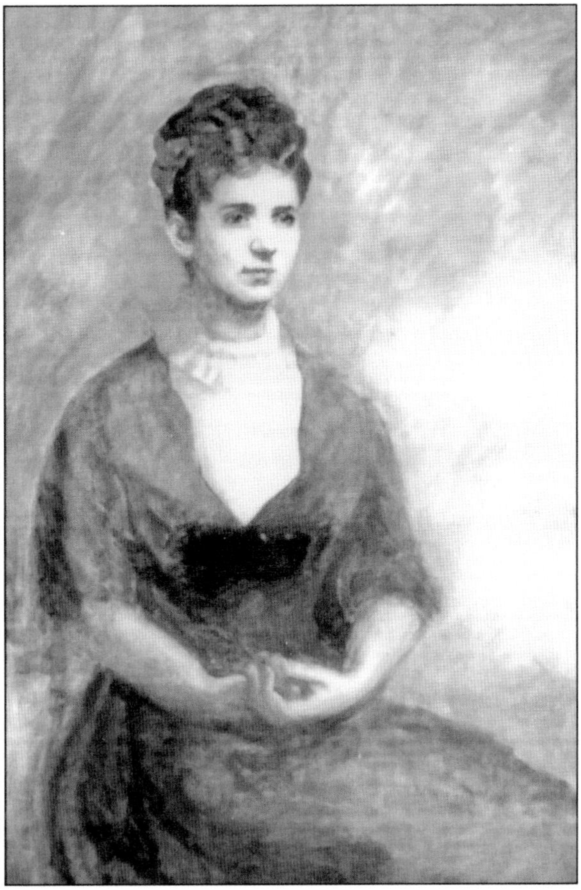

Annie Coleman Peyton was instrumental in founding the Mississippi State College for Women, now known as Mississippi University for Women. She was born in 1852, the youngest child of Mary Gilchrist and Elias Hibben of Madison County. She graduated from Whitworth College in 1872, married Chancellor Ephraim Geoffrey Petyon of Gallatin, and lived there until the late 1870s, when they moved to Hazlehurst. She was concerned about her daughters' education. She felt that many Mississippi girls were being deprived by poverty and had little education beyond the most elementary. Church schools were limited in endowment. She wrote numerous articles under the name "A Mississippi Woman" and lobbied the legislators, among other things; she was finally able to see legislation passed which created the institution in 1884. (Courtesy of MDAH.)

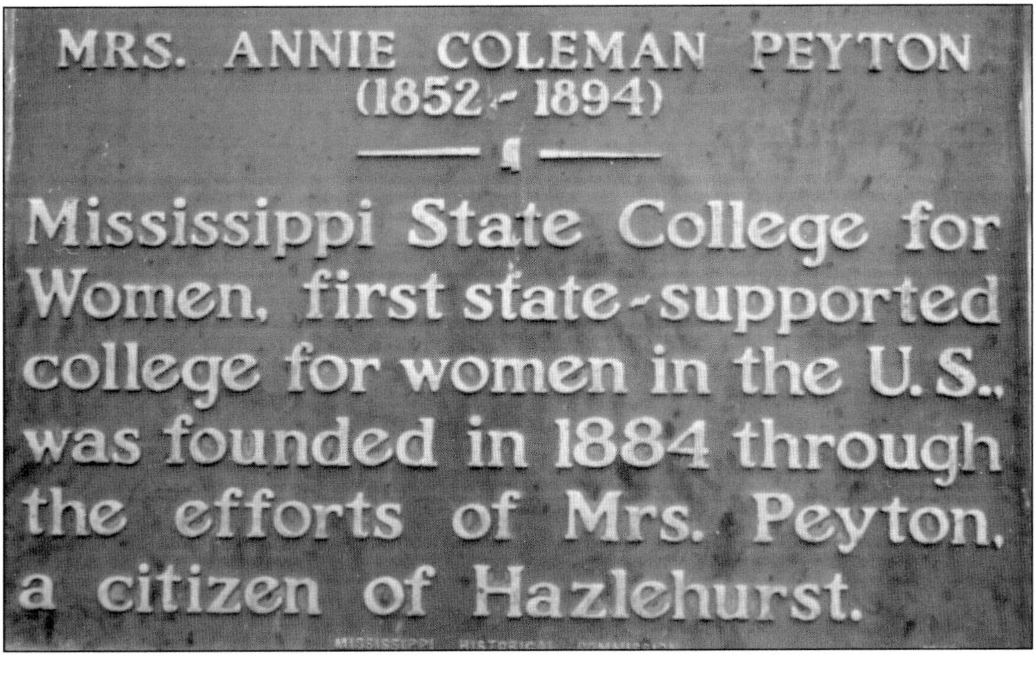

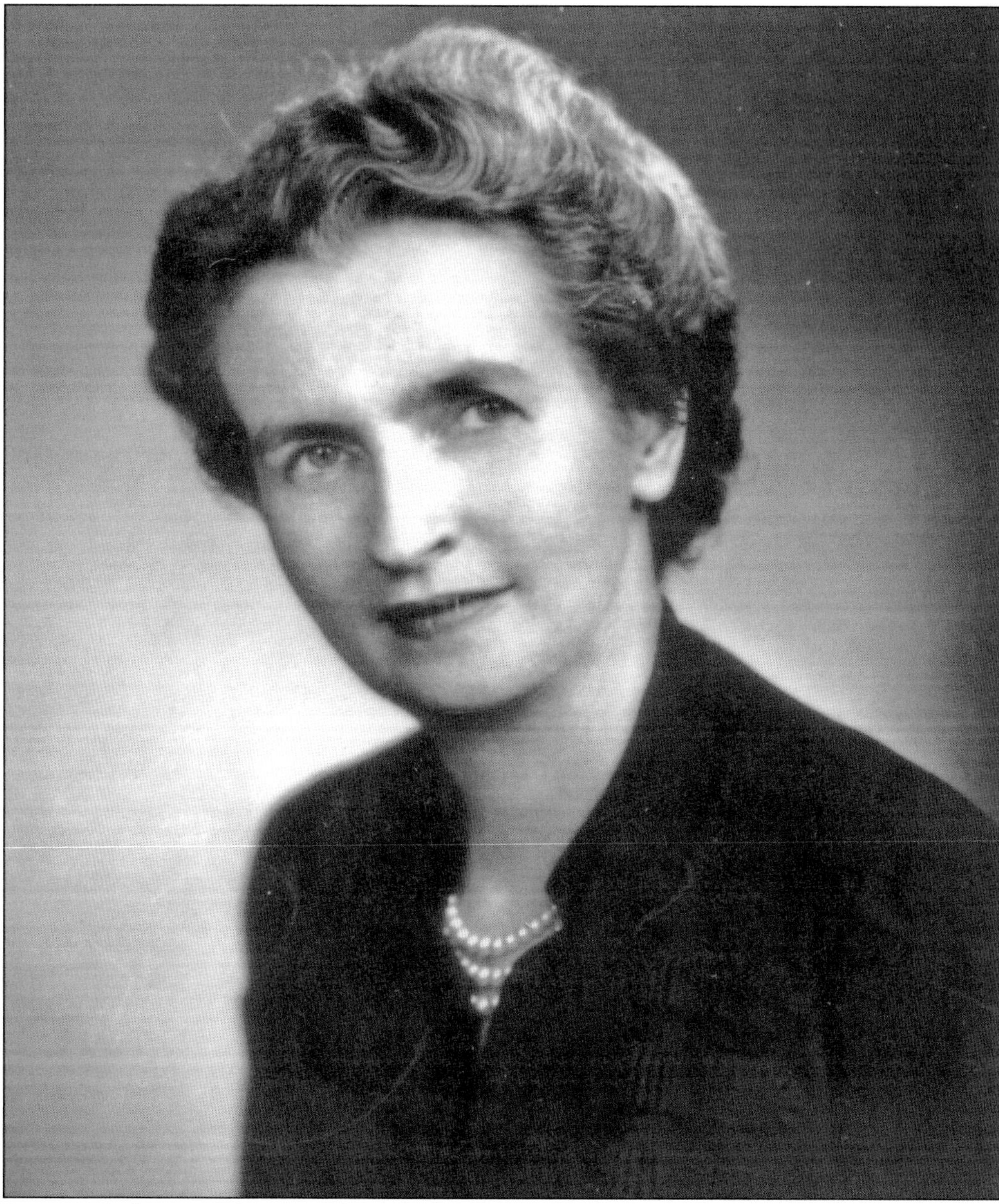

Burnita Shelton Matthews was born near Hazlehurst on December 28, 1894. Burnita's father, Burnell, served as the clerk of the chancery court and tax collector of the county. Hoping Burnita would avoid the legal field, her father sent her to the Cincinnati Conservatory of Music. She taught music lessons in Georgia for a while and then met her husband, Percy Ashley Matthews, who supported her dream of attending law school. They married in 1917, which was the same year Burnita started law school at what is now George Washington University. Burnita went on to accomplish many things throughout her life. She most wished people to remember that, in 1949, she was the first woman appointed to the federal district court bench, and she was an "author of laws advancing the status of women." She spent many years advocating women's rights and often took on work for no pay. When she died in 1988, these two facts were noted on her headstone in the Shelton family cemetery in Copiah County. (Courtesy of MDAH.)

Frances Addine "Fannye" Cook was born July 19, 1889. She graduated from the Mississippi State College for Women and taught school for a short time before she moved to Washington, D.C., where she was an auditor for the IRS. She spent most of her time doing research and preparing specimens for the Smithsonian Institute. In 1926, she moved back to Mississippi. In 1927, she organized the Mississippi Association for the Conservation of Wildlife, which eventually led to the establishment of the Game and Fish Commission. In the 1930s, she supervised a state plant and animal survey funded by the federal WPA. She wrote numerous articles and several books. She also helped organize the Mississippi Ornithological Society. Cook became the first director of the Mississippi Wildlife Museum. (Courtesy of Mississippi Museum of Natural Science.)

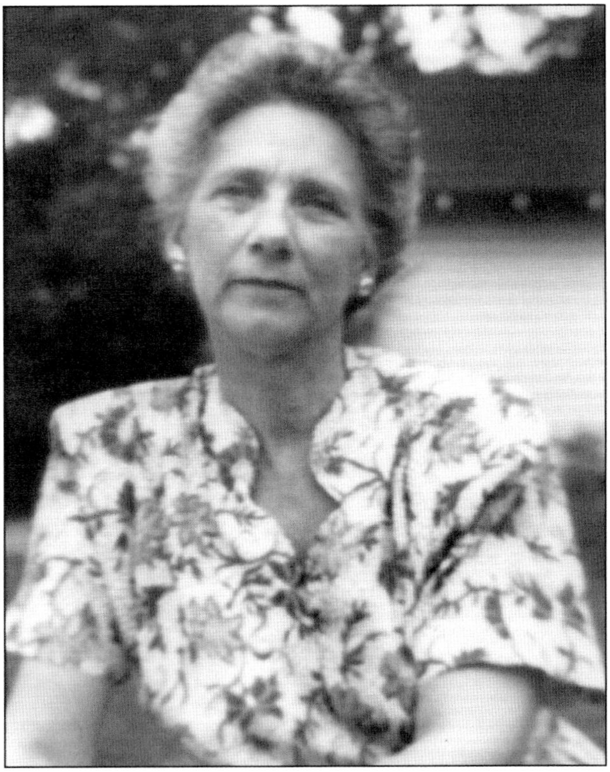

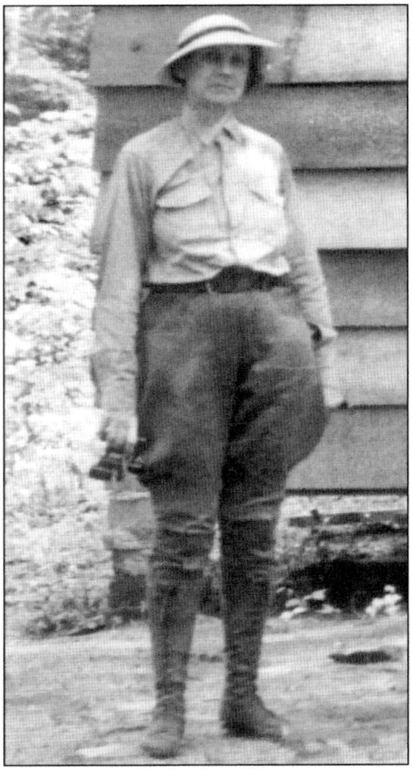

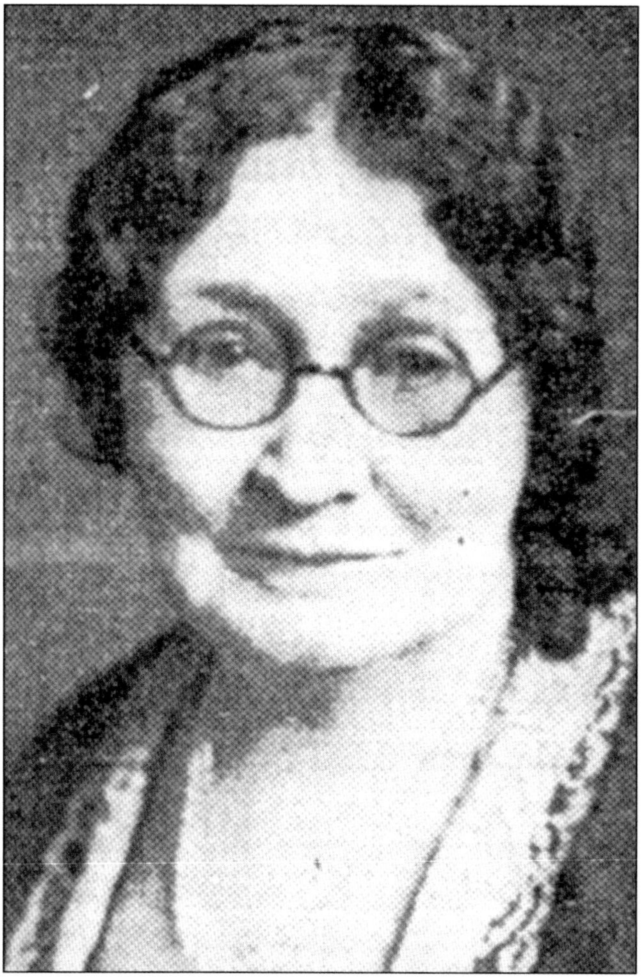

Bessie Lackey Stapleton formed the Mississippi Parent Teacher Association (PTA) in 1909. Born in Crystal Springs, her mother was the niece of Gov. John J. McRae of Mississippi. Her father, Prof. J. J. Lackey, was educated by Henry Ward Beecher, a great American Congregational minister. She was educated in New Orleans and at Hillman College in Clinton, Mississippi. It was while living in Hattiesburg that she began efforts to start the Mississippi PTA. On September 5, 1905, she called a small meeting in her home to discuss the idea. Her efforts came to fruition at Lake Chautauqua in 1909, when she was elected president of the association and her sister, Margaret Lackey, was elected secretary. She served as president until 1914. (Courtesy of CCHGS.)

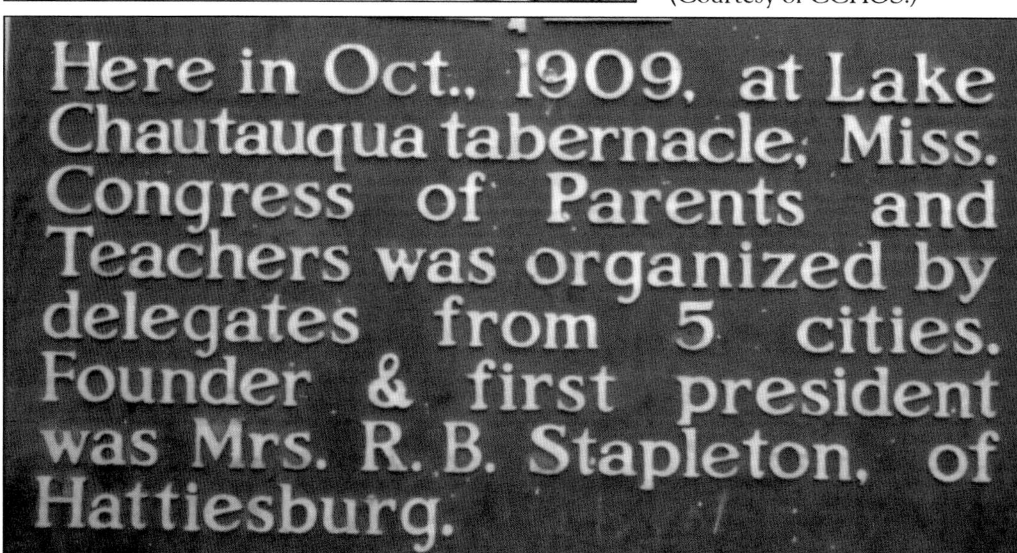

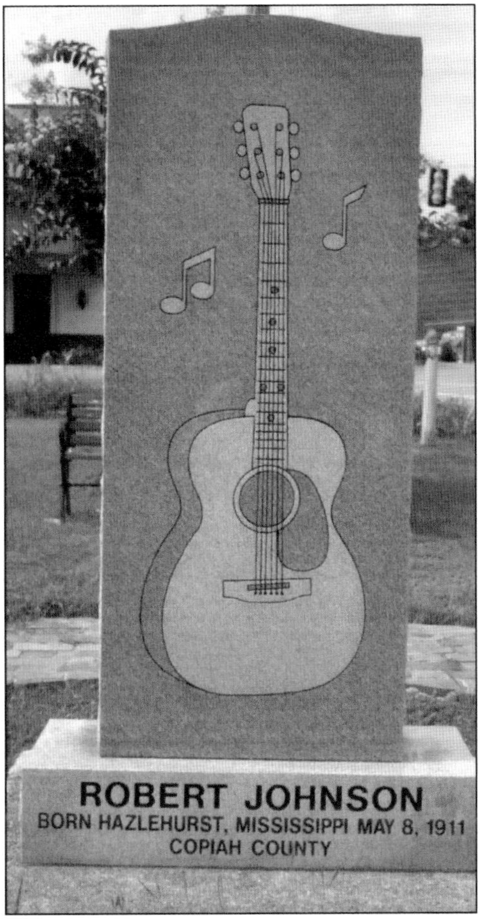

Houston Stackhouse, born in 1910 in Wesson, and Robert Johnson, born in 1911 in Hazlehurst, were noted bluesmen. Johnson spent most of his life in the Delta. He died on August 16, 1938. Although he only recorded 29 tracks, his style was so unique that he was considered by some to be the "Grandfather of Rock and Roll." He was a master of the guitar, and soon rumor had it that he had made a pact and sold his soul to the devil. In 1986, the film *Crossroads* was produced based on Johnson's career. Johnson was inducted into the Blues Foundation's Hall of Fame in 1980 and the Rock and Roll Hall of Fame in 1986. There are three grave markers devoted to Johnson, but he is actually buried at Little Zion Missionary Baptist Church in Greenwood, Mississippi. (Courtesy of CCHGS.)

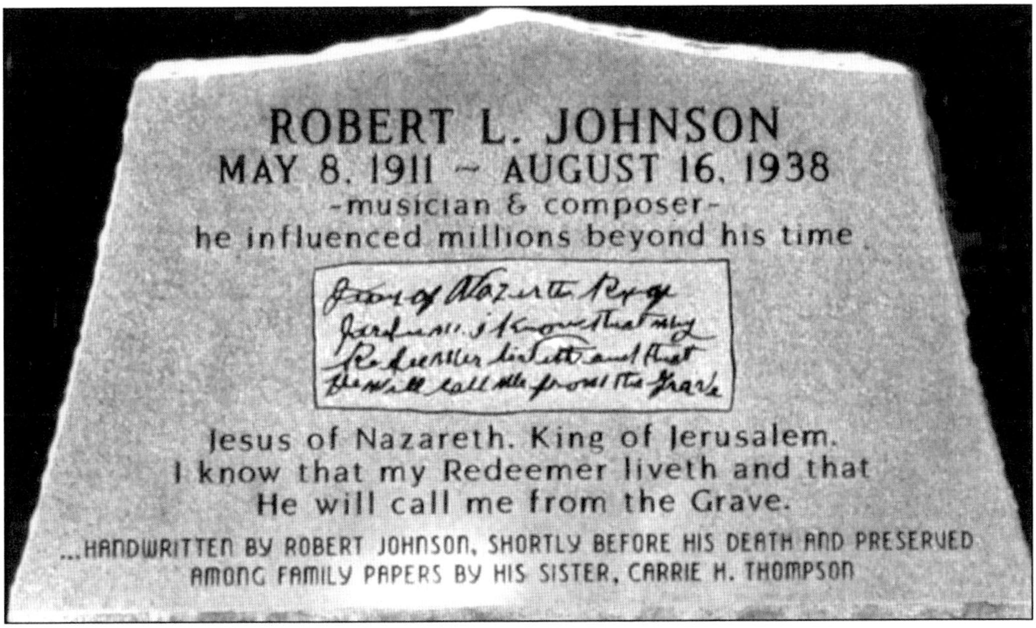

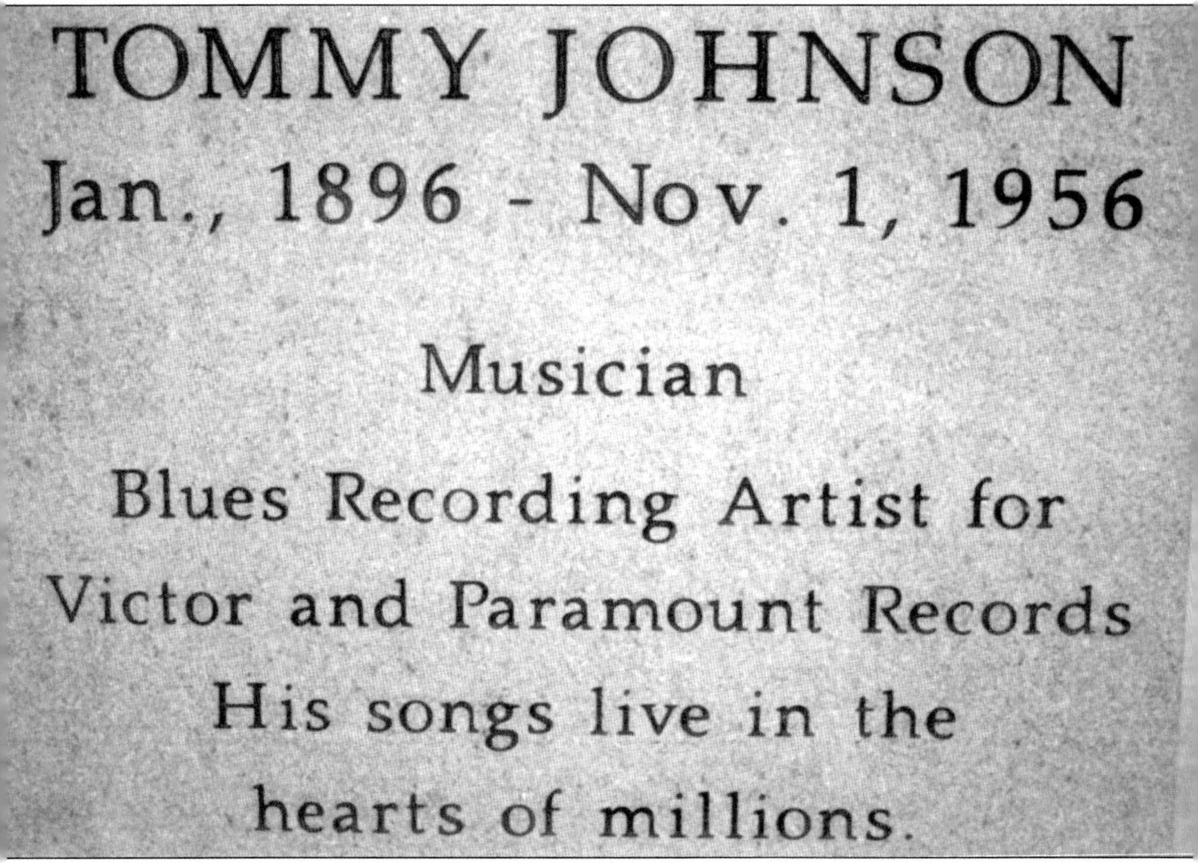

Tommy Johnson, another great bluesman, was born in Terry, Mississippi, in 1896 on the George Miller plantation. The family moved to Crystal Springs in 1910, and soon thereafter, Tommy, aged 16, ran away to begin his career as a professional musician. Tommy openly admitted to going to the crossroads to sell his soul to the devil to learn how to play the guitar. This was further perpetuated by the Coen brothers' movie *O Brother, Where Art Thou?* He recorded from 1928 to 1930 but began to decline and was seen playing juke joints and small house parties thereafter. He was playing one such party when he died from a heart attack on November 1, 1956. He is buried in the Warm Springs Methodist Church Cemetery in Crystal Springs. Pictured is an inscription on a statue of Tommy Johnson commissioned by Bonnie Rait that sits at the J. T. Biggs Jr. Memorial Library in Crystal Springs until it can be placed on his grave. (Courtesy of CCHGS.)

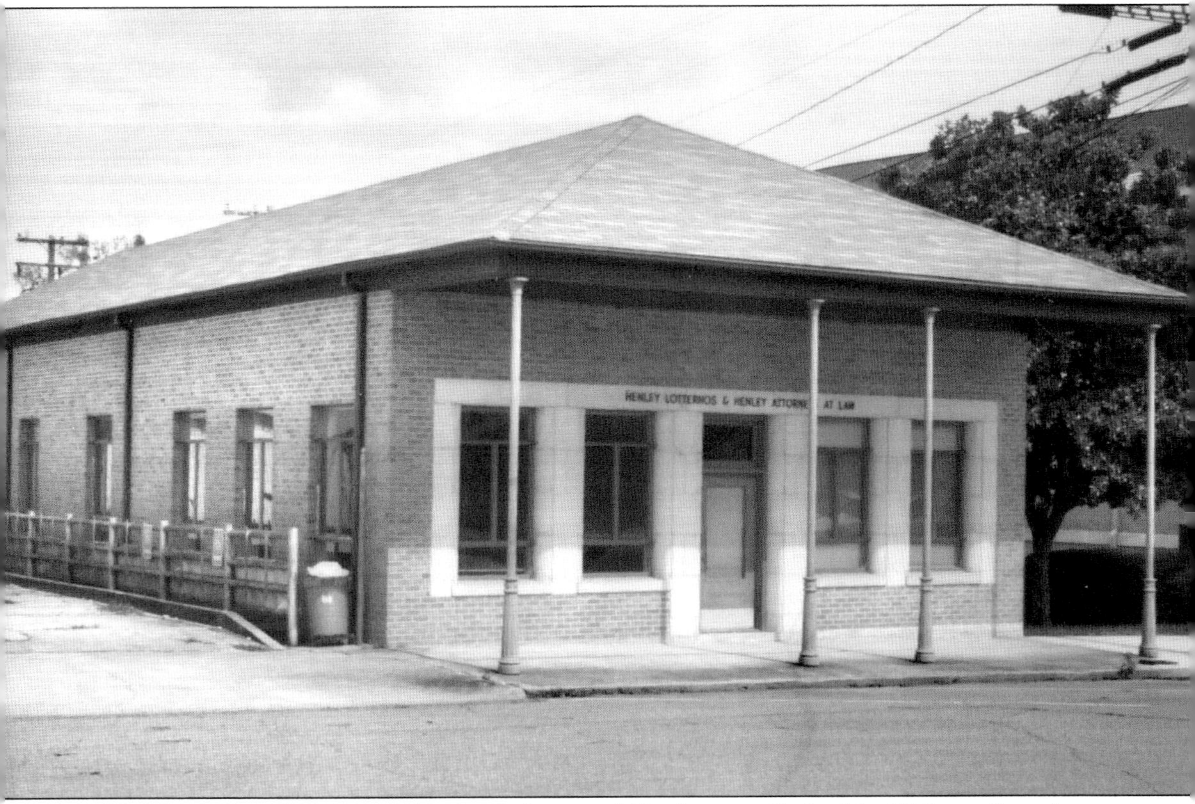

Pictured is the law firm of Henley, Lotterhos, and Henley, established by William Saunders Henley in Hazlehurst in 1925. Henley served one year as president of the Mississippi State Bar, one term in the state legislature, and over 50 years on the board of trustees of Co-Lin Community College. His son, Charles Boyce, was educated in Hazlehurst and was the father of Beth Henley, a playwright and actress. Charles served in World War II and practiced law with his father. He also served as a county judge for Hinds County and served as a representative and senator in the state legislature. In 1978, Beth wrote *Crimes of the Heart*, a tragic comedy set in Hazlehurst about three sisters surviving a crisis in a small Mississippi town. She was the first woman to win the Pulitzer Prize for drama in 23 years, and her play was the first ever to win before opening on Broadway. The law firm of Henley, Lotterhos, and Henley is still going strong. (Courtesy of CCHGS.)

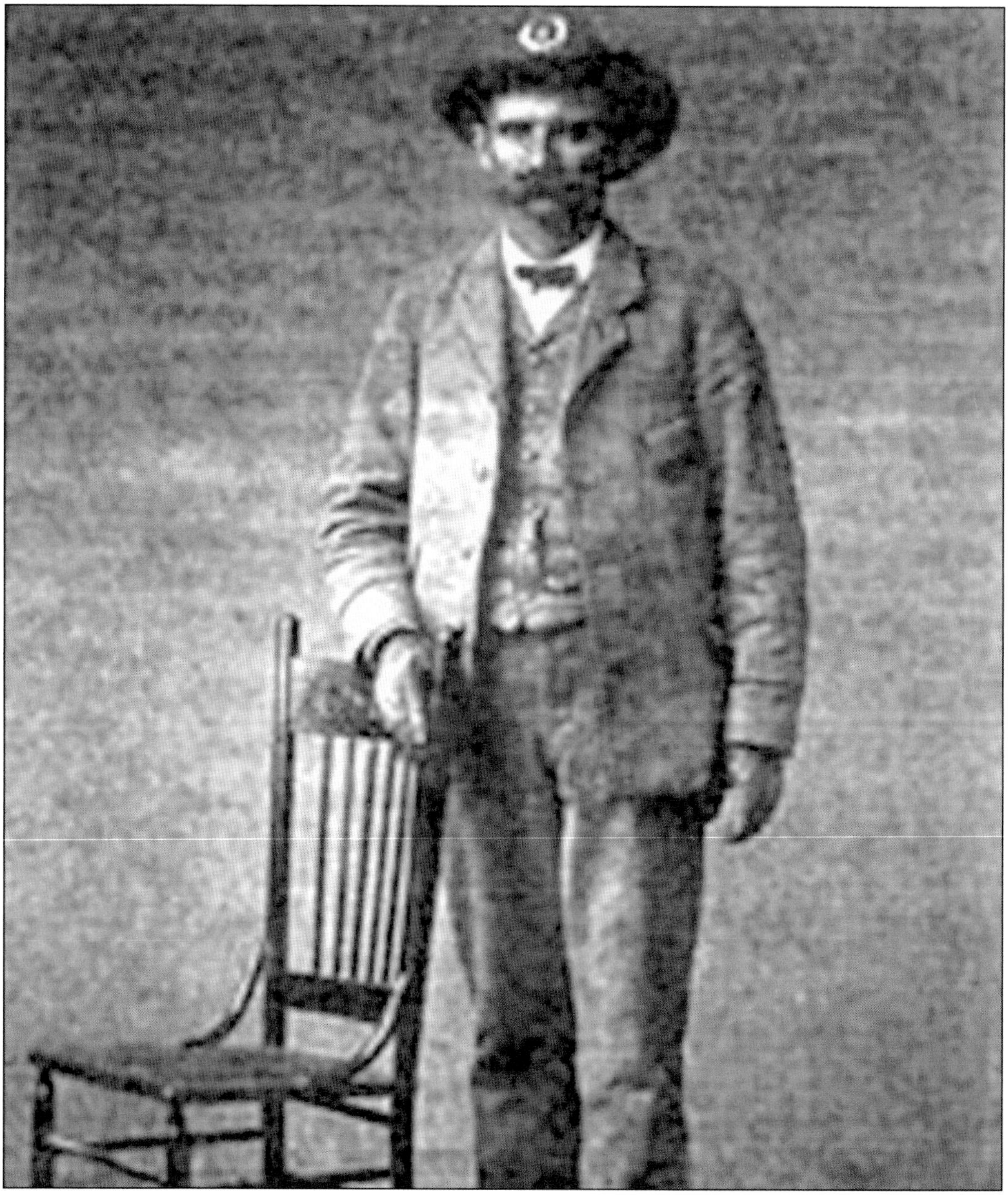

Rural carrier service around Crystal Springs began in 1901 with "Babe" Fleming and his substitute, R. C. "Cornelius" Taylor, serving Route One. Later Taylor was given permission to organize Route Two. The mail was delivered using a horse and buggy, but once in 1905, when the roads were impassable due to the weather, he walked the entire 31-mile route. Well-wishers greeted him with hot soup, coffee, and words of encouragement. Taylor was twice the president of the Mississippi Rural Letter Carrier's Association and was a delegate to the National Rural Letter Carrier's Convention several times. It was through his efforts at the Kansas City Convention that Christmas Day became a national holiday for rural carriers. He delivered the mail for over 31 years. He bought one of the first automobiles in Crystal Springs and was the first to deliver mail in a car in the county. Frequently he would take orders for necessities from people on his route, make the purchases in town, and deliver them the next day. (Courtesy of Mary Taylor Guy.)

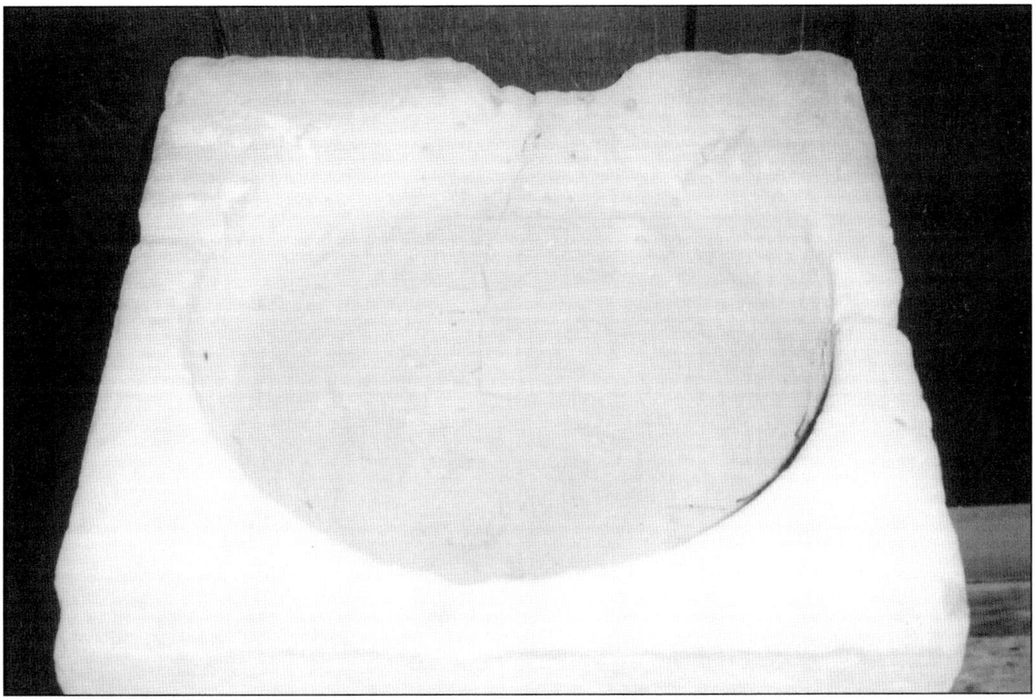

This limestone rock, hollowed out in a bowl shape in the center, was placed in a spring to capture the cold clear water for the Johnson family. Revolutionary War patriot and pioneer Daniel Johnson and family lived on a hill located just off of today's Blocker Road. Today many descendants still reside in the county, many on Johnson Road east of Crystal Springs. (Courtesy of Dan H. Johnson.)

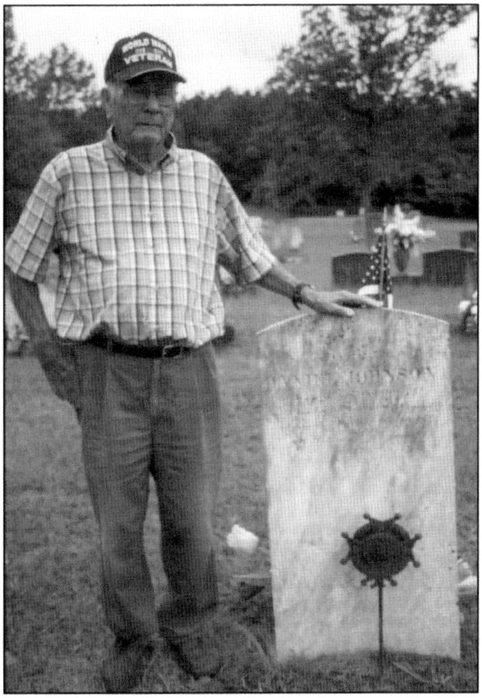

Daniel Johnson's grave is located in Johnson Cemetery, where he was the first person buried in 1854 when he died at the age of 102. The Daughters of the American Revolution placed a marker at his grave on October 13, 1935, and the Sons of the American Revolution dedicated a marker on May 6, 2001. Pictured at Daniel's grave is great-great-great-grandson John Harding Johnson. (Courtesy of Dan H. Johnson.)

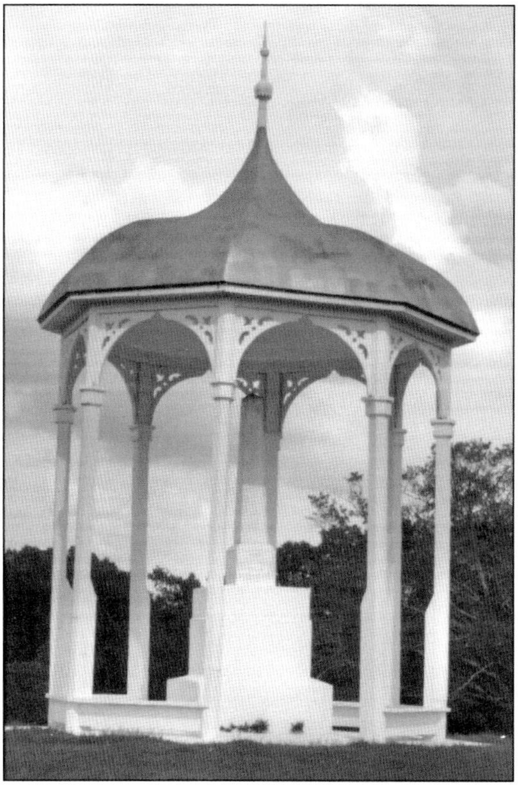

The Confederate Memorial in the Crystal Springs Cemetery pays tribute to the veterans men who fought in the War Between the States. The bodies of 20 unknown soldiers are buried here. The memorial was placed by the "Ladies of Crystal Springs Miss. 1876." The cupola was erected from funds raised by students at Newton Institute. The Sons of the Confederate Veterans help maintain the memorial. (Courtesy of CCHGS.)

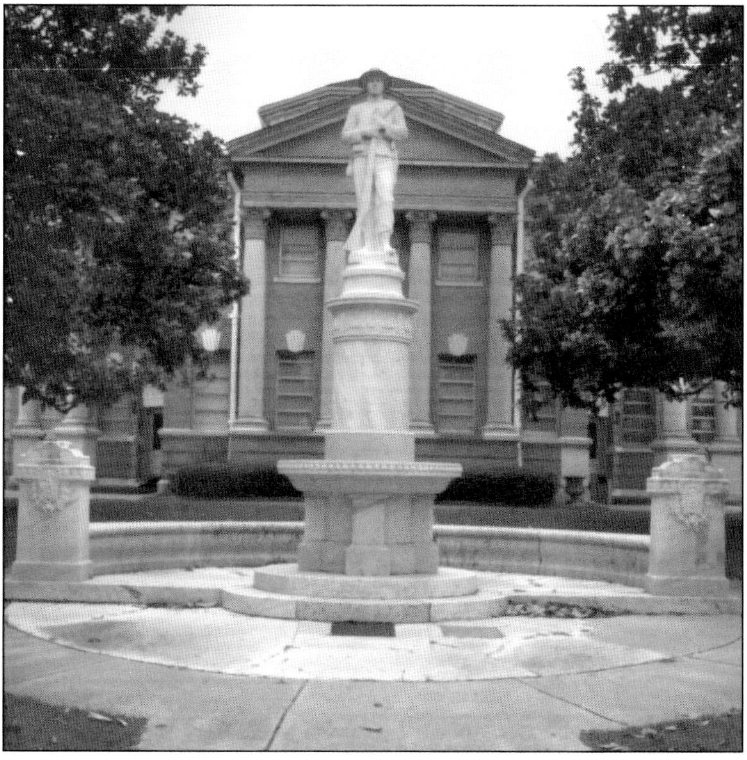

Another tribute to Copiah County's fallen soldiers is the statue of a confederate soldier in front of the Copiah County Courthouse in Hazlehurst. Erected by Copiah County and the Charles Edward Hooker Chapter of the United Daughters of the Confederacy in 1917, the following is etched on the memorial: "[i]n honor of those who fought and died and those who fought and lived." (Courtesy of CCHGS.)

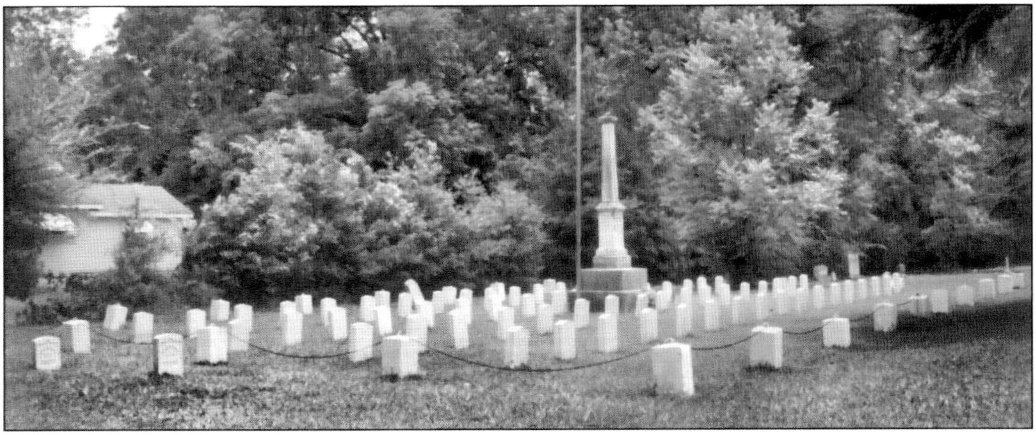

Pictured is the Confederate soldiers section of the Hazlehurst cemetery. Sixty-eight unknown Confederate soldiers are buried there. Heavy chains outline the area in which they are buried. Two Union soldiers were buried outside of the chains on the left. This goes to show the sentiment of the people in the South at the time. (Courtesy of CCHGS.)

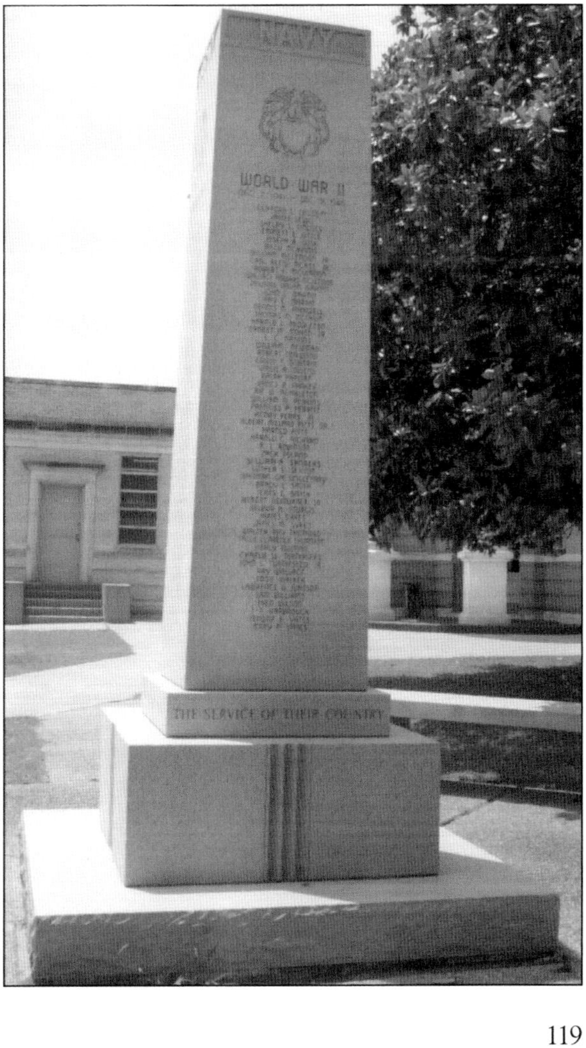

Another monument dedicated to the veterans of Copiah County is this one located at the Copiah County Courthouse. This four-sided obelisk lists the names of Copiah County citizens who were killed in action in World War I, World War II, Korea, and Vietnam. There is a similar memorial in Railroad Park in Crystal Springs. (Courtesy of CCHGS.)

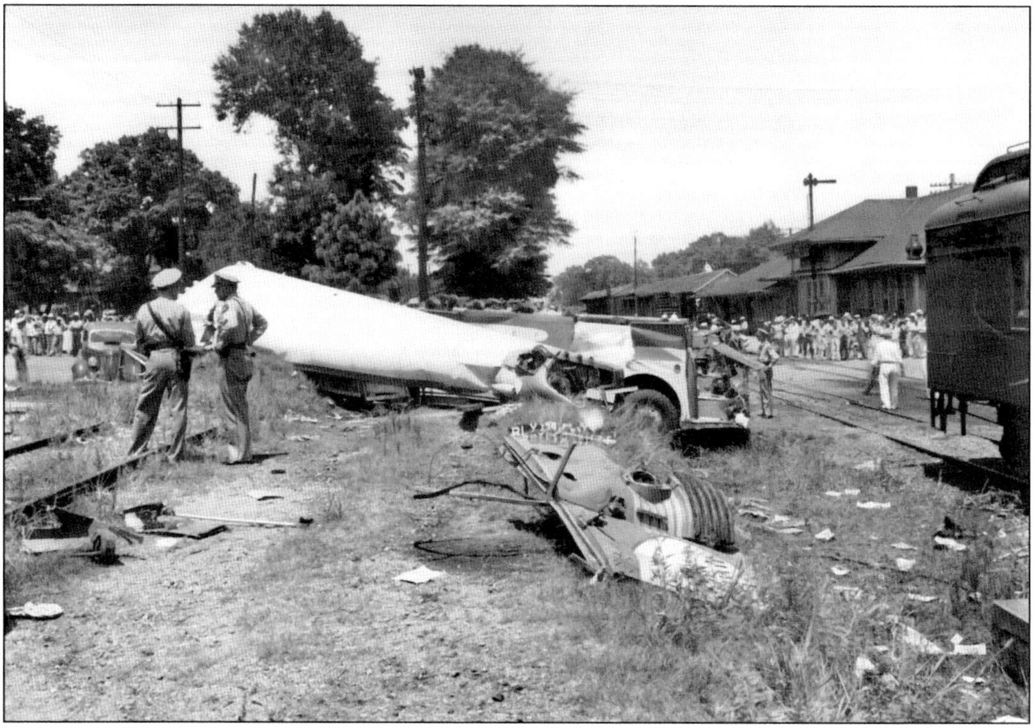

One of the saddest pages in Copiah's history happened in Crystal Springs on August 5, 1942. A Greyhound bus on its New Orleans-to-Jackson run received passengers at Thaxton's Drug Store. It then proceeded onto Marion Avenue to make its way to Highway 51. The bus stopped at the Marion Avenue railroad crossing to await the passing of a northbound passenger train. As the train passed, the driver immediately began crossing the tracks, realizing too late that an Illinois Centra Railroad southbound special troop train on the other set of tracks was coming toward them. The train collided with the bus, which had its roof ripped away and its 52 passengers (26 of whom were aviation cadets) strewn along the tracks. By the next day, 13 casualties were listed. (Courtesy of MDAH.)

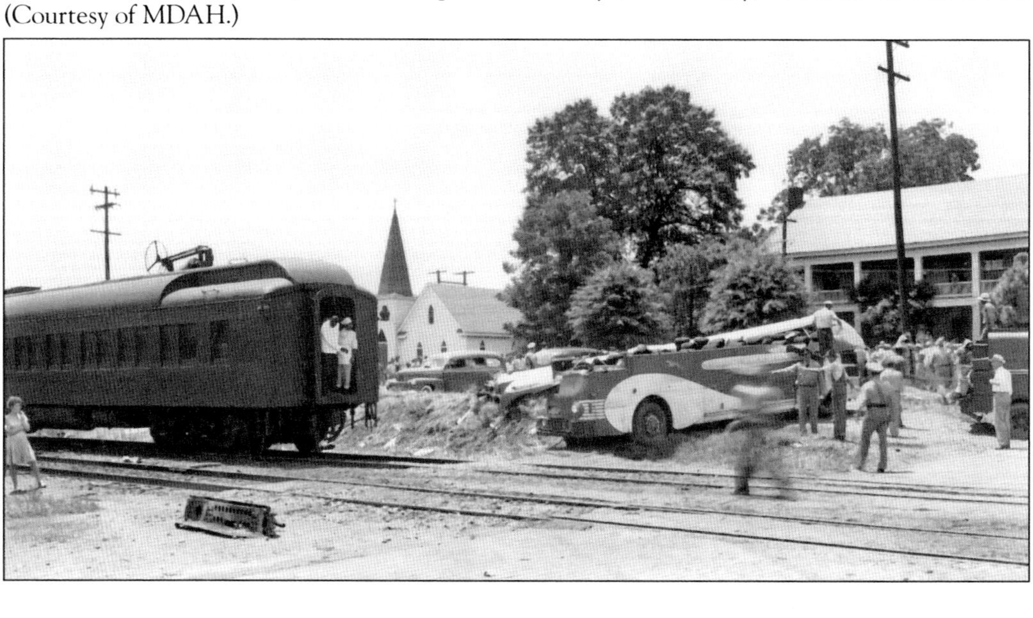

Seven

ENTERTAINMENT

It can only be left to the imagination to think of the number of activities that one would have to choose from in a time when there were no televisions, computers, major roadways, or even electricity. Popular attractions were Brown's Wells and the lakes. There were plenty of other activities as well.

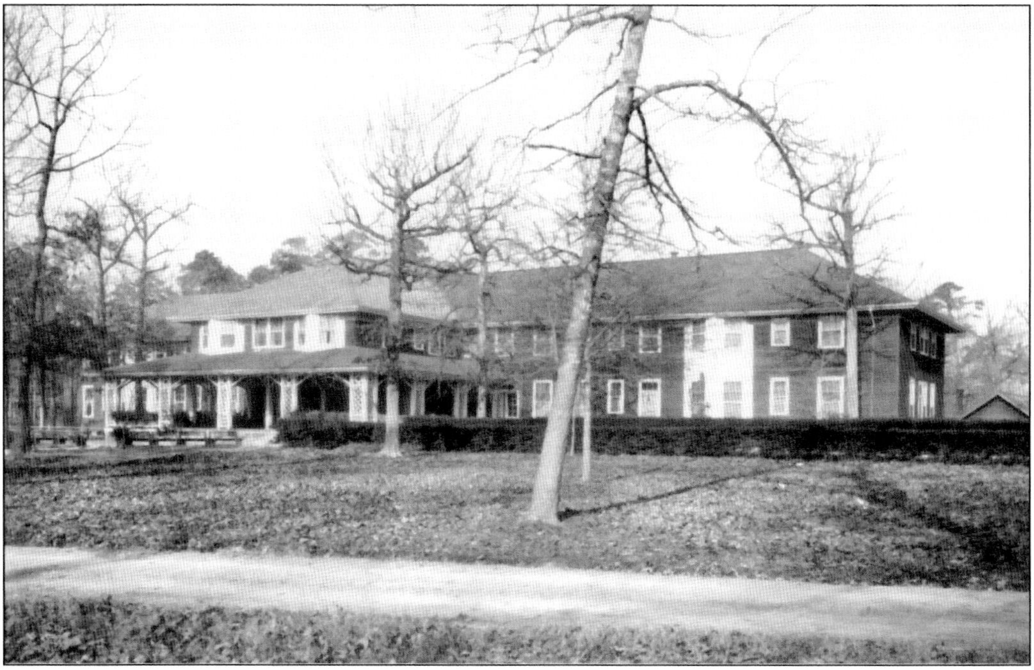

In 1852, William Brown purchased from the federal government the land on which Brown's Well Health Resort was located. By 1865, he had discovered the mineral waters of the wells. Brown eventually built a hotel. In the early 1880s, many prominent people were entertained and came to drink the marvelous curative mineral waters at Brown's Wells. (Courtesy of MDAH.)

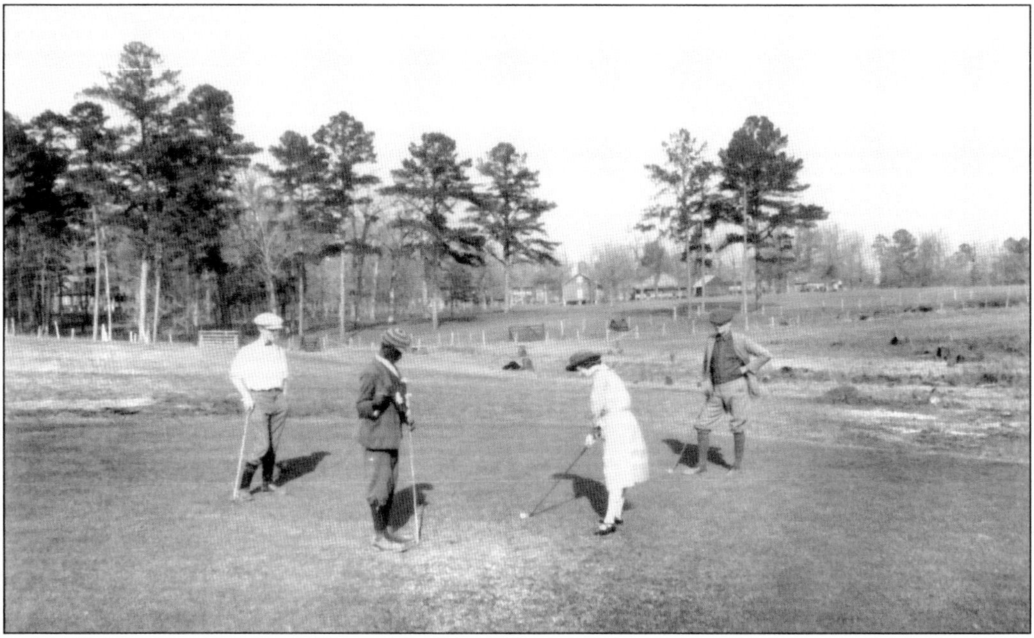

In the early 1900s, the property was acquired by several businessmen, mainly from Hazlehurst and New Orleans. The new owners spent about $50,000 to greatly improve Brown's Wells. The hotel had electric lighting and was equipped with a complete system of sewage and water, as were the cottages. Guests could hunt, play golf, or just relax, among other things. (Courtesy of MDAH.)

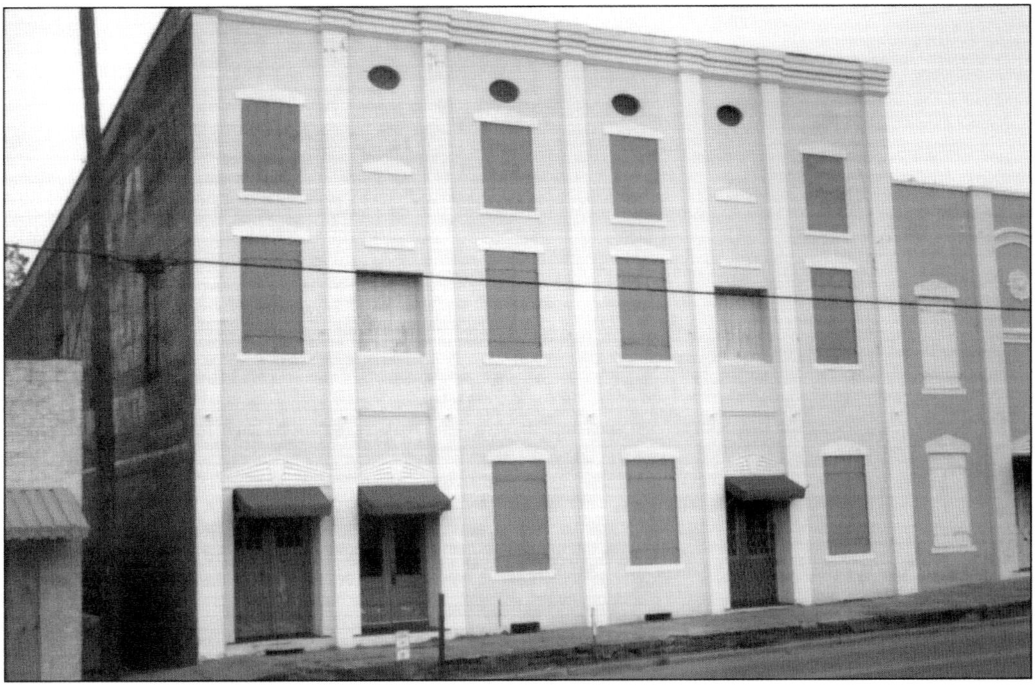

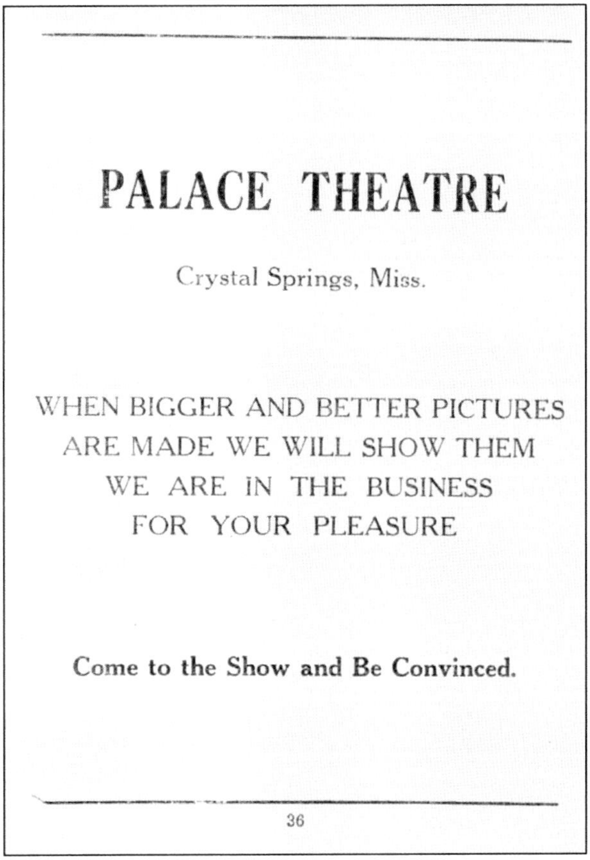

PALACE THEATRE

Crystal Springs, Miss.

WHEN BIGGER AND BETTER PICTURES
ARE MADE WE WILL SHOW THEM
WE ARE IN THE BUSINESS
FOR YOUR PLEASURE

Come to the Show and Be Convinced.

36

Faler Opera House in Hazlehurst was built by Martin Faler in 1883. The building was constructed of the finest materials money could buy. There was a stage at one end and a gallery for servants at the other end. Many activities took place in the building, such as plays, dances, public speaking, flower shows, beauty and baby contests, and talent shows. The building is waiting to be restored. Besides the opera house, there were several places to watch a movie: Pictureland Theatre in Crystal Springs, Crystal Theatre on Front Street (East Railroad Avenue), the Folly on Back Street, and the Palace Theatre, which was in operation in the 1930s. S. B. Ford, who was the manager of the movies at Chautauqua, was also the manager of Pictureland Theatre. (Courtesy of J. T. Biggs Jr. Memorial Library.)

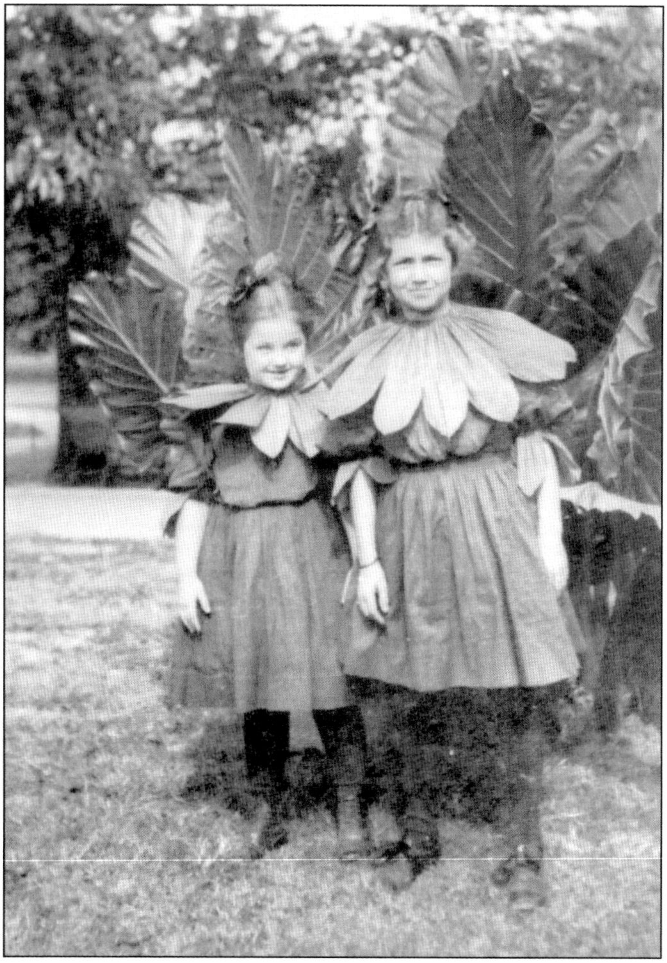

Each year, on the first day of the Copiah County Fair, Hazlehurst held a Floral Parade. Many merchants had floats, and there was a carnival and prizes for the best livestock. There were also competitions for homemaking crafts such as canning, quilting, and tatting. The home demonstration encouraged home canning and preserving. Burnley Drug Store gave an award each year for the biggest watermelon. Also each year, a girl was selected the "Prettiest Girl in Hazlehurst." Pictured are Susan and Dorothy Covington in the 1907 Floral Parade in their sunflower costumes, which matched Mamie Colie Covington's 3rd-place-winning buggy. (Courtesy of George W. Covington Memorial Library.)

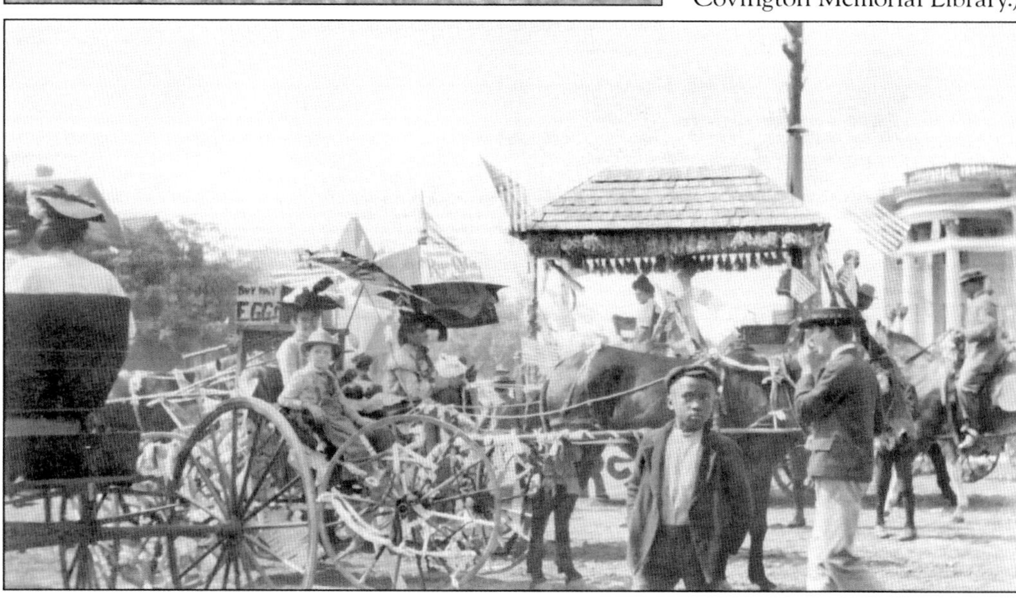

John A. Wise managed the first professional baseball team in Hazlehurst in 1903. In the early 1950s, Durr and Robert Wise donated the land for a ballpark. It was designed by Willis Hudlin, a former major-league pitcher. Marshall Nesmith Sr., a former semi-professional baseball player and coach, and other interested citizens helped. The Jackson Senators baseball team changed the team name to the Hazlehurst Senators and finished the season in Hazlehurst when a tornado destroyed their grandstand. For several years, the baseball park was a second home for the Memphis Red Sox. These cleats were donated by Nesmith to the Hazlehurst Depot Museum. Willie Mays, Henry Aaron, Ernie Banks, Don Newcombe, Junior Gilliam, and Satchel Paige all played at the park. In 1968, it was named Wise-Nesmith Field and became the property of the Hazlehurst School System. (Courtesy Hazlehurst Depot Museum.)

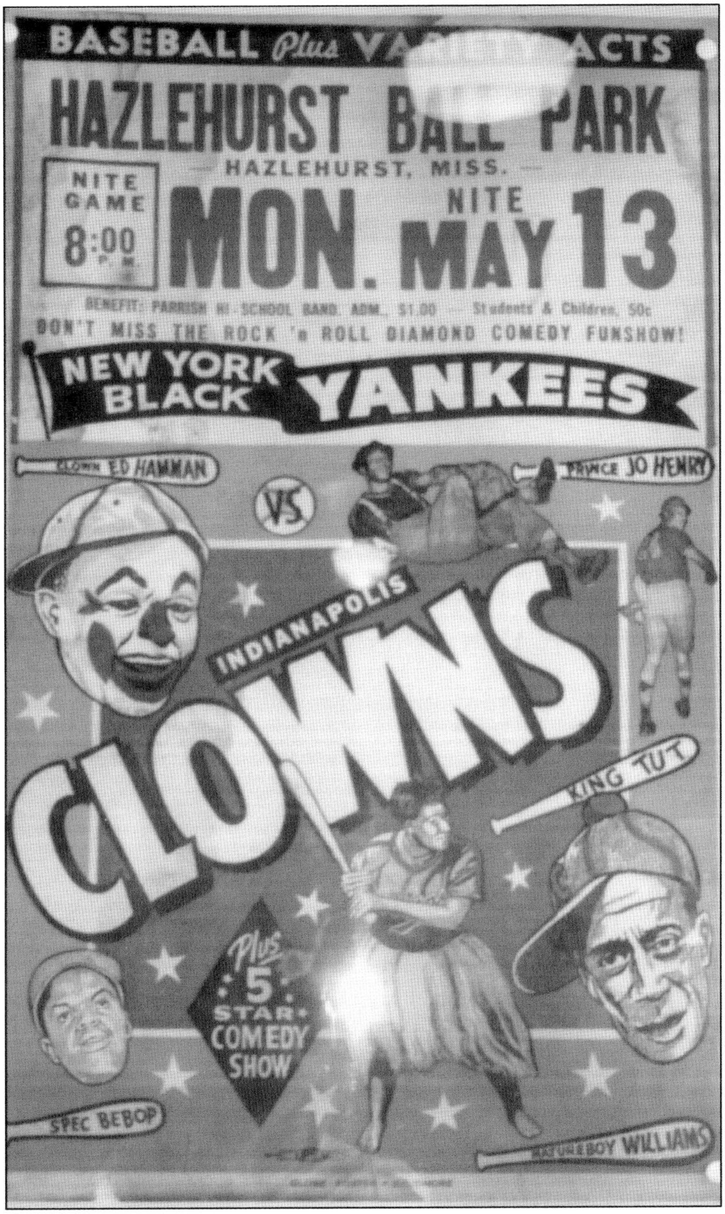

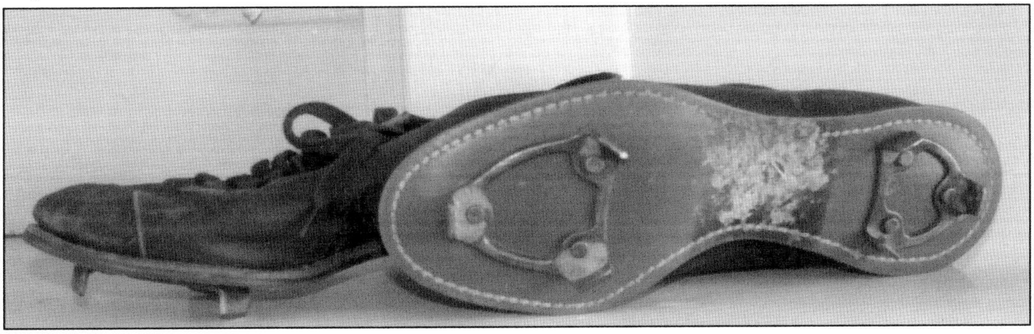

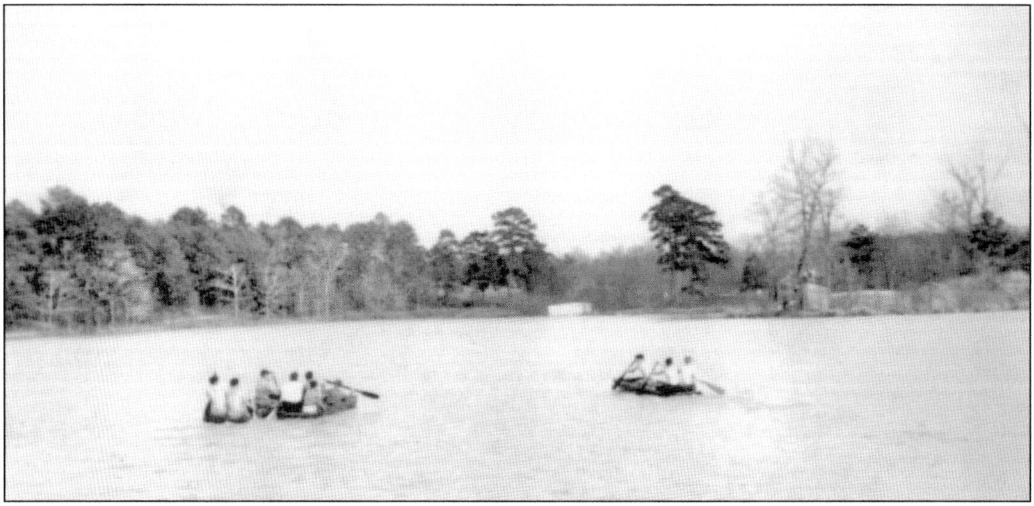

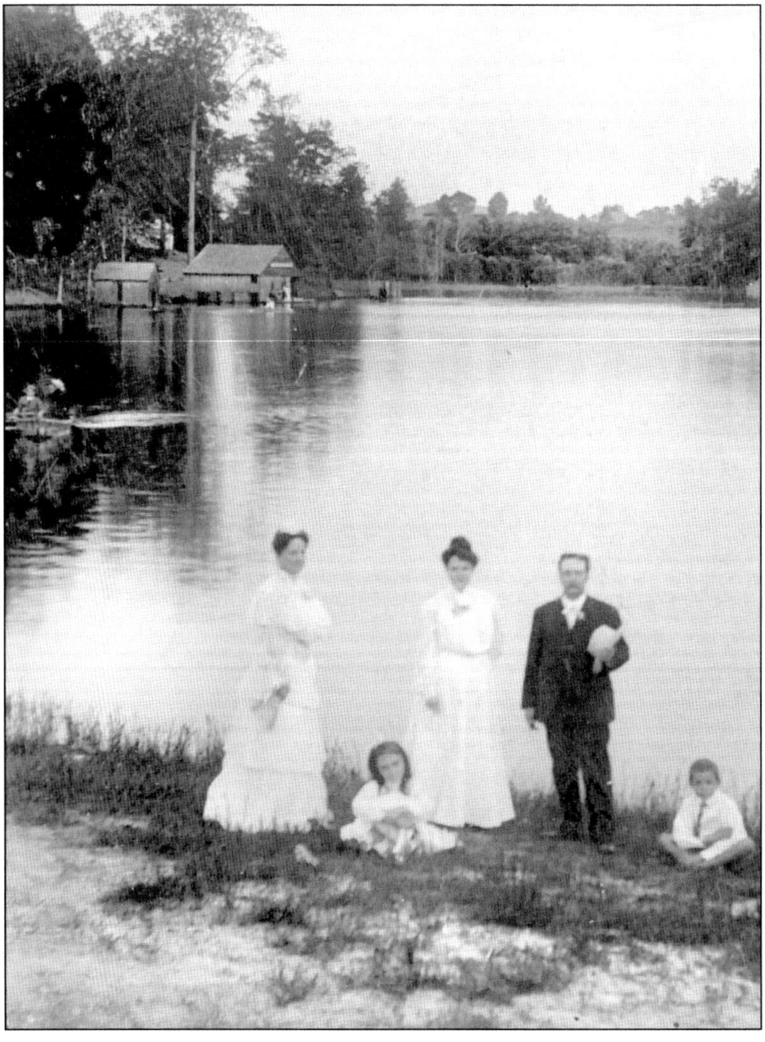

Lake Hazle was in Hazlehurst. Built in the early 1900s, the lake cost $20,000. In Crystal Springs, Lake Chautauqua was a fun place to go as well, as seen here. There was a large boathouse at the lake and rowboats could be rented by the hour. A kerosene-operated boat called a "Coal Oil Johnny" was operated and was later replaced by a gasoline launch, the *Dixie*, that gave rides at 25¢ per passenger. The boathouse, located on the north shore of the lake, had 12 dressing rooms, and a large swimming area was fenced in for the swimmers to enjoy. (Courtesy of George W. Covington Memorial Library and J. T. Biggs, Jr. Memorial Library.)

BIBLIOGRAPHY

Alford, Dorothy Moore. *Reflections and Recognitions: Crystal Springs, Mississippi (1820–1972)*. Unpublished, 1972.

Biographical and Historical Memoirs of Mississippi. Vol. II. Chicago: The Goodspeed Publishing Company, 1891.

Cook, Hartwell. *Hazlehurst, Copiah County, Mississippi*. Jackson, MS: AAA Printing and Graphics 1985.

"Crystal Springs' Centennial Celebration: 1858–1958." *The Meteor*, September 11, 1958. Centennial Edition.

Hazlehurst: A View of the Past. Hazlehurst, MS: Hazlehurst Historical Society, 1976. (Reprint of *Hazlehurst Courier*, February 26, 1907.)

Scrapbook of Information about Georgetown at the Georgetown Public Library.

Scrapbook of Information about Hazlehurst at the George W. Covington Memorial Library.

Scrapbook of Information about Wesson at the Longie Dale Hamilton Memorial Library.

Sims, Mary Helen. *Gallman, Mississippi*. Unpublished, no date.

Vertical files about Crystal Springs. J. T. Biggs Jr. Memorial Library, Crystal Springs.

Walker, Durr and David H. Higgs. *Wesson: Industrial City of the South*. No publisher, 1995.

WPA Historical Research Project for Copiah County. On file at Mississippi Department of Archives and History, Jackson.